Engaging the Sociological Imagination:
An Invitation for the Twenty-First Century

Dedicated to Peter Berger and C. Wright Mills:

Inspiration, not imitation, is the sincerest form of flattery.

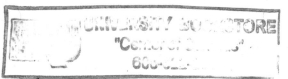

John Curra

Paul Paolucci

Eastern Kentucky University

KENDALL/HUNT PUBLISHING COMPANY
4050 Westmark Drive   Dubuque, Iowa 52002

Table of Contents

Preface

A popular saying, perhaps wrongly attributed to the Chinese, goes, "May you live in interesting times." The twentieth century was indeed interesting *and* consequential. Like all centuries, it was the best of times and the worst of times, filled with momentous events. It was a time during which the world experienced the most radical social, technological, and political change the planet has yet seen. The century in which we now find ourselves promises to be as interesting. The concerns over war, terrorism, cultural clashes (based on racial, religious, and/or ethnic differences), inflation, and economic inequalities are ever-present. If we are to cope with the confusion and uncertainty that modern society brings with it, we must possess a way to make sense out of our seemingly chaotic world. We live in a time of uneasiness and/or indifference, and public issues and personal troubles have not yet been widely defined as problems for social science to address and solve. Without a focused and systematic approach, we are left confused and unsure about where we are, where we have been, or where we might be going. These concerns have not been formulated in such a way that human reason and sensibility can be used to understand them (Mills 1959:11). Now more than ever, what is needed is sound, logical thinking and a commitment to a scientific understanding of the social world.

This book is an invitation to learn more about the scientific study of society. Few things, in our opinion, are as intellectually stimulating or as personally enriching. The sociological imagination promises to help us in grasping the relationship between the events of history and those of our own biographies and how both are acted out in society (Mills 1959:6). This quality of mind allows its possessors to appreciate their placement in and experience of the world and to see it in a new light. Those possessing the sociological imagination are able to provide themselves with adequate summations, cohesive assessments, and comprehensive orientations in their thinking (Mills 1959:8). In the sociological imagination, old or traditional modes of thought may begin to appear incorrect or muddleheaded, and things that once seemed ordinary or commonsensical might be seen in new ways (Mills 1959:7-8). The sociological imagination promises to provide a significant contribution to understanding the problems we face as a global society, as a species, and as a planet. We hope that by the end of this book you, our readers, will agree with this assessment.

As the discipline of sociology enters a new century, it is still struggling to understand the nature of all the social changes initiated during the twentieth century. As sociology continues its tradition of producing groundbreaking ideas and cutting-edge research, it brings with it a long history of valuable theories, leading personalities, and classic texts. When contemporary sociologists reflect on the most significant personalities and texts that influenced their development, two of the most commonly cited authors are C. Wright

Mills and Peter Berger. Most sociologists today often find it necessary to position their own views in relationship to Berger's and Mills's ideas and works. Each has each made substantial contributions to our understanding of what a sociological imagination means and entails. They agreed that a sociological imagination (Mills) or sociological consciousness (Berger) is the best way (Mills 1959:14) or one good way (Berger 1963:17) for humans to achieve the requisite understanding of events in the wider society and also in their own lives. We are confident that a sociological imagination is the most satisfactory way to come to grips with the rapidly changing world as we enter the twenty-first century.

Mills and Berger pursue different themes and emphasize different ideas, even while they are in agreement about many fundamental matters. Mills's (1959) *The Sociological Imagination* has been highly influential, being read by both undergraduates in sociology classes and by their professors (often, again and again). His book is used across the full range of courses offered in sociology. Its writing style is elegant, its meaning is clear, and its call for social responsibility and clarity in sociological explanations is inspiring. Mills's work provides a broad framework for an understanding of how an individual's personal biography is shaped by his or her place in a society that is constantly changing. Mills's call for a sociology that understands and can explain in scientifically correct ways the interplay between biography, history, and society—and is able to move effortlessly from one level of explanation to another—fits nicely with Berger's (1963) *Invitation to Sociology*. Berger's book has also enjoyed a wide popularity. It provides great insight into the processes by which humans see the social world and their place in it. According to him, sociology is a frame of reference that understands human societies and relationships, and the sociologist is the individual who understands human experience in a disciplined way. Sociologists try to suspend whatever biases, predispositions, and prejudices that they may have in the hopes of describing social events as objectively and dispassionately as possible. Berger (1963:24) argued that sociology will be the most satisfying to those individuals who can think of nothing more entrancing than watching human beings in order to understand them better. Both Berger and Mills were fascinated with sociology. For Berger (1963:21) it was because sociology makes it possible to see the familiar world in a new light, and for Mills (1959:8) it was because it makes it possible for us to acquire a new way of thinking and to experience meaningful participation in the construction of our own values. For each, sociology held the promise of providing the knowledge people needed to make sense of their world.

The aforementioned books are not the only two by these authors to leave an indelible mark on the discipline of sociology. In 1956, Mills published his groundbreaking and controversial work, *The Power Elite*. Ten years later, Berger and Thomas Luckmann (1966) published their equally groundbreaking and controversial work, *The Social Construction of Reality*. These two works – the former about the upper echelons of power in American society and the latter on the sociology of knowledge—do not seem immediately related. They do inform each other in important ways, however. Few sociologists deny that a relationship exists between wealth and power in a society. Mills argued that in the United States these had become particularly united and concentrated, a situation that was threatening to undermine the meaningful participation of the public in the decision-making process. Many sociologists agree that the social institutions that prevail in the modern world have been shaped in ways that serve some groups over others. The groups that dominate these institutions can profoundly influence what passes for knowledge in society. While Berger and Luckmann's work provides great insight into the processes by which humans come to see the world and think of their place in it, it tends to underplay the relationships of power involved in the process. Mills's work provides a broad framework for understanding how the destinies of uncountable individuals have been shaped by the distribution of power within the historically changing social structure of the United States. *The Social Construction of Reality* fails to incorporate the question of inequalities and power in the social construction of reality just as *The Power Elite* leaves this latter issue underdeveloped. Nevertheless, these two approaches to sociological research, presenting different traditions and perspectives, can be used to inform one another.

We urge readers of our book to follow the lead of these two sociologists. We believe they will benefit from what we have to add and feel "invited" to develop their own sociological imagination. We also hope that our readers will cultivate and pursue their own sociological imaginations as they learn more about the discipline of sociology and about the power of human groups and the nature of social relationships. The sociological imagination has the potential to make a difference—as Mills insisted it could—in the quality of life in our times.

This book has three main goals. First, *it introduces students to a sociological view of the world so that they might develop a sociological imagination.* Like Berger's *Invitation to Sociology*, this book is meant to be read more than it is to be studied. It reflects our view of what's important to understand about the human experience as developed through our personal engagement with the discipline of sociology and the ideas of Mills and Berger and Luckmann. Berger, Luckmann, and Mills all wrote what are considered classic statements, designed for both the beginning student and the seasoned professional. We hope our book is able to add to the discourse their work initialed. Second, the book *introduces readers to a range of sociological concepts and principles representative of the field as a whole.* From this point of view, this book is less a plea for others to become students of Berger, Berger and Luckmann, or Mills and more an attempt to use their work to introduce students to the basics of the discipline of sociology. Third, this book attempts to *provide the reader an orientation about both the state and trajectory of the world and the state and trajectory of the discipline of sociology.* Our book presents some of the key ideas and findings that subsequent researchers have developed—essential knowledge if you will—to explain the world of the present while exploring its past and discussing its future directions.

Though this work reflects its authors' encounter with Mills and Berger and Luckmann, it also attempts to introduce readers to a way of understanding the world through the eyes of several generations of sociologists. It tries to do this in a manner fit with coming to grips with our social reality as we enter a new century. We hope that this book demonstrates to its readers how a sociological imagination makes it possible to understand our historical roots and to develop sensible explanations of both our social structure and the changes it has gone through. It is founded on a belief in the value of integrating the perspectives of Berger and Luckmann and Mills, while taking seriously their call for a commitment to a scientific analysis of our social world, steered by a sociological imagination. You are invited to join us so that you, too, can make better sense of your life and times.

NOTE TO READERS: Throughout this work, gender neutral terminology is favored. However, often when citing others one encounters conventions of a prior period. This often includes the gender bias contained in language use, more so when those quoted are from generations long past. In order to both retain continuity in meaning and as a way to reflect these historical realities, when a direct citation is used, the gender bias found in its presentation is kept.

References

Berger, Peter. 1963. *Invitation to Sociology: A Humanist Perspective*. Garden City, New York: Anchor Books / Doubleday Company.

Berger, Peter and Thomas Luckmann. 1966. *The Social Construction of Reality*. Garden City, New York: Anchor Books / Doubleday & Company.

Mills, C. Wright. 1956. *The Power Elite*. New York: Oxford University Press.

_____. 1959. *The Sociological Imagination*. New York: Oxford University Press.

Chapter One: Getting Started

Social Facts and Personal Experiences

Traps and Tribulations

Public Issues and Private Troubles

The Sociological Imagination

An Invitation

The Tradition of Sociology

Sociological Insights

Origins

Sociological Motifs

Social Actors in a Social World

Sociology and Human Nature

The Social World

Society and Social Control

Overintegrated and Oversocialized?

The Social Construction of Reality

Dialectical Relationships

Habitualization, Institutionalization, and Social Reality

Ideologies and Contested Spaces

Science and Sociology

The New Know-Nothings

The Know-It-Alls

Stalking the Sociological Imagination

Conclusion

References

Chapter One: Getting Started
Social Facts and Personal Experiences

Jean Jacques Rousseau (1712-1778) claimed in *The Social Contract* that humans are born free but live out their lives bound by chains ("Man is born free, but everywhere he is in chains."). His words are still useful today. The social groups or collectivities within which most of us spend the duration of our lives—family, school, community, workplace, nation—define us in the eyes of others, while they envelop and define us to ourselves as well. We become the roles we play: son, daughter, husband, wife, student, teacher, parent, and so on. In some ways, our roles are liberating. We find great pleasure and fulfillment, for example, in being parents or students. We delight in our children, and we like to learn new things. In other ways, however, our roles are imprisoning, and we play them with disinterest or even dislike. Collective experiences that are characterized by alienation, exploitation, or insecurity are detrimental to personal growth and self-fulfillment. Sometimes, it becomes difficult for us to maintain a sense that life is under our control and that we will be better off next year than we are today.

Traps and Tribulations

The groups to which we belong can seem more and more confining (Mills 1959:3). They may seem to be places to escape *from* rather than to escape *to*. Max Weber (1968), a founding father of sociology, hypothesized that societies would come more and more to resemble "iron cages" in which practically all features of life would be efficient, predictable, *and* incredibly repetitive and boring. We would each become parts of a multitude of large, bureaucratic, social machines—at school, at work, in the community—and individual wants and needs would become increasingly less important. C. Wright Mills (1959:12), a mid-twentieth century sociologist, had no trouble agreeing with this dismal assessment of the direction of modern society. He thought that we were living in a time of pervasive uneasiness and indifference, but our problems, collective or personal, had not yet been defined in terms of values and threats to them. We are now in the twenty-first century, and things are not all that different from when Mills wrote. Public issues and private troubles are still not widely viewed as problems for social science to address and solve (Mills 1959:11).

One good way to escape a sense of entrapment is to understand as much as we can about the sociocultural forces that shape and influence us. By understanding how society works, we will come to an increased sense of control. Automobile mechanics, for example, understand cars in ways that the rest of us do not. They know what things to worry about and what things to ignore. They know what things have to be taken care of immediately and what things can wait until later. When it comes to human experience, we also need a quality of mind that makes it possible for us to use reason to develop concise summaries of what is happening in the world; we need to understand the relationship between social forces and our own personal experiences (Mills 1959:5). A systematic understanding of how things work in a society has both enormous power and incredible promise for anyone willing to take the time and trouble to acquire the knowledge.

Public Issues and Private Troubles

In order to start to understand what is happening in our lives and how things affect us, it is necessary to separate "personal troubles of milieu" from "public issues of social structure" (Mills 1959:8). A **personal trouble** exists when an individual's cherished values are threatened. Personal troubles occur in those areas of life over which an individual has some control, such as dating, marriage, childrearing, or work. If an individual could be taught to cope more effectively with the situation he or she faces, the individual's personal trouble would disappear. A **public issue** is something that threatens the cherished values of a large number of people such as war, poverty, terrorism, divorce, crime, or unemployment. A public issue involves the organization of a society and its network of institutions. Because public issues are caused by crises or contradictions in institutional arrangements, they cannot be eliminated by the actions of a lone individual (Mills 1959:9). The cause and the correction of a public issue is only to be found in the structure of a society.

As institutions have grown in number and complexity, and as the speed of both social and cultural change has accelerated, social institutions have exerted an ever greater impact on our lives. Consequently, to understand both personal troubles and public issues—or human experience itself—it is necessary to look beyond an individual and his or her immediate environment.

> When a society is industrialized, a peasant becomes a worker; a feudal lord is liquidated or becomes a businessman. When classes rise or fall, a man is employed or unemployed; when the rate of investment goes up or down, a man takes new heart or goes broke. When wars happen, an insurance salesman becomes a rocket launcher; a store clerk, a radar man; a wife lives alone; a child grows up without a father. (Mills 1959:3)

We must come to understand how changes in society, and the interconnections between its institutions, affect or even determine individual experiences. It is impossible to separate an individual's life from the life of his or her society, because nothing—no human action, thought, or feeling—exists in a social vacuum.

Individuals are very often inclined to view their experiences as personal, as unrelated to social structure and social change. However, much of what we are and will become is a result of the forces of our society itself, which alter and transform the aims and conditions of people's lives (Mills 1959:13). If only one child were having trouble at school or if only one couple were to have an unhappy marriage, we could easily consider these as personal troubles unrelated to social conditions. However, most problems individuals experience are something other than simply personal. For example, educational experiences in U.S. schools can themselves produce apathy, boredom, cynicism, or stifling obedience; and while families are the site of love and affection, they are also the site of discord and unhappiness. The happenings in any one group or social institution reflect what is happening in other groups and/or institutions in a society, as well as the interconnections among societies all across the world.

The Sociological Imagination

Mills (1916-1962) described what he called the **sociological imagination**. This imagination allows its possessor to understand the interconnections between individual biography, historical change, and institutional contradictions as they are played out in a society. In other words, the sociological imagination is a vivid or clear awareness of the relationships between the wider society and individual experience.

> It [the sociological imagination] is the capacity to range from the most impersonal and remote transformations to the most intimate features of the human self—and to see the relations between the two. Back of its use there is always the urge to know the social and historical meaning of the individual in the society and in the period in which he has his quality and his being. (Mills 1959:7)

Most people, Mills insists, are unaware of the interconnections between their own lives and social change. They do not possess the state of mind that allows them to comprehend the linkages between individual and society, between biography and history, between self and world (Mills 1959:4). Not only does a lack of a sociological imagination make it impossible for individuals to understand personal troubles and public issues, it makes it far less likely that they will be able to deal successfully with the structural factors or historical changes that they confront.

The sociological imagination, curiously enough, requires a knowledge of more than just sociology. It also requires a knowledge of history, anthropology, psychology, social psychology, political science, economics—the whole range of the social sciences—even though its possessor will want to specialize in sociology and become a sociologist. For Mills, himself a sociologist, the sociological imagination is neither fad nor fashion.

> It is a quality of mind that seems most dramatically to promise an understanding of the intimate realities of ourselves in connection with larger social realities. It is not merely one quality of mind among the contemporary range of cultural sensibilities—it is *the* quality whose wider and more adroit use offers the promise that all such sensibilities—and in fact, human reason itself—will come to play a greater role in human affairs. (Mills 1959:15)

Sociologists study human relationships wherever and whenever they find them. You don't have to study only movers and shakers in social life such as politicians or corporate executives. You can also, if you like, study potato farmers, prostitutes, clam diggers, or circus clowns. Sociologists regularly occupy themselves with concerns that others regard as too trivial or boring, too sacred, or too distasteful for serious investigation (Berger 1963:19). Sociologists are not principally concerned with the ultimate significance of what individuals do, think, feel, or remember; they are, however, principally concerned with human experience and its interconnection with the structure of society. What distinguishes the mature use of the sociological imagination is a commitment to exploring how the interplay between biography, history, and society impacts the collective and individual experiences of human beings.

An Invitation

As valuable as Mills's exploration of the sociological imagination is—in fact, his book on the subject is one of the most influential sociology books ever written (Phillips, Kincaid, and Scheff 2002)—he neglected to emphasize that sociology is much more than a quality of mind. It is something you do; something you are; and something you share with others. In the pages ahead, we will tell you more about how we conceive of sociology, sociologists, and the human experience. Although it is probably too soon for you to accept, we invite you to consider becoming a part of the sociological tradition by developing *your own* sociological imagination. This will make it possible for you to formulate your own questions and discover your own understandings about the relationships between individuals (biography), sociocultural change (history), and society. You will reach the point where you are able to recognize the linkages between the wider society and personal experience. You will be able to move or shift from one perspective to another and build up a picture of society and its parts and processes. You will develop the ability to analyze the linkages between things that at first seem unrelated. What do gasoline prices have to do with terrorist attacks? What does political organization have to do with sexual expression? What does art have to do with patterns of social deviance? You will learn to tolerate the sloppiness and ambiguity of your initial thoughts about social processes so that you can work through them and cultivate ideas of your own that are new and original. The entire world is your laboratory, and your time frame is the entire course of human history (Mills 1959:224-5). Your sociological imagination will eventually help you to understand *your* place in society.

Those individuals who possess the sociological imagination view themselves as part of the classic tradition (Mills 1959:195-226). This means that they view themselves as individuals at work on problems of substance and importance. For classic sociologists—Comte, Marx, Weber, Durkheim, Mead, Simmel—their work was part of everything they did. Their sociology gave meaning to their lives, and their lives defined their sociology. When they looked at people acting together, they saw the influence of groups, institutions, and organizations. Their passion for sociology—doing it, thinking it, and sometimes even teaching it—was the center of their personal identity. What they were and their dedication to sociology were inseparable. While the sociological imagination can be learned, its acquisition is not like learning how to bake bread or drive an automobile. It will take some time to acquire the knowledge and learn the methods of the sociologist. In the final analysis, the sociological imagination requires a playful and open quality of mind, coupled with a strong commitment to a better understanding of the world (Mills 1959:211). This playfulness—in which new ideas are developed and old ideas are combined in new ways—and the drive to make sense of human experience make sociologists more than reporters. While both sociologists and reporters must have the courage and determination to find the truth and publicize their findings, sociology is a far greater undertaking (Mills 1959:224). Sociologists are often in a position to call into question conventional or taken-for-granted views of the world.

Auguste Comte is considered to be the father or founder of sociology, because he coined the term **sociology** (in 1839) to name the scientific study of societies, groups, and social relationships. He believed that sociology was the apex of the social sciences by being the umbrella under which the totality of human experience could be studied. He probably overstated the case. As we told you already, the sociological imagination requires a knowledge of more than societies and social relationships; it requires knowledge of biology, psychology, anthropology, history, and so on. It is true, however, that sociology is a broad and inclusive social science, and not many things that impact human experience have been neglected by sociologists in their scientific studies. Sociology is the only social science that offers a coherent and scientifically informed view of societies, institutions, groups, and individuals and the linkages between them. While acquisition of the sociological imagination is difficult—it is not easy to develop a comprehensive understanding of biography and history and how they intersect in a society—it is highly rewarding.

We must not only learn sociology, we must also learn *from* sociology (Bell 1999:295-7). A sociological imagination can bring us to a point of enlightenment so that we can view others, as well as ourselves, with a measure of detachment. We must come to accept both our successes and our failures with grace and understanding. Use your sociological imagination to change what you can, accept what you can't, and know the difference to avoid frustrating yourself needlessly.

> The development of objectivity in the student . . . involves a systematic attempt to expand self-centered awareness beyond the parochial situation in which everything in society is judged according to whether it fulfills or frustrates our desires. The wealthy student must learn to see the society through the eyes of the poor . . . the young must understand how the world looks to the old. This is not a purely intellectual process, but it involves learning how the other feels by becoming, if only momentarily, the other. (Bell 1999:296)

This mental projection into the position of another sets the foundation for empathy and, perhaps, even sympathy. It also sets the foundation for understanding. It will help us to manage those areas of life most directly under our control: our immediate social surroundings and our own individual experiences. The ways of enlightenment seek to liberate us from the capricious authority of society and those who dominate it (Bell 1999:298). If you are the kind of person who can—or who can learn to—think outside the box and come to appreciate the power and promise of the sociological imagination, consider becoming a part of the sociological tradition. Work to develop your own sociological imagination and become the best sociologist that you can be—the best sociologist that *anyone* can be.

The Tradition of Sociology
Sociological Insights

The first lesson of sociology is that human experience can only be understood by locating individuals within a particular place and period (Mills 1959:5). Individuals can really only know themselves by recognizing their connections with other individuals who share their circumstances. No human is an island. He or she is a historical social actor, and the things that happen in his or her society powerfully form each and every human on earth. A second lesson is that things are not always what they seem (Berger 1963:23). A sociological imagination makes it possible for us to see a world that was once taken for granted in a new and different light. The people, places, and experiences that once seemed familiar will now seem foreign.

> The experience of sociological discovery could be described as "culture shock" minus geographical displacement. In other words, the sociologist travels at home—with shocking results. (Berger 1963:23)

Just as travelers to another land may experience a sense of uneasiness, disorientation, or surprise when faced with people whose customs are different from their own (and from what they find normal, natural, or healthy), so can we be equally shocked by seeing new things in our own land or familiar happenings in a new way. Sociology will make it possible for you to learn things about human experience that you never knew or even thought possible. The sociological imagination could even make it possible for you to experience a sense of astonishment as you acquire new understandings about your society and your social relationships (Mills 1959:8).

The "social shocks" that can occur from encountering cultural variation can be appreciated by examining some of the features of the home-birth culture in the United States. As home birthing became more popular, a unique home-birth culture evolved that attached new meanings to old processes. A home birth not only leaves parents with a new baby, it leaves them with a new placenta. When a birth takes place in a hospital, the placenta may be treated by hospital staff as one more piece of biological waste and incinerated, or it may be sold to drug or cosmetic companies. Pharmaceutical and cosmetic companies extract the hormones and proteins from placentas for use in manufacturing drugs or beauty products. Sometimes hospitals will keep placentas for their own medical research.

When a birth takes place at home, however, different options present themselves. The placenta or afterbirth may be dumped in the garbage, flushed down the toilet, buried in the back yard, or planted at the base of a fruit tree bought to celebrate the child's birth (the tree grows right along with the child). Another option is for the proud and happy parents to follow the custom of **placentophagia** and eat the afterbirth of their newborn (Janszen 1981:366).

> Placenta is eaten raw or cooked, depending on the sensitivity of diners' palates and stomachs. When cooking it smells like liver frying and even tastes like liver or kidney but is sweeter and milder. It is tender meat. Cooking preparations range from simple to gourmet, limited only by the imaginations of the chefs—usually the new fathers. Placenta can be boiled in salted water, pan fried in butter and garlic, stir fried in soy sauce with vegetables, sautéd in wine and spices, or sun dried in strips for jerky. Placenta stew is an old favorite; a recipe can be found in the *Birth Book*, a popular collection of first-person accounts of home birth. (Janszen 1981:367)

Eating placenta or afterbirth is usually viewed by parents who do it as the natural culmination of the very natural process of bringing new beings into the world, and placentophagiasts take nature very seriously. While no universal consensus exists on what is "natural," what does exist is widespread consensus that eating afterbirth qualifies. It is defined as a healthy food, and eating it allows parents to celebrate both a new child and a successful home delivery. Even vegetarians may still find the placenta good to eat (Janszen 1981:367). Little doubt exists that many parents—maybe most—would find the prospect of eating the afterbirth of their newborn as distinctively unattractive. Because such a wide array in human experience exists, it is imperative to develop a sociological imagination to be able to make sense of it.

Humans construct social situations that allow things to occur that would ordinarily be forbidden. They temporarily suspend one set of rules and adopt very different ones. During the New Orleans Mardi Gras, actions that would normally be forbidden become customary (Douglas, Rasmussen, and Flanagan 1977:238), indicating that human experience is powerfully impacted by social arrangements. One of these is "parade stripping," in which females expose their naked breasts to people on parade floats so that they will be thrown glass beads and trinkets. These women—referred to as "beadwhores" by people not so accepting of the practice—and their benefactors on the floats are part of a social world that gives a nondeviant meaning to their otherwise deviant activities

(Forsyth 1992:395). Parade stripping is not simply unbridled, carnal exhibitionism. It is a ritualized exchange of things of value. The float rider gets to see naked breasts, and the woman receives beads, trinkets, and confirmation that her breasts warrant a bestowing of gifts (Shrum and Kilburn 1996:444).

Sociologists explain why people act, think, feel, and remember as they do by starting with the groups within which people do their acting, thinking, feeling, and remembering. Groups have significant power over us. We all have had the experience of entering an unfamiliar group to find that everyone else is interacting and having a good time, though we feel very uneasy and uncomfortable because we're outsiders. We'd rather be anywhere else. Sociologists keep groups and social relationships foremost in every explanation of human experience that they develop. Societies institutionalize ways to ensure that they will attract (or make) the kinds of people best suited to their needs and discourage the development of the kinds of people who will do them no good (Gerth and Mills 1953). The processes of socialization and social control encourage individuals to be what societies need most.

> The sociologist stands on its head the commonsense idea that certain institutions arise because there are certain persons around. On the contrary, fierce warriors appear because there are armies to be sent out, pious men because there are churches to be built, scholars because there are universities to be staffed, and murderers because there are killings to be performed. It is not correct to say that each society gets the men it deserves. Rather, each society produces the men it needs. (Berger 1963:110)

During the lifelong process of socialization, not only do social forces influence what we do (or *want* to do) but also to a remarkable degree what we know, feel, and remember. Groups and relationships shape everything about us, and the structure of society becomes the structure of individual consciousness. We come to be, from the standpoint of a society, what we must be: workers, consumers, husbands, wives, daughters, sons, students, and so on. "Intelligence, humor, manual skills, religious devotion and even sexual potency respond with equal alacrity [i.e., enthusiasm] to the expectations of others" (Berger 1963:101). Humans create social arrangements as they act together, and they themselves are changed in the process.

The sociologist is an individual who is passionately interested in the workings of humans, especially their social relationships in groups, institutions, organizations, and societies. Whenever or wherever relationships are found—in big groups or small, in this time or a thousand years from now—the sociologist will have an interest in them. By using the tools of science, the sociologist maximizes his or her chances that sociological explanations will be based on observation rather than speculation or common sense, which can mislead us. The scientific method, if followed responsibly, makes it possible for scientists to increase their odds of being objective and of seeing things clearly rather than having their conclusions and observations tainted by prejudice, self-interest, or just plain sloppy thinking. The use of science is the way for sociologists to ensure that their explanations of the social world fit the facts. Without science it would be too easy for individuals to find whatever they wanted to find, and sociology would very likely be reduced to what was trendy or hip rather than what was logical and observable.

Origins

It is impossible to identify a precise date when sociological theory began (Ritzer 2000:4). People have probably always thought about their relationships to others and the nature of their society. Some individuals, however, have done it more thoroughly and formally, and they have developed a coherent view of both social structure and social change. These individuals attained their understandings through more than logic and observation. They also used imagination and intuition. They were able to develop sketches of society that are both inspired and inspiring (Nisbet 1966:18-20). Rationalism was the cornerstone of the Enlightenment, an eighteenth-century philosophy that powerfully affected the growth of the sciences. Rationalists believed that the road to understanding came from the use of logic and observation. Influenced by such views, sociologists developed scientific explanations of social behavior so that it could be objectively examined and rationally explained (Martindale 1960:29).

Early U.S. sociologists shared a rural and small-town background and this encouraged them to view a social problem as anything that was *not* small-town and rural (Mills 1943). This meant that they worried about both urbanization and industrialization, and they often displayed an uncritical acceptance of the status quo (Eisenstadt 1976:40). U.S. sociology also developed as a response to both bureaucracy and capitalism (Adams and Sydie 2002:3-57; Ashley and Orenstein 2001:23; Hinkle and Hinkle 1954:2-3). Large-scale organizations, economic competition, industrialization, and urbanization all worked together to give a distinctive form to U.S. social organization, patterns that sociologists wanted to understand and explain. Even though U.S. sociology was influenced by the thoughts of European social theorists like Comte and those who followed his tradition (Morgan 1997), it was still distinctly American (Hinkle and Hinkle 1954:7). U.S. sociologists combined both logic and science to make sense of the dynamic nature of a rapidly changing society.

Sociological Motifs

Peter Berger (1963) identified four motifs or themes that characterize the sociological imagination. Knowledge of these motifs will help you to understand more about the distinctiveness of sociology in comparison with other social scientific disciplines and the power and potential of possessing a sociological consciousness.

(1) The **debunking motif** (Berger 1963:38). The sociological imagination does—and must—work to reveal and illuminate the facades or screens that individuals use to cloak or hide their actions and intentions from one another. Because socially created roles are used to justify acts of cruelty, cowardice, incompetence, stupidity, insensitivity, or self-interest, we must look for the lies, distortions, or pretensions that individuals use to lead their lives. The debunking motif requires sociologists to penetrate verbal and institutional smoke screens to get at the real mainsprings of human action (Berger 1963:41-2). They are unremittingly suspicious of what most other people take for granted and of what passes for "official" truth.

(2) The **unrespectability motif** (Berger 1963:43). Sociology must avoid becoming too respectable because, if it does, it will lose its sharp edge and capacity for critique and criticism. Sociology must reserve its place as the one discipline that can call into question the status quo and offer theoretically sound and empirically correct analyses of customary practices in the official world. It can become neither too complacent nor too comfortable or it will lose its critical spirit. (Berger's use of the word "unrespectability" seems an unfortunate choice of terms. It makes it sound like sociologists are dishonest or untrustworthy. A better term might have been "outsider motif" or "iconoclast motif.")

(3) The **relativizing motif** (Berger 1963:52). An important feature of sociological consciousness is the recognition that identities, ideas, and customs are specific to a particular time and place. The sociological imagination makes it possible for—in fact, requires—an individual to alternate from one perspective to another and to take account of meaning systems that stand in opposition to one another. At one level, this alternation may be alarming. But at a deeper level, this alternation from one worldview to another, without moral judgment, is what distinguishes professional social scientists. You have to be able to jump from one perspective to another without judging other people by standards of your own group or time.

(4) The **cosmopolitan motif** (Berger 1963:52). The sociologist must be familiar with the whole world, both present and past. What this invites is an openness to other people and their experiences regardless of where or when they live. "The sociologist, at his best, is a man with a taste for other lands, inwardly open to the measureless richness of human possibilities, eager for new horizons and new worlds of human meaning" (Berger 1963:53). Sociologists avoid both ethnocentrism and egocentrism in their quest to understand human social experience better.

These four motifs overlap with one another so much that it is practically impossible to have one without some element of all the others. When your discipline obligates you to alternate from one view to another, it becomes far easier to unmask or uncover the propaganda and prejudices that humans use to conduct their affairs and the meaning systems they use to justify what they do. Both relativity and debunking require an observer to be able to adopt the role or view of the outsider or stranger, which is really what unrespectability is all about. In order to maintain a relativistic, unrespectable, and debunking view of the world, it helps to be aware of, and open to, the wide range of experiences found among humans in other lands and at other times, which is cosmopolitanism. In a nutshell, sociologists are inclined to maintain a skeptical gaze, allowing them to go beyond surface appearances and expose latent structures and explain puzzling events (Portes 2000:6). The motifs of sociology make it possible for us to identify and understand alternate systems of meaning and contrasting social arrangements in ways that other disciplines cannot.

A good example of how sociological motifs can work together to uncover something unexpected is found in the distinction between **manifest functions** and **latent functions** (Merton 1968:114). These two terms allow us to distinguish our reasons or intentions for what we do from their objective consequences or functions. For example, while people may marry because they are in love, the institution of the family provides a whole host of functions for societies from regulating sexual conduct to socializing the young. While social arrangements have clear and intended purposes or functions (manifest), they can also have hidden or unintended functions (latent) (Merton 1968:117). For example, schools teach the "three R's" (manifest function), but they also give teachers and administrators jobs and keep youngsters occupied for many hours a day, allowing parents to do things other than supervise their children (latent function). The concepts of manifest function and latent function show that things are not always what they seem and that humans can be unaware of the consequences their intended actions produce. Social arrangements that seem silly, irrational, or even dangerous may, in fact, continue to perform important functions for a group, functions that may be far removed from their intended purpose (Merton 1968:118). Emile Durkheim (1938) offered the novel idea that crime is for a society what pain is for an individual. Pain, within limits, is both normal and functional because it tells individuals that they are exhausting their bodies by, for example, exercising too much. Similarly, crime, within limits, is both normal—an integral part of all healthy societies—and functional.

> Crime, for its part, must no longer be conceived as an evil that cannot be too much suppressed. There is no occasion for self-congratulation when the crime rate drops noticeably below the average level, for we may be certain that this apparent progress is associated with some social disorder. (Durkheim 1938:72)

It is surprising but true that in certain respects crime is functional for both police and U.S. society. Crime gives police officers jobs, and criminals are convenient scapegoats upon which to blame some of the ills of a society. By focusing public attention on crime and criminals, it sanctifies the status quo and benefits those who have the most invested in it (Reiman 2001:4).

Studies of the unintended functions of social arrangements or cultural beliefs challenge common sense or what everybody takes for granted (Merton 1968:122). Kingsley Davis's (1937) study of prostitution is a good example of the benefits that can come from a **functionalist analysis**. He wanted to know why something that is both widely disapproved of and against the law continues to be found in so many places. Davis's study indicated that the legal and moral proscriptions were not strong enough–never could be strong enough–to eradicate prostitution because of the functions it fulfills. Prostitution, by providing a sexual outlet for individuals whose sexual appetities cannot be satisfied within a family, performs a function that no other institution can (Davis 1937:755). Davis fell short of saying that prostitution sustains the family, but he did insist that it was no danger to it.

At times Davis's analysis was insightful, but at other times it was simple-minded, sexist, and culture-bound. He came dangerously close to attributing prostitution to the human female's physical nature and her capacity for continuous sexuality (Davis 1937:744-5). He claimed—without benefit of any data whatsoever—that some women enjoy the intercourse they sell (Davis 1937:750). He equated the prostitute with the artist who receives a "generous reward" from painting but loves painting so much that receipt of payment is unnecessary (Davis 1937:750). No responsible scientist would make claims like these nowadays. However, his functionalist analysis did make it possible for us to understand things about prostitution that would have been otherwise impossible to understand. If you don't look at latent functions, you will never be able to fully understand social relationships.

Social Actors In A Social World
Sociology and Human Nature

One thing that sociologists have shown about human nature is that it is broad and constantly changing.

> But in our time we have come to know that the limits of "human nature" are frighteningly broad. We have come to know that every individual lives, from one generation to the next, in some society; that he lives out a biography, and that he lives it out within some historical sequence. By the fact of his living he contributes, however minutely, to the shaping of this society and to the course of its history, even as he is made by society and by its historical push and shove. (Mills 1959:6)

Individuals do, of course, bring to the world certain characteristics such as anatomical structure (e.g., genitals), skin color, body shape, and many other things. However, these features of personal identity really only become important as they become relevant to the flow of social interaction; what is most important is how our personal characteristics are recognized and evaluated by others. Human nature does not—cannot—exist in a social vacuum. The self is not a solid, fixed entity that an individual carries from one social situation to another. It is rather a process, continuously created and re-created in each social situation that one enters, held together by the slender thread of memory (Berger 1963:106). Personal identity is socially bestowed, socially sustained, and socially transformed (Berger 1963:98). While we can become habituated to certain features of our personal identity, displaying them practically everywhere we go, we can also be nudged in new directions by those individuals with whom we interact.

The Social World

Humans confront a social world that seems, and in many ways is, overwhelming. We may get the idea that all society sits on us. We should not dismiss this as some paranoid delusion, because in many ways it *does* sit on us. Durkheim (1938:1-13) was right to believe that society is more than the sum of the individuals who make it up. When people get together, a new level of reality, the social level, emerges that has its own patterns. It has both an ideational component and a relational component. The ideational component refers to an individual's personal identification with a particular group or category. The relational component refers to the actual connections between members of some group (Moody and White 2003:104).

Many living creatures are born with instincts. These preorganized and predetermined responses to external stimuli prepare an organism to act in ways that maximize its chances to survive in a place where survival is never guaranteed. When food-gathering, defense, or reproductive strategies are under the control of instincts, it means that creatures don't have to be smart in order to survive. They simply have to follow their instincts. Humans, however, lack instincts, so we need different ways to survive and develop. This is where social institutions become so important.

Social institutions are habitual or enduring patterns of human interaction, organized around important or central tasks in a society. Social institutions consist of shared knowledge (values and norms), groups, statuses, and roles, organized around fundamental social tasks, which have important social consequences. Families, schools, businesses, churches, synagogues, mosques, athletic teams, and political parties are all parts of institutions. As an individual matures in a society, he or she participates in more and more institutions and is transformed in the process. He or she will become a parent, a boss, a worker, a student, a teacher, a firefighter, a police officer, a son or daughter, a physician, a basketball player, or one of countless other things. Participation in institutions, of course, brings each of us in contact with others who are also participating in them. We are then able to cooperate with them by fitting our lines of behavior together into some relatively coordinated whole (Mark 2002:324). The groups that form in institutions and the relationships that take place there are the lifeblood of a society and a major determiner of what each individual can and will become.

Society and Social Control

While society is an objective fact, something that constrains and coerces (Durkheim 1938:3), that is not all it is. It is also something that gets inside each of us. The structure of society shapes the structure of individual consciousness, and we come to do, think, feel, and remember what we must do, think, feel, and remember from the standpoint of a particular society at a particular point in time. Society penetrates us as much as it envelops us, and our link to society is not so much established by conquest as by collusion (Berger 1963:121). Sometimes we are forcibly controlled, but most times we supervise ourselves and cooperate in our own regulation. We desire just that which society expects of us. We are made to *want* to obey the rules, at least most of them, most of the time. We want to play the parts that society has assigned to us. Society not only determines what we do and who we are but also what we cannot do or become (Berger 1963:93).

Social groups have many ways to control their members. Sometimes **social control** is external and coercive, close to raw power. We don't rob banks, even though that's where the money is, because we fear the sanction would be swift, certain, and most unpleasant. No society, however, can rely exclusively or even principally on coercive forms of social control. They would be too expensive and just too difficult and exhausting to use all the time. A far more important—and effective—mechanism to ensure that enough individuals conform often enough to a society's standards is socialization.

Socialization refers to the lifelong process of developing human abilities and learning the way of life of a society (Macionis 2001:115). It is in the context of socialization that each of us develops a self or personality while we internalize thoughts, feelings, and remembrances that are necessary for members of the groups to which we belong. While the things that we bring to the world—reflexes and drives, for example, or our upright posture or brain size—certainly help to customize our socialization experiences, it is our relationships to others in our lives that account for what we are. Of paramount importance is the influence that others have on our thoughts and feelings. In the early days of life, children are characterized by a high degree of egocentricity in which they are separate and apart, enclosed in their own point of view (Piaget 1932:26). However, day by day, week by week, month by month, and year by year, children are nudged away from their egocentricity as they mentally project themselves into the positions of others and learn to see the world through their eyes (Mead 1934).

Human development is inextricably tied up with the acquisition and mastery of language. A child's first words almost always refer either to concrete objects (e.g., a toy or pillow) or specific individuals (e.g., mother or father; brother or sister). Once children realize that things have names and that names are associated with objects, people, situations, and experiences, they learn new words at a rapid pace. All studies of language development show that at about eighteen months children experience a "naming explosion" during which they become interested in naming objects and people, and their vocabulary increases substantially (Lieberman 1991:145).

> . . . from the age of 18 months to six years, the child reaches a lexicon of 9,000-14,000 words at a clip of approximately nine words per day. (Hauser 1997:338)

Language was built upon physical gestures as a way to promote cohesion and solidarity within social groups (Massey 2002:9).

Symbols are conventional sounds (e.g., words) or gestures that stand for, or represent, something else, because two or more individuals agree to let that happen. The word "pizza" stands for a fast-food treat, and the word "frog" stands for a small amphibian. A child acquires meanings by observing and learning what particular sounds, words, or physical gestures will do in terms of how others respond to them. In time, these sounds, words, or physical gestures come to evoke in the child the same response that they have evoked in others.

> We are all heirs of symbolic forms that were passed from one generation to the next and from one group to another, forming a single unbroken tradition. We derive all our symbolic "traits" from this common pool and contribute to its promulgation. Being a part of this symbolic information lineage is in many respects a more diagnostic trait for "humanness" than any physical trait. (Deacon 1997:341)

A child can complete an act mentally and predict what is likely to happen because he or she has observed and learned what others have done. During peak or critical periods, a child may learn a great deal of new information about self and others; at other times, much less is learned. At the heart of the process of **symbolic interaction**, then, is the ability to take the role of others and look at the world—and one's own self—through their eyes (Mead 1934).

Because symbols can be invented—*are* invented—to describe anything that needs to be described, symbols are at the heart of humans' ability to respond flexibly and yet very precisely to different stimuli. Symbols make it possible to name and categorize the world and human experiences in ways that would be impossible without them. "Through vocabulary, syntax, and grammar, languages inevitably created categories of perception for time, objects, and events in the real world" (Massey 2002:9). You never have to meet a hungry shark face to face to know that it is an experience best avoided, because the details of a shark attack can be imagined, symbolized, and passed from individual to individual. Our symbols constitute the lens through which we interpret the world and that we use to relate to others and even to judge and evaluate ourselves. We construct our actions based on the anticipated consequences of those acts, taking account of others and using our definitions of situations.

Overintegrated and Oversocialized?

We may have given you the impression that human beings are quite pliable, becoming whatever they are supposed to become during the process of socialization. This is true up to a point, but the story is just beginning. Humans are not completely at the mercy of social expectations and institutional pressures. Society is neither an oppressive prison system nor some malevolent puppet stage (Berger 1963). It is a bounded area populated by people who act both consciously and self-consciously. This does not mean that humans are totally free from the constraints imposed by the physical world (e.g., gravity), the social world (e.g., the law of the land, custom, role expectations), or the internal demands and drives of individual biology (e.g., hunger, thirst, sexuality). What it does mean, however, is that humans are neither prisoners nor puppets, and they have a range of options from which to choosein deciding how to lead their lives.

> . . . [humans] have options—of playing their parts enthusiastically or sullenly, of playing with inner conviction or with "distance," and, sometimes, of refusing to play at all. . . . Social reality now seems to be precariously perched on the cooperation of many individual actors—or perhaps a better simile [sic] would be that of acrobats engaged in perilous balancing acts, holding up between them the swaying structure of the social world. (Berger 1963:138)

If *we* create groups, organizations, institutions, and societies, then *we* can also change them. We are neither totally nor rigidly determined by the groups to which we belong. While humans are socialized, they are not entirely social (Wrong 1961). Socialization does not guarantee that we will always do what we are expected to do, and its effects can be modified or altered. Socialization can be, and often is, a conflictual process that can transform children who once were happy and spontaneous into tense and emotionally mutilated adults (Bell 1999:289).

In all likelihood, the first human groups were loose-knit and fluid, inclined toward low-density networks, low sociality, and strong individualism (Maryanski and Turner 1992:13). Cultural components (e.g., values, norms, and symbols) and social institutions developed that worked together to produce cohesive human social connections or bonds. In other words, sociocultural evolution created "social cages" in the form of social groups and institutions that imposed constraints upon our basic biological propensities toward individualism and autonomy (Maryanski and Turner 1992:165-6). Millions of years of evolution have created humans who have a remarkable capacity for cognitive and rational behavior. We also have intricate emotional lives.

> Emotionality remains a strong and independent force in human affairs, influencing perceptions, coloring memories, binding people together through attraction, keeping them apart through hatred, and regulating their behavior through guilt, shame, and pride. (Massey 2002:20)

A great deal of overlap exists in emotions and cognitions, and it is impossible to separate them from our experiences in groups. Thinking and emotion are not opposite processes. Rather they are separate names for parts of a continuous psychosocial process (Barbalet 1998:45). Emotions change when meanings change, and meanings are socially constructed and embedded in relationships. No human experience can be only emotional, and no emotional experience can be strictly physiological (Lindesmith, Strauss, and Denzin 1999:132).

Another unique difference between humans and other living creatures that comes from human symbolic abilities is our ability to **role play** and to manage impressions for the sake of others. Each of us, for a good portion of each and every day, tries to present a favorable image of self to others (Goffman 1959). We may want to be thought of as trustworthy, loyal, helpful, friendly, courteous, kind, obedient, cheerful, thrifty, brave, clean, and reverent, and we do what we can to convince others that we embody these traits. We manipulate impressions so that others will be convinced that we really are what we claim to be. Deception, fabrication, and impression management are central features of this process. You must be able to fool some of the people most of the time, and they you, or society will become less and less manageable. These mutual improvisations show us just how negotiated and fabricated—and therefore fragile—our social order really is. Humans have a great deal of influence over how they act and what they are—even how they are treated by others. We make and remake our own roles in many ways (Turner 1962:21-2).

The Social Construction of Reality
Dialectical Relationships

All creatures from the large to the small help to create the environments within which they live, and these creatures are then, in turn, transformed by their relationship to the environment and to other living creatures. Biology alone does not determine behavior (Miller and Costello 2001:597). What happens is that a living organism's range of responses is influenced by what it brings to the world, which includes elements of heredity and personal identity (Piliavin and Lepore 1995:21).

> Just as there is no organism without an environment, there is no environment without an organism. Organisms do not experience environments. They create them. They construct their own environments out of the bits and pieces of the physical and biological world and they do so by their own activities. (Lewontin 1991:109)

Features of the world are made relevant to organisms by what these creatures do and by what they are. Living organisms make, modify, or even destroy features of the external world by their own activities (Lewontin, Rose, and Kamin 1984:273). In this **dialectical relationship** between organism and environment, both are changed in the process. Even the so-called law of gravity is really no law; it, too, depends on characteristics of an organism and its relationship to the external world.

> A bacterium living in liquid does not feel gravity because it is so small and its buoyant properties free it from what is essentially a very weak force. But the size of a bacterium is a consequence of its genes, and so it is the genetic difference between us and bacteria that determines whether the force of gravitation is relevant to us. (Lewontin 1991:117)

The relevance of the physical facts of nature to an organism is always a consequence of the nature of the organism itself.

One way that humans make their world is by selectively perceiving the stimuli to which they will respond. We don't experience the world exactly as it is but rather how we are prepared to perceive it (Kumbasar, Romney, and Batchelder 1994). For example, if you're hungry, the outside world isn't to you what it would be if you were stuffed from eating a big meal. Just because two individuals are sharing what seems to be the same experience, it does not mean that they are responding in the same way. They may actually be receiving different sensory information, and their brains may be processing the information in different ways. Just as individuals perceive the world differently if they are hungry rather than full, so do people from different groups and societies. They may have different sensory experiences, partly because their sensory apparatus is programmed differently, and partly because cultural differences allow certain kinds of information to filter through and other kinds to be screened out (Hall 2003:52). The Solomon Islanders can recognize nine types of coconut, and Eskimos can recognize over thirty kinds of snow. Americans can recognize neither nine coconuts nor over thirty kinds of snow, principally because their culture does not prepare their sensory apparatus for this kind of experience.

Humans also construct their world through collective intentionality. This does not simply mean that we do things together. What this means is that we share beliefs, desires, and goals that make it possible for us to do things together that we could never do alone. "The crucial element in collective intentionality is a sense of doing (wanting, believing, etc.) something together, and the individual intentionality that each person has is derived *from* the collective intentionality that they share" (Searle 1995:24-5). It is collective intentionality that allows us to overcome, at least in part, the determinism of both biology and the physical environment. No individual human being could fly by flapping his or her arms, nor could a group of human beings—even if it numbered in the millions—fly even if all its members flapped their arms at the same time (Lewontin 1991:121; Lewontin, Rose, and Kamin 1984:286). However, we can get airborne by using planes flown by pilots with the assistance of flight attendants. We may not be able to leap over buildings in a single bound, but we can make elevators and escalators to get to the top so that jumping will be unnecessary. We may not be able to control the elements, but we can plan for them and build structures that will make that control unnecessary. We may not like the kind of nose, hairline, or body shape that we inherited from our parents, but through surgery, exercise, and diet, we can alter those features of our personal appearance. Collective intentionality and the social organization based on it makes it possible for us to be the kind of people who can do or be practically anything we want.

Habitualization, Institutionalization, and Social Reality

Social order is a human product and an ongoing human production (Berger and Luckmann 1966:52). It will cease to exist without sufficient human interest and activity to produce it (Sarbin and Kitsuse 1994:2). Much of what humans do becomes habitual and subject to a certain degree of institutionalization so that it can be repeated with a minimum of effort (Berger and Luckmann 1966:53). Humans must find food to eat, water to drink, and companions with whom to live; they must socialize their children; they must learn skills and knowledge from one another; and they must deal with death (their own and that of others). Once human relationships and activities become patterned, it is likely that they will occur again and again in what seems a very natural, almost automatic, way. The institutionalization of human relationships makes it unnecessary for individuals to define each new situation all over again and to figure out new ways of acting appropriate to each new situation. Who would want to reinvent the wheel every day, especially if it is unnecessary?

Institutions evolve over time, and they control human conduct by channeling it in some directions rather than others (Berger and Luckmann 1966:54-5). Teachers *could* do things differently in a class from what they ordinarily do. They could enter the room and sleep on the floor, brush their teeth, eat a bowl of cereal, work a crossword puzzle, fix the chain on a bicycle, iron a shirt, or mop the floor. Humans can do all these things. However, none of these is likely to occur in a classroom. Institutions are created by people acting together—they cannot be created instantaneously—but they then *seem* to be something other than a human creation. Institutional practices, even new ones, are usually justified by an appeal to history and tradition, making them look more natural and normal than they really are (Hobsbawm 1983:12). Once social forms are created, however, they resist further efforts to transform them (Berger and Luckmann 1966; Soeffner 1997).

It is wrong to think that institutions are cast in stone and uniformly supported and followed by everyone in a society. Some groups have more power to advance their interests and preferences in a society's culture and institutions than do other groups. Powerful people try to convince everyone else that what the powerful have created is actually an objective, inevitable fact of life (Martin 2002:885-86). Over time, the interests of the few may become the customs of the many. However, no power is absolute. Members of a society show different degrees of support for their institutions, and some groups will try to create new institutions, or modify old ones, to suit their needs. In some cases, these alternate institutional forms will attain their own claims to moral validity, and they may be added to the existing institutional structure or even supplant older institutional forms (Merton 1968:176). Humans can and do create a social world that they then experience as something other than a human construction (Berger and Luckmann 1966:61).

Ideologies and Contested Spaces

Ideas are almost always created by individuals or groups to benefit themselves, making them **ideologies** (Merton 1968:546-548). One of the best ways for individuals to get ideas they support adopted by others is to get them into the culture of the group as quickly as possible, thus institutionalizing them. The ability to control institutions and to create cultural knowledge increases the likelihood that what are actually the values of the few will become the customs of the many. Ideologies can worm themselves into the lives of people who do not recognize that their way of life has been fashioned in the interest of someone other than themselves. It is even possible for groups to be "taken in" or seduced by their own ideologies until they come to believe their own propaganda. If blue-eyed kids are told often enough that they are best, it will be easier for them to come to believe it. Liars know that they are lying, but ideologues do not recognize just how distorted or self-serving their ideas are (Berger 1963:112). Those groups that benefit most from the status quo are probably not the most objective and informed about what is really happening in a society.

Ideologies are—or can be—fragile things, and crises of legitimacy regularly occur. What were once viewed as natural, normal, or self-evident truths can come to be seen as arbitrary rationalizations (Berger 1995). The discredited view that women are "naturally" suited to housework and child care is now seen as ideological claptrap and a belief system that was created by men in order to benefit themselves. Members from different social worlds often collide with each other in particular locations or sites in a society (Clarke 1998).

> We define "contested spaces" as geographic locations where conflicts in the form of opposition, confrontation, subversion, and/or resistance engage actors whose social positions are defined by differential control of resources and access to power. . . . Spaces are contested precisely because they concretize the fundamental and recurring, but otherwise unexamined, ideological, and social frameworks that structure practice. (Low and Lawrence-Zùñiga 2003:18)

When controversies and conflicts occur over cultural knowledge, one group's ideological control is challenged. This sets the foundation for the institutionalization of new cultural understandings and social practices (Miller and Hoffmann 1999).

Science and Sociology

Sociologists' commitment to understand the human experience through the methods of science is at the foundation of sociology's many successes. Sociology without science would just look like common sense; it would look like it is doing little more than elaborating the obvious or cataloguing what everyone already knows. While science is a set of procedures, it is more than that. It is a set of understandings or values that scientists share with one another regardless of their discipline.

> Such values are humility before the immense richness of the world one is investigating, an effacement of self in the search for understanding, honesty and precision in method, respect for findings honestly arrived at, patience and a willingness to be proven wrong and to revise one's theories, and, last but not least, the community of other individuals sharing these values. (Berger 1963:166)

The core value can be called "scientific integrity." This is a commitment to develop theories or explanations that are logical and based on empirical research, uncontaminated either by political pressures or personal prejudices. By following the strict rules and procedures of the scientific method—to be empirical, rational, honest, precise, and objective—and then by publicizing information on both procedures and findings to others in the scientific community, sociologists maximize the likelihood that their explanations of the social world will actually fit the facts.

The New Know-Nothings

More and more, scientific findings about human behavior and, by implication, human nature are met with resistance and sometimes outright attack. Some of this skepticism regarding scientific findings is healthy and beneficial. However, what is occurring more and more is that various groups have organized attacks on research projects (or simply *proposed* research projects) because they believe they could be hurt by any of the findings that *might* emerge from the study. These groups are often articulate, well-connected, and influential. They have been able to interfere with, and sometimes stop entirely, research projects that could have made substantial contributions to our understanding of human experience (Hunt 1999:xi). These "new know-nothings," as Hunt (1999) calls them, are like the proverbial ostrich with its head in the sand; they don't want to know any more than they already know. They certainly do not want to know anything that might hurt their interests, values, or positions in a society.

> Today's "New Know-Nothings," as I have called them, dogmatically assert that certain kinds of new knowledge will have dire consequences or that the social costs of the knowledge will greatly outweigh the possible benefits, but their predictions are based on political and religious beliefs, not on empirical evidence. While they have a right to their beliefs, they do not have a right to force scientists to abstain from seeking knowledge that may challenge those beliefs. (Hunt 1999:344)

Advocacy groups are probably doing more harm than good in their efforts to suppress both proposed research and research findings that have already been discovered only because they find them potentially damaging to their interests (Hunt 1999:24-25). The only way that we can advance our understanding of the human condition is through free and open inquiry. Censorship of research, especially before it is even started, is far more damaging to us than is the possibility that scientific research will be used to damage the reputation of members of some particular group (Halpern 1994). While politics, religion, and philosophy are important to us in many ways, it is social science that offers us the best chance to understand ourselves and the world within which we live (Hunt 1999:19).

The Know-It-Alls

Just as the "new know-nothings" pose a threat to anyone who values freedom of speech and freedom of research—and chronic curiosity—we can identify another threat to science. This threat is posed by the "know-it-alls," those individuals who claim far more for their scientific findings than is warranted from the data. Social scientific knowledge is far from perfect knowledge. Things can and do go wrong in research projects, even well-meaning and well-designed ones (Collins and Pinch 1998). Variables may be defined incorrectly, empirical indicators may be invalid and unreliable, theories may be improperly applied, hypotheses may be wrongly deduced, data may be poorly collected or incorrectly analyzed, and results may be just plain wrong. The direction of causality may be unknown, and the findings may be unrepresentative. It is even possible for fraud to occur where the results are fudged by unscrupulous or unethical researchers.

Every science has a certain degree of knowability (Lewontin 2000:254). A social science like sociology cannot be transformed into a natural science like physics or biology simply by using similar methods of data collection and analysis. Humans are capable of a wide range of behaviors, from those that are totally self-conscious and reflexive, to those that are totally irrational and mysterious, even to individuals themselves. Sociologists must be able to deal with—and construct theories that make sense of—the ambiguity and disorder of social life (Perrow 1981:2). Nothing is wrong with trying to understand as much as we can about human experience and social relationships, but it is possible that some of the happenings in the social world will never be fully explained. Social scientists hurt themselves and set their disciplines up for criticism if they claim a level of knowledge and understanding that they do not have.

Simplicity in theories, ironically enough, may be the best way to make sense of the complexities of social life (Smith-Lovin 2000:302). After all, a **theory** is just a concise and systematic explanation that makes sense of relationships in ways that fit our observations of how things really work. Good theories allow us to see things that we had not seen before (or see familiar events in a new or different light), and they allow us to explain what we see in a direct and rational way. Theories must be crafted well enough that simple and direct statements of relationships can be deduced from them **(hypotheses)** and compared against observations of the real world. Theories must be clear enough that it can be determined when, or if, they are wrong.

Stalking the Sociological Imagination

Sociology has not only been attacked by the "new know-nothings" and plagued by the "know-it-alls." It has also been attacked by individuals who view its built-in potential for criticism and skepticism as disruptive.

> . . . sociological understanding is always potentially dangerous to the
> minds of policemen and other guardians of public order, since it will
> always tend to relativize the claim to absolute rightness upon which such
> minds like to rest. (Berger 1963:48)

Some U.S. sociologists experienced both personal and professional setbacks because of their politically incorrect views of U.S. society. They were vexed by its high levels of social inequality, racism, and oppressive social control. Edward A. Ross, for example, was once dismissed from his teaching position at Stanford University, because his political views were considered too radical (Eisenstadt 1976:40). He was fearful that powerful groups could use the forces of social control to get what they wanted. Edwin H. Sutherland, a prominent and influential U.S. criminologist, was pressured to behave (or at least write) in more politically correct ways. His study of white-collar crime revealed that major U.S. corporations were responsible for perpetuating harmful acts against an unsuspecting public. His plan to publish the names of the offending companies and to brand them as persistent criminals made administrators at his university nervous. They feared that donations to the university from these businesses could be lost as a result of Sutherland's negative publicity (Geis and Goff 1983). He capitulated to the pressure and removed the names of the offending companies from the published work (Sutherland

1949). (It was not until decades later that an uncut version of his work was published that revealed the names of the companies [Sutherland 1983].) These are not isolated cases. The entire discipline of sociology was attacked by powerful adversaries in the United States who seemed to think that anyone who was not flagrantly supportive of the status quo was a traitor.

Many prominent sociologists came under the surveillance of the Federal Bureau of Investigation for what J. Edgar Hoover, its director from 1924 until 1972, defined as radical or unAmerican activities (Keen 1999:6-8). In some cases, individuals gleefully snitched on their colleagues to the FBI. In other cases, the FBI became suspicious about a particular sociologist, and agents instigated their own investigation by collecting as much information as they could from fellow sociologists about his or her patriotism and loyalty. While loss of jobs did not usually occur—most of the targeted individuals had enough clout and prominence to survive an FBI investigation—the investigations still had a damaging effect. They created embarrassment, anxiety, worry, and fear among some of the brightest and the best that sociology has had to offer. Some prominent African American sociologists (e.g., W.E.B. Du Bois and E. Franklin Frazier), principally because they were outspoken in their condemnation of the racist policies and discriminatory practices of the United States, were viewed as communist sympathizers and conspirators. They were the target of intrusive background checks, defined as security risks, and disallowed to leave the country (e.g., they were not able to get passports). Other prominent sociologists were also defined as security risks and investigated and harassed. Sometimes rumor or innuendo was all that was needed to get an individual singled out for attention by the FBI and labeled as unAmerican. At other times, the spark that initiated an investigation was nothing more than an expressed interest in Russia or Cuba, or simply an affiliation, no matter how slight, with an organization that was viewed as a communist front by the FBI. Even the ability to speak Russian or the wish to travel abroad was suspect. The FBI declared war on both the discipline of sociology and sociologists, administered by a tyrannical and racist director, under cover of a fight against world communism (Keen 1999:203). The activities of FBI agents stifled dissent, subverted the principles of a democratic society, and nudged mainstream sociology—at least temporarily—more in the direction of uncritical support of the status quo (Keen 1999:207). The discipline, however, survived quite well, and it provided scientific understandings of both human society and human experience.

Conclusion

The sociological imagination can help us understand the interconnections between public issues of social structure and private troubles of individuals. This imagination maintains a vivid awareness of the relationship between the wider society and personal experience. It ties together history, biography, and society to provide rational and scientific explanations of human experience. We hope this introductory chapter has given you enough information about societies, social relationships, and human beings that you are inclined to accept our invitation to learn more about collective experiences and come to possess a sociological imagination for yourself.

Human experience can really only be thoroughly understood by locating or contextualizing it in a particular place and time. People construct their actions together, taking account of one another, using their definitions of situations. We come to be what we must be from the standpoint of a society. Every group, in every institution, in every society contains social pressures that work together to nudge individuals in some directions rather than in others. In the lifelong process of socialization, humans acquire selves and minds. In this way, societies interpenetrate our personal, subjective experiences, while they influence our relationships to others. Human nature, however, is broad and constantly changing because of the impact of social relationships on individual biography. A society is both an objective fact as well as something that gets inside of each individual. A society penetrates and envelops humans as they live out their lives together.

Sociological consciousness is characterized by four distinctive motifs or themes. The debunking motif means that things are not always what they seem. It is necessary to look behind the masks that people use to hide their actions, intentions, and identities. The unrespectability motif means that sociologists must play the role of the stranger or outsider to be able to question what other people take for granted. The relativizing motif means that sociologists know that customs and ideas reflect particular places and times and are specific to them. What is correct and proper in one place and time will be incorrect and improper at some other place and time. The cosmopolitan motif means that sociologists view the whole world as their laboratory, and they must be familiar with the experiences of people who live in different lands and/or times. Sociology's skeptical or contrarian view is responsible for many of its insights and intellectual excitement.

Humans, like all other creatures, do not simply live in the world. They make a world through their activities. The relevance of the physical facts of nature is always a consequence of the nature of the organism itself. By filtering some information in and screening some out, humans selectively perceive the world within which they live and then shape it. Their collective intentionality makes it possible for humans to share objectives and goals, which transforms individual intentions into social forces as they act together. Collective intentionality makes it possible for us to be or do almost anything we want. Humans create social institutions, which then channel relationships in certain directions rather than others. This guarantees that important social activities—reproduction, socialization, food-gathering, protection—are accomplished by the members of a society. Once human relationships and activities become patterned, it is likely that they will occur again and again with a minimum of effort. However, institutions change over time, and they shape human relationships into relatively stable patterns.

The skepticism of sociology and its commitment to the methods of science have upset powerful individuals in the United States, and they have stalked the sociological imagination and harassed prominent sociologists. Some activist groups have tried to stop important research projects or suppress the findings of those they could not stop. Why? They thought they would be hurt by sociologists' findings. Other groups have been unnerved by sociological findings, and they tried to stop sociologists from fulfilling their obligation to provide scientific knowledge about the workings of societies and groups. The FBI's war on both sociology and sociologists was administered by a tyrannical director under the cover of a fight against communism. Mainstream sociology was nudged temporarily in the direction of supporting the status quo and its constellation of social institutions and groups rather than debunking and explaining them. The discipline, however, survived quite well, and it continues to provide scientific understandings of human societies and groups.

References

Adams, Bert and R.A. Sydie. 2002. *Classical Sociological Theory*. Thousand Oaks, CA: Pine Forge Press.

Ashley, David and David Michael Orenstein. 2001. *Sociological Theory: Classic Statements*, 5th edition. Boston, MA: Allyn and Bacon.

Barbalet, J. M. 1998. *Emotion, Social Theory, and Social Structure: A Macrosociological Approach*. Cambridge, UK: Cambridge University Press.

Bell, Inge. 1999. "Buddhist Sociology: Some Thoughts on The Convergence of Sociology and The Eastern Paths Of Liberation." Pp. 287-300 in *This Book Is Not Required: An Emotional Survival Manual for Students*, revised edition, edited by Inge Bell and Bernard McGrane. Thousand Oaks, CA: Pine Forge.

Berger, Bennett. 1995. *An Essay on Culture: Symbolic Structure and Social Structure*. Berkeley, CA: University of California Press.

Berger, Peter. 1963. *Invitation to Sociology: A Humanistic Perspective*. Garden City, NY: Anchor/Doubleday.

Berger, Peter and Thomas Luckmann. 1966. *The Social Construction of Reality*. Garden City, NY: Doubleday.

Clarke, Adele. 1998. *Disciplining Reproduction: Modernity, American Life Science, and "the Problems of Sex."* Berkeley, CA: University of California Press.

Collins, Harry and Trevor Pinch. *The Golem at Large: What You Should Know About Technology*. Cambridge: Cambridge University Press.

Davis, Kingsley. 1937. "The Sociology of Prostitution." *American Sociological Review* 2:744-55.

Deacon, Terrence. 1997. *The Symbolic Species: The Co-Evolution of Language and the Brain*. New York: W. W. Norton and Company.

Douglas, Jack, Paul Rasmussen, and Carol Flanagan. 1977. *The Nude Beach*. Beverly Hills, CA: Sage.

Durkheim, Emile. 1938. *The Rules of Sociological Method*, 8th edition, translated by Sarah Solovay and John Mueller and edited by George Catlin. New York: Free Press.

Eisenstadt, S. N., with M. Curelaru. 1976. *The Form of Sociology—Paradigms and Crises*. New York: John Wiley and Sons.

Forsyth, Craig. 1992. "Parade Strippers: A Note on Being Naked in Public." *Deviant Behavior* 13:391-403.

Geis, Gilbert and C. Goff. 1983. "Introduction." Pp. ix-xxxiii in E. H. Sutherland, *White Collar Crime: The Uncut Version*. New Haven, CT: Yale University Press.

Gerth, Hans and C. Wright Mills. 1953. *Character and Social Structure: The Psychology of Social Institutions*. New York: Harcourt, Brace and World.

Goffman, Erving. 1959. *The Presentation of Self in Everyday Life*. Garden City, NY: Doubleday Anchor.

Hall, Edward. 2003. "Proxemics." Pp. 51-73 in *The Anthropology of Space and Place: Locating Culture*, edited by Setha Low and Denise Lawrence- Zùñiga. Malden, MA: Blackwell.

Halpern, Diane. 1994. "Stereotypes, Science, Censorship, and the Study of Sex Differences." *Feminism and Psychology* 4:523-30.

Hauser, Marc. 1997. *The Evolution of Communication*. Cambridge, MA: MIT Press.

Hinkle, Jr., Roscoe, and Gisela Hinkle. 1954. *The Development of Modern Sociology: Its Nature and Growth in the United States*. New York: Random House.

Hobsbawm, Eric. 1983. *The Invention of Tradition*. Cambridge: Cambridge University Press.

Hunt, Morton. 1999. *The New Know-Nothings: The Political Foes of the Scientific Study of Human Nature*. New Brunswick, NJ: Transaction.

Janszen, Karen. 1981. "Meat of Life." Pp. 366-371 in *The Social World*, edited by Ian Robertson. New York, NY: Worth.

Keen, Mike. 1999. *Stalking the Sociological Imagination: J. Edgar Hoover's FBI Surveillance of American Sociology*. Westport, CT: Greenwood Press.

Kumbasar, Ece, A. Kimball Romney, and William Batchelder. 1994. "Systematic Biases in Social Perception." *American Journal of Sociology* 100:477-505.

Lewontin, Richard. 1991. *Biology as Ideology: The Doctrine of DNA*. New York: HarperPerennial.

_____. 2000. *It Ain't Necessarily So: The Dream of the Human Genome and Other Illusions*. New York, NY: New York Review Books.

Lewontin, Richard, Steven Rose, and Leon Kamin. 1984. *Not in Our Genes: Biology, Ideology, and Human Nature*. New York: Pantheon.

Lieberman, Philip. 1991. *Uniquely Human: The Evolution of Speech, Thought, and Selfless Behavior*. Cambridge, MA: Harvard University Press.

Lindesmith, Alfred, Anselm Strauss, and Norman Denzin. 1999. *Social Psychology*, 8th edition. Thousand Oaks, CA: Sage.

Low, Setha and Denise Lawrence-Zùñiga. 2003. "Locating Culture." Pp. 1-47 in *The Anthropology of Space and Place: Locating Culture*, edited by Setha Low and Denise Lawrence-Zùñiga. Malden, MA: Blackwell.

Macionis, John. 2001. *Sociology*, 8th edition. Annotated Instructor's Edition. Upper Saddle River, NJ: Prentice-Hall.

Mark, Noah. 2002. "Cultural Transmission, Disproportionate Prior Exposure, and the Evolution of Cooperation." *American Sociological Review* 67:323-344.

Martin, John Levi. 2002. "Power, Authority, and the Constraint of Belief Systems." *American Journal of Sociology* 107:861-904

Martindale, Don. 1960. *The Nature and Types of Sociological Theory*. Boston, MA: Houghton Mifflin.

Maryanski, Alexandra and Jonathan Turner. 1992. *The Social Cage: Human Nature and the Evolution of Society*. Stanford, CA: Stanford University Press.

Massey, Douglas. 2002. "A Brief History of Human Society: The Origin and Role of Emotion in Social Life: 2001 Presidential Address." *American Sociological Review* 67: 1-29.

Mead, George Herbert. 1934. *Mind, Self and Society*. Chicago, IL: University of Chicago Press.

Merton, Robert. 1968. *Social Theory and Social Structure*, enlarged edition. New York: Free Press.

Miller, Alan and John Hoffmann. 1999. "The Growing Divisiveness: Culture Wars or a War of Words?" *Social Forces* 78:721-52.

Miller, Eleanor and Carrie Yang Costello. 2001. "The Limits of Biological Determinism." *American Sociological Review* 66:592-598.

Mills, C. Wright. 1943. "The Professional Ideology of Social Pathologists." *American Journal of Sociology* 49:165-80.

_____. 1959. *The Sociological Imagination*. New York: Oxford University Press.

Moody, James and Douglas White. 2003. "Structural Cohesion and Embeddedness: A Hierarchical Concept of Social Groups." *American Sociological Review* 68:103-127.

Morgan, Gordon. 1997. *Toward an American Sociology: Questioning the European Construct*. Westport, CT: Praeger.

Nisbet, Robert. 1966. *The Sociological Tradition*. New York: Basic Books.

Perrow, Charles. 1981. "Disintegrating Social Sciences." *New York University Education Quarterly* 12:2-9.

Phillips, Bernard, Harold Kincaid, and Thomas Scheff. 2002. *Toward a Sociological Imagination: Bridging Specialized Fields*. Lanham, MD: University Press of America.

Piaget, Jean. 1932. *The Moral Judgment of the Child*, with the assistance of seven collaborators. Translated by Marjorie Gabain. New York: Harcourt, Brace and Company.

Piliavin, Jane Allyn and Paul Lepore. 1995. "Biology and Social Psychology: Beyond Nature versus Nurture." Pp. 9-40 in *Sociological Perspectives on Social Psychology*, edited by Karen Cook, Gary Alan Fine, and James House. Boston, MA: Allyn and Bacon.

Portes, Alejandro. 2000. "The Hidden Abode: Sociology as Analysis of the Unexpected." 1999 Presidential Address. *American Sociological Review* 65:1-18.

Reiman, Jeffrey. 2001. *The Rich Get Richer and the Poor Get Prison: Ideology, Class, and Criminal Justice*, 6th edition. Boston, MA: Allyn and Bacon.

Ritzer, George. 2000. *Sociological Theory*, 5th edition. New York: McGraw-Hill.

Sarbin, Theodore and John Kitsuse. 1994. "A Prologue to *Constructing the Social*." Pp. 1-18 in *Constructing the Social*, edited by T. Sarbin and J. Kitsuse. Thousand Oaks, CA: Sage.

Searle, John. 1995. *The Construction of Social Reality*. New York, NY: Free Press.

Shrum, Wesley and John Kilburn. 1996. "Ritual Disrobement at Mardi Gras: Ceremonial Exchange and Moral Order." *Social Forces* 72:423-458.

Smith-Lovin, Lynn. 1999. "Core Concepts and Common Ground: The Relational Basis of Our Discipline," Presidential address given April 9, 1999, at the Southern Sociological Society Meetings in Nashville, Tennessee. *Social Forces* 78:1-23.

Soeffner, Hans-Georg. 1997. *The Order of Rituals: The Interpretation of Everyday Life*, translated by Mara Luckman. New Brunswick, NJ: Transaction Publishers.

Sutherland, Edwin H. 1949. *White Collar Crime*. New York: Dryden.

_____. 1983. *White Collar Crime: The Uncut Version*. New Have, CT: Yale University Press.

Turner, Ralph. 1962. "Role-Taking: Process versus Conformity." Pp. 20-40 in *Human Behavior and Social Processes: An Interactionist Approach*, edited by Arnold Rose. Boston: Houghton Mifflin.

Wrong, Dennis. 1961. "The Oversocialized Conception of Man in Modern Sociology."

American Sociological Review 26:183-93.

Weber, Max. 1968. *Economy and Society: An Outline of Interpretive Sociology, Volume III*, edited by Guenther Roth and Claus Wittich. New York: Bedminster Press.

Chapter Two:
The Dialectic of Humans and Society— Creating that Which Creates Us

The Internal Relationships between Society and the Individual

Thinking Dialectically in Sociology

Social Facts and Social Structure

Thinking Dialectically in Sociology

> The Internal Relationship between History, Social Structure and
> > Sociological Knowledge
>
> The Dialectic of History, Structure, and the Sociological Imagination
>
> The Internal Relationship between Materialism and Idealism
>
> The Dialectic of Materialism, Idealism, and the Sociological Imagination:
> > Entertainment Industries
> >
> > Sex, Violence, and Television: Idealism versus Materialism
> >
> > The Rise of Pop Music: Idealism and Materialism

Marx and Engels: The Dialectic of Society and the Individual

> The Individual and Material Reality
>
> The Individual and History
>
> The Individual in Capitalism
> > Ideology and the Camera Obscura

C.W. Mills and the Sociological Imagination

> Putting the Sociological Imagination to Work:
> > History, Social Structure, and the Rise of Racism

Berger and Luckmann: The Social Construction of Reality

The Social Construction of Gender

> Becoming Male and Female

Chapter Two: The Dialectic of Humans and Society—
Creating that Which Creates Us
The Internal Relationships between Society and the Individual
Thinking Dialectically in Sociology

In many ways our experience of the world is a deeply personal affair, something guarded so jealously that it becomes something rarely reflected upon: *why do I experience the world just as I do?* In thinking about this question, we often lack the tools to understand the **interconnectedness** our experience has with wider human dramas. A moment's reflection reveals a truism that often remains unthought: our sense-of-self is reliant on our interaction with others and the larger social world.

> [T]he individual is not separable from the human whole, but a living member of it, deriving his life from the whole through social and heredi-tary transmission as truly as if men were literally one body. . .A separate individual is an abstraction unknown to experience, and so likewise is society when regarded as something apart from individuals. The real thing is Human Life, which may be considered either in an individual aspect or in a social, that is to say a general, aspect; but is always, as a matter of fact, both individual and general. In other words, "society" and "individuals" do not denote separate phenomena, but are simply collective and distributive aspects of the same thing. (Cooley 1964:35-37)

It is for such reasons that sociologists hold that our individual experience of the world is dependent on our membership in social groups. Individuals' experiences teach them the meaning of realities appropriate to their cultural context.

Within modern society's media-drenched culture, citizens can be made bored quickly when things are no longer entertaining, while Arctic peoples' lives are more often scheduled by weather, agricultural cycles, and cultural events. In modern society, one is free to contemplate things such as philosophy, art, science, sport, leisure and/or grow spoiled and fat. In a nomadic society, one is forced into matters of daily practicality where the search for food is the most important knowledge and activity that guides daily considerations. America's culture of rampant **individualism** and relatively open cultural spaces brings Americans an experience of personal body-space that differs radically from those in Central America or Tokyo, where people are more comfortable standing closer to one another. Within America, where bathing is a daily cultural expectation, the smell of a "normal" human being is actually no smell at all, quite a peculiar standard by world-historical norms.

Social Facts and Social Structure

Assumptions about social life and our interpretations of others are deeply sociological affairs. Whether individuals are apt to see this or not, much of human perception is shaped by **social facts** that are *external to* and *coercive of* the individual (Durkheim 1982:50-51). Social facts are external in the sense that they exist outside of individuals and function independently of human will. They are coercive in the sense that they compel individuals to perform behaviors lest they suffer social penalties for failing to adhere to prescribed social norms. Humans are creative thinkers but are also dependent on social conditioning in order to acquire and cultivate the tools that make thought possible. We learn our society's language and think in its terms. If we ignore the standards of economic laws and sexual propriety of our **culture**, we subject ourselves to punishments that range from ostracism to incarceration. Through socialization, a culture's standards are reproduced as individuals learn "the shared understandings that people use to coordinate their activities" (Becker 1982:517).

Whether it be language, customs, religion, food, or what have you, people are socialized into a set of **norms** and this often sets the framework for their tastes, desires, aspirations, vocations, and personal moralities. Norms are cultural rules for acting, thinking, feeling, and remembering. These define the range of behavior that is allowed or not allowed. For example, money developed as a mode of facilitating economic exchanges. In modern society, the investment of money for the purpose of expanding its value becomes the ultimate goal of the economic system. Over time, the primary goal of the entire political-economic system is increasing money, the magnitude of this abstract symbol of value. In fact, we are learning more and more that this goal can be pursued to the point that it threatens the health of the basic ecological conditions upon which the production and exchange of goods and services is made possible (Foster 1995, 2002). In viewing a society where human sacrifice was practiced, say the Incas, a typical modern response might be, "What were *they* thinking? Certainly we are more rational and sane, right?" However, to a people 1000 years from now, our failure to curb our dependence on fossil fuel, our perpetual appeal to war, or our lackluster response to global warming will look equally irrational. The claim that we need to balance the needs of cleaning up the environment with "business friendly" solutions will appear tantamount to idol worship and human sacrifice.

For its unit of analysis, sociology prioritizes facts that are larger than, and exist prior to, the personal life of the individual. It often appears to newcomers that sociology claims all aspects of reality in the world are the product of sociological variables. Sociologists, however, do not claim only sociological realities exist and readily admit up front that there are multiple layers of reality, not all of which are the product of social facts. The power and effect of sociological processes themselves are variable, and their causal properties and relationships cannot be determined with a high degree of precision and predictability. Humans, unlike inanimate matter, have a will, act on their opinions, and reflect on those actions. This is so even if those opinions and actions have been shaped by external forces. Thus, it is not this will of the individual in the abstract that interests sociologists, but rather those phenomena in human life that are the product or indication of **supra-individual** social forces.

34

A supra-individual phenomenon is a patterned set of human relationships or collective actions that cannot be reduced to the level of the individual in the abstract. The central supra-individual concept sociologists work with is the idea of **social structure**. What is a social structure? This is an institutionalized and patterned set of practices backed by rules, law, custom, and/or the functioning of other forms of social organization. Things that sociologists conceive as social structures might include an economic system that provides goods and services, a language that facilitates communication, norms that regulate the interaction between individuals, a system of education that teaches the basics of math, language, and history, a male-to-female ratio that shapes the market for marriage partners, forms of familial organization that provide early childhood socialization, and the distribution of wealth and political power that shapes other social institutions. The concept of social structure is meant to capture in thought a collection of structures comprising a relatively coherent system. By extension, the social structure of the United States can be said to be comprised of various **sub-structures**, including linguistic traditions, relations of power such as patriarchy and/or the class system, the educational apparatus, the mass media, the industrial system and its class structure, the institutions of state, the methods of dealing with health, illness, and death. Such social structures are relatively stable over a period of time, though they can and do change internally. Their various changes interest sociologists because they believe that changes in social facts cause changes in other social facts (Durkheim 1982). Because of this, a systematic study and explanation of sociological phenomena is possible.

Thinking Dialectically In Sociology

In philosophy, the concept of **dialectic** was most famously developed by Aristotle and the German philosopher Georg Hegel. In the social sciences, this term is most closely associated with Karl Marx and Frederick Engels, though a host of unsettled debates exist on what they meant by the term **the dialectical method**. Dialectic should not be confused with the term *dialect*, a variation on a language. As used here, the term *dialectic* refers to mutually dependent, reciprocally interactive, and creating/destroying/creating relationships between two or more things. The growth of vegetables, their transformation and consumption as food, the growth of the body, and the elimination of waste can be said to involve relationships that are interrelated, interacting, reciprocal and changing. Thus, a **dialectical relationship** exists between the production of individuals, food, and the decay and regeneration of both. Dialectical relationships also exist between individuals, social institutions, and the dynamics of social stability and change. Individuals are born into a society within a pre-existing institutional framework into which they are socialized and taught the rules of interacting with other similarly socialized individuals. "In this connection the human personality is both a continually producing factor and a continually produced result of social evolution, and this double relation expresses itself in every elementary social fact" (W.I. Thomas 1966:11). Society and individuals, then, are dependent on one another and their mutual interconnections result in each being created, destroyed, and re-created by the other.

One central notion of Marx's dialectical method was the acceptance that reality is composed of **internal relations** (Ollman 1971, 1993). If it is true, as dialecticians hold, that "the whole is revealed in certain standardized parts" (Ollman 2003:45), then individuals' lives and experiences are internally related to cultural forms of knowledge and the historical development of social structures. To understand the world sociologically and dialectically, then, it is extremely important to understand these internal relationships.

The Internal Relationship between History, Social Structure, and Sociological Knowledge

Sociology flourished as a systematic discipline only with the onset of the modern era and then only somewhat *after* capitalism's initial period of development. Capitalism is an economic system reliant on the systematic exchange of **commodities**, that is, anything that can be bought and sold. Within this system, there are markets for wage-laborers and markets for goods, each of which is paid for in precise measurements called "money." An institutionalized set of practices related to this system has become highly systematic and regularized. The search for profit requires a general search for maximum efficiency in the process of buying and selling of labor and commodities. This means that hours, days, weeks, prices, levels of supply and demand, population dynamics, and overall trends each must be carefully measured and calculated. With the state functioning as to provide hospitable conditions for profit making, there tend to be laws and specified policies, publicly recorded, that delineate the rights and responsibilities of individuals, property holders, and state bureaucrats. The growth and spread of the market unites many different social locations—within and across class, gender, race, geography—into a regularized set of rhythms, including cycles of the workday, the work week, holidays, etc. This unification of people within a social structure links them across a geographically dispersed division of labor, resulting in many people in different cultures being subject to common forces. Because of the internal ties between social structures, as their interactions change each other over time they change the details that make up human events and human culture. The dialectic between history and structure, then, is a central focus in the search for sociologically causal variables that shape human behavior.

The Dialectic of History, Structure, and the Sociological Imagination

Sociologically speaking, history is not dealt with simply as the total catalogue of events that have occurred over a time and a space. In sociology, history is seen as a casual **variable** in its own right. What happens at one point in time allows for a range of possible alternatives at another. There have been many different types of social structures in history, from methods of producing and distributing goods and services, to kinship systems and household structures containing family units, to institutions that regulate and administrate affairs of policy and power, to the dictates of religious knowledge and authority. These parts often fit together in an order that represents systems containing causal properties. These relations shape the individual's experience of life. Food is one of the best ways to demonstrate this. Everyone has encountered something that has made him or her nauseated, whether it be a flu-bug, the sight or smell of a dead animal, or eating something that has spoiled. In terms of food, there are certain images and odors one might find repulsive. Such repulsion in response to something "gross" is experienced as a very visceral thing. That is, it feels "inborn" or "natural," as if nausea *should* happen because the object causing the nausea is perceived in its absolute truth as something that *is* "gross." Culturally speaking, to not be nauseated is to be abnormal. This is how it is experienced. However, many of the things we find distasteful we are conditioned to find that way. Children eat bugs but later learn from adults this is "gross." Dogs in some parts of the world are viewed similarly to how Americans and Europeans view pigs: as farmed animals fit for consumption and not meant for household domestication. Grounded bovine shoulder, pressed into patties and served with melted cheese, lettuce, tomato, onion, mustard on an onion roll is "lunch" for many Americans, but it is offensive for many people of traditional India where cows are not to be eaten (Harris 1974). As a carrier of symbolic cultural meaning, food functions in important ways. Jews have a Passover dinner; Muslims exchange nuts and candies during Ramadan; eggs are hunted during Easter in the Christian world. We might get a bit queasy at seeing a pride of lions huddled around an antelope's carcass, but we wax nostalgic at a Norman Rockwell painting of Grandma's presentation of her holiday turkey. Such **symbolic meaning** comes from social, not biological, roots.

> The meaning, or value, of a symbol is in no instance derived from or determined by properties intrinsic in its physical form. . .The meanings of symbols are derived from and determined by the organisms who use them; meaning is bestowed by human organisms upon physical things or events which thereupon become symbols. (White 1949:25)

Symbols are products of the human mind and do not derive their meaning from things external to our social relationships. Meanings individuals hold are therefore internally related to both their culture's history and the social structures in which culture is contained.

Take beer. Old as civilization itself, beer has not always functioned as either a social drink or an intoxicant, but rather originated as a way to prepare, store, carry and preserve grains, that is, it was used as a food. Beer was part of the regular provisions of the workforce tasked with building the pyramids. It was often a mainstay in the long-distance journeys undertaken by many a migrating culture, in the life of many a soldier on bivouac, and in the daily activities of many a pilgrim in his or her wanderings.[1] Like other foodstuffs, brewing of beer was often women's work. It became a cultural mainstay in many European provinces and early states, each region having beers with their own flavor and style. Dutch, German, Belgium, English, Italian, and Irish beers are all somewhat different from one another. Like cheese, each country has its own local variants and specialties. This pattern of unique regional brews was reproduced in the United States up until Prohibition and just after World War II, when a distinctly Americanized version—a light-colored and light-bodied pilsener-lager style of beer not very common in comparison to world-historical standards (one of about 20,000 different types of beer)—became dominant (Papazian 1991). In order to mass produce and mass market American beer, brewers were moved to sacrifice taste, body, and uniqueness (Rhodes 1995:43). As American culture has spread worldwide, so has its form of beer.

Before Prohibition, European and American beer drinking was often associated with men's activities. Prohibition caused thousands of breweries to close. It also severely curtailed the traditional practice of home brewing. After Prohibition's repeal, the larger breweries, many of which had survived by converting to production of malt products for food industries, were able to secure the best market position and began to mass market beer in a way to gain a greater share of the national market. In attempting to appeal to the greatest number of consumers as possible, "many of the richer styles of American beer were not brewed in an attempt by the breweries to market beer that would appeal to women," that is, a beer with less body and a more watery taste (Andersen 1987:96). During World War II, with women providing significant amounts of labor for the war effort and the need to ration foodstuffs during the wartime economy, the elements were in place to push lighter beers even further to the front of American culture. The rise of the advertising industry and mass marketing prior to World War II required knowledge of consumptive behavior patterns. "After Prohibition, brewers found themselves increasingly marketing to women. Studies showed that the female of the household, generally responsible for the family's grocery shopping, was increasingly purchasing beer, just as she purchased butter and bread, as a grocery item for at-home consumption" (Andersen 1987:6). Producers wanted to capture this emerging female market, a significant portion of which was a result of women's increased participation in the industrial workforce.

> [T]he real impetus to lightness was provided during World War II by the at-home army of "Rosie the Riveter" female war workers. . .Exposed to considerable beer drinking for the first time, "Rosie" would literally cut her beer with water. Brewers, pressed with stringent wartime grain quotas as they were, got the message and began to brew it that way, with less barley malt, more corn and/or rice. (Andersen 1987:96)

As women emerged as a marketing demographic cohort with greater household spending power, producers concluded they could sell them more beer if it was lighter in effervescence and color. The combination of mass production, opening of new plants and the consolidation of the brewing industry through driving smaller brewers from the market set the stage for the largest producers to capture markets and grow into national brands. Beer in the United States lost almost all of its European-regional characteristics and took on a distinctively American flavor and style. These historical roots and its transformation by social structure are among the sociological meanings of beer.

The Internal Relationship between Materialism and Idealism

There are two dominant approaches to sociological explanations of human events: materialism and idealism. **Materialist** explanations account for patterns of social behavior by appealing to such things as class relationships, economic processes, changes in technology, and/or other physical-spatial considerations. Materialist approaches prioritize economics, the class structure, and organizational relationships as providing the most explanatory power in understanding collective behaviors and experiences. For example, materialists tend to reject claims that hold war is part of "human nature" but rather argue that war is the result of conflicting political and economic structures between societies, or within them. **Idealist** explanations of social behavior focus on dispositions of individuals, an ethos of a group or era, or a form of knowledge that is otherwise socially regular and geographically dispersed. Idealists are likely to look at war and focus on how religious beliefs or ethnic prejudices lead groups into armed conflict. Sometimes materialist and idealist approaches offer competing explanations where one is more scientifically accurate and satisfying than the other. Other times, materialist and idealist approaches are elegantly compatible with one another. Comparing materialist and idealist explanations demonstrates their differences and points of compatibility.

The Dialectic of Materialism, Idealism, and the Sociological Imagination: Entertainment Industries

Both television and pop music are modern phenomena that can be understood through materialist and idealist explanations. Being able to grasp the relationship between them is an exercise in the sociological imagination.

Sex, Violence, and Television: Idealism versus Materialism

The quality of television has been a topic of discussion for years. By the early 1960s, television had already been described as a "vast wasteland."[2] The quality and quantity of sex, violence, and coarseness in programming are often interpreted as evidence of television's low quality. "If television is reflecting what the public wants, then it is a good barometer of popular tastes and desires," goes the conventional wisdom of its apologists and critics alike. By claiming that they are only responding to market demand, executives offer similar reasoning. These outlooks imply television programming is an emblem of the decline in our social norms and values. This view expresses an idealist explanation by targeting as primary explanatory variables the attitudes and opinions of a collection of individuals. Despite its intuitive appeal, such an explanation has little to do with how this state of affairs came to be. A materialist explanation makes a more powerful case.

A materialist explanation of television would focus on the economic, class, and technological forces involved in producing and consuming television products. Understood organizationally, television executives make the decisions that ultimately decide which programs stay on the air. If the organizations employing executives do not make profits, executives may lose their jobs. Most profits in the entertainment industry come from air time sold to advertisers. From the advertisers' point of view, the number of viewers a program receives, especially in a "target audience," is the main concern. Ideal target audiences have money available for spending, whether they be those that are retired and over 60, teenagers still in high school, or white males between 20 and 40. Ultimately, television producers must secure a large enough target audience for their programs so that advertisers will buy air time to maximize profits. To keep profits up, entertainment industries constantly search for new markets. Billions of dollars have been invested in technologies for the home such as new satellite dishes, VCR's, DVD's, production and distribution of cassettes and disks, high-definition technology, cable wiring, and mega-antennas. These technologies have had a profound impact on the dynamics of television viewing. For example, with the creation of the remote control and the rise in satellite and cable television with their overwhelming number of channels, the viewer now gives each program less time to catch his or her attention than previously, more so as competition for viewers increases. These material conditions play an important role in the quality of programming.

The essential thing for executives is to get and maintain an acceptably large audience, and today this audience is global in scope. Programmers, therefore, must find a universal language that captures viewers' attention. With cable television and remote controls in ever more households, they must do this as quickly as possible. Given the wide range of various tastes, languages, religions, styles, foods, value systems, etc., in a global viewing public, executives have learned that sex and violence are easily interpretable, communicate well across cultures, and are also relatively cheap to make (Gerbner 1995). These factors—the profit motive, the needs of advertisers, the search for global audiences, the competition for audiences across hundreds of channels, and the fickleness of viewers—put media executives in a difficult position. How can they catch and retain a large enough audience to satisfy enough advertisers who will pay enough monies to keep the show on the air? Incorporating both images and plot themes that are instantly recognizable, titillating, and translatable across cultures solves some of this problem. These material forces account for the presence and persistence of sex and violence on television much better than the idealist explanation that audiences want them.

The Rise of Pop Music: Idealism and Materialism

An idealist explanation about the rise and popularity of rock and roll would first focus on those personalities associated with its creation. Though the terms "rock" and "roll" are found in an early Blues recording by Trixie Smith (1922)—"My Daddy Rocks Me (With One Steady Roll)"[3]—the genre of music known as rock and roll is more closely associated with people such as Les Paul, Alan Freed, Bill Haley, Buddy Holly, Chuck Berry, Little Richard, Elvis Presley and, of course, The Beatles. Though rock and roll originated in Rhythm and Blues and Jazz circles as a term for sex, in 1951 Cleveland disk jockey Alan Freed started playing the new type style over the radio after he observed white youths buying the music at record stores. He was later to call it "rock and roll" during his radio show at WINS in New York City. Bill Haley's widely popular hit, "Rock Around the Clock," brought the new style of music to an even wider audience. Buddy Holly increased the music's commercial appeal, especially for white teenagers. Chuck Berry found new potential in the electric guitar, and he produced music with a faster backbeat and dance-friendly rhythm. Little Richard added flair and showmanship. Music executives understood the market appeal of the music, and the spirit of the times was ready for something new in mass culture. Elvis made the whole package acceptable to white, affluent audiences. An industry was ready to be born from this musical "fad." Soon, an explosion unalterably changed mass culture with the popularity of The Beatles. The social unrest of the 1960s produced a sense of alienation among youth. Rock and roll both reflected and encouraged, in dialectical form, a social critique of, and rebellion from, a society that was involved in an unpopular war abroad and was wrestling with problems of race, gender, and sexual inequalities at home. The rise of rock and roll met with the revival of folk music, which was attracting middle-class students and other artists. This transformed rock and roll from pop-oriented jingles and dance tunes to political criticism and social commentary. Rock and roll became a central feature of American life, and eventually world culture. The ideas of musical innovators, intersecting within the ethos of a wider cultural climate, caused the rise of rock and roll music. While all of this is true, it does not tell us the whole story.

A materialist approach would inquire into the historical-social roots of rock and roll (Friedlander 1996). The Blues was a cultural phenomenon long before rock and roll came on the scene and it influenced many, if not most, of rock's originators (Podell 1987).[4] Blues music originated in places like Chicago, Kansas City, Memphis, New Orleans, and Mississippi. Four of these geographical areas are connected to each other by water and connected to Kansas City by railroads and highways. The Blues came from these blue-collar towns, and its first artists came from the fields and the factories. The music originated in juke joints and ramshackle makeshift bars near work places. The music's themes echoed the concerns and experiences of the working class, such as exhausting labor, alienating or unrewarding jobs, and problems with authority. The experiences of black men, often their sexual prowess and/or romantic relationships, also predominated. The transportation routes connecting these regions allowed for cross-pollination of styles (e.g., Chicago Blues) and personalities (e.g., Robert Johnson, Muddy Waters, Lightning Hopkins, Buddy Guy, B.B. King).

The Blues met the city and the electric guitar, and it was irrevocably changed. As Blues fans and musicians learned to play the electric guitar (invented by Les Paul), some started putting a faster beat and different timings to the style. In terms of mass production, mass marketing, and mass culture, both Blues and early rock and roll players were, in industry executives' eyes, from the wrong racial category. This reflected, in part, blatant racism. However, from the vantage point of an executive making decisions in the marketplace, it made economic sense. Trying to sell records to black audiences, audiences with fewer numbers and less money to spend on records, was not an attractive prospect. While executives concluded that more money could be made from white audiences, they assumed—correctly or not—that white audiences would not buy the music of black singers. What was needed was a white blues singer who could also play the new music and who sounded like a black singer. Elvis was "discovered," packaged, and sold like any other commodity by the record industry.

Other things were going on in terms of technological changes and economic development. The ability to broadcast music in homes and cars and to produce inexpensive records to be played on cost-affordable jukeboxes accelerated. The earliest rock and rollers had a growing audience and a means to reach them unavailable to Blues artists of the previous generation. At the same time, there was a growing, affluent middle class, an affluence that was, in part, bought through adventurism in foreign countries. This adventurism moved the United States to thwart anti-systemic movements in Southeast Asia. During this period, the United States relied on a draft that hit the middle and working classes the hardest. As the Vietnam War became less and less popular, protests against it collided with other social movements centered on the distribution of power and money in American society. The working-class roots of the Blues and the rebellious nature of rock and roll dovetailed nicely with larger social currents and each played off the other, giving each greater strength and power than it would have had alone. As seen here in the sociology of the history of rock and roll, structural and historical analyses can be made ever more richer when the appropriate relationships between material and ideal forces are recognized.

Marx and Engels: The Dialectic of Society and the Individual

Marx and Engels wanted to understand the ways in which human behavior is rooted in the interplay of **material** and **ideological** conditions (Marx and Engels 1846). Given their view that "the ideal is nothing else than the material world reflected by the human mind, and translated into forms of thought" (Marx 1873:29), they tended to stress material relationships in their research. Their working hypothesis was that changes in material conditions tend to create changes in forms of ideological knowledge (Marx 1959). Thus, even thinking itself can be understood as a product of material conditions (Marx, in Seve 1978:128). As a society changes over time, so do humans' experience of it and the knowledge they use to understand it. Modern capitalist society in particular creates unique types of human individuality and sets of social relationships (Seve 1978). These three social facts—humans' relationship to material reality, their relationship to history, and their relationship to capitalism—require special consideration.

The Individual and Material Reality

As a materialist, Marx believed the "concept of the human species, [should be] pulled down from the heaven of abstraction to the real earth" [Padover 1979:35]. Sociologically speaking, human existence must be understood in the context of its entire set of social relationships. Thus, in the dialectical view, "the human essence is not abstraction inherent in each single individual. In its reality, it is the ensemble of social relations" (Marx 1845:145). This existence ranges from total social systems, to modes of production, to classes, to individuals. Human individuals are made through their interrelationships with social institutions, as well as each other. Among the different material and social relationships that form the individual, for Marx and Engels, **labor** plays *the* crucial role.

> [T]he first premise of all human existence and, therefore, of all history, the premise, namely that men must be in a position to live in order to be able to "make history." But life involves before everything else eating and drinking, housing, clothing and various other things. The first historical act is thus the production of the means to satisfy these needs, the production of material life itself. (Marx and Engels 1846:41-42)

Humans' core feature as a unique animal in relation to nature (including other animals) is that they are a **species-being** (Marx 1844:75-76). Humans' central reality as a species is as a social animal. This vision of humans as a species assumes that a level of self-consciousness as social creatures is possessed by all people, even if only at a rudimentary level (McLellan 1973:111). As opposed to psychological models, it is therefore within material and social relationships that humans must be understood first.

The Individual and History

Dialecticians think that human existence can be treated as an object of inquiry if one begins with humanity's material and historical roots. Societies rise and fall, others take their place, and what seemed ancient and inviolable is swept away in the rush of history. From such observations, dialecticians conclude that "generally, *everything* which is *specifically human*, in the developed social sense of the term, is a product of history and not a natural given" (Marx, in Seve 1978:102-103). When an individual is born, usually it is within a social structure. This always involves relationships to other social structures as well as their historical development. Political alliances and participation in culture are two very powerful sources of meaning of the human individual, and each is made possible by human labor (Gould 1978:42). Labor—the act of transforming nature into usable human goods and services—creates the basis of our social world. For instance, both nomadic and sedentary societies across the world (i.e., wandering bands and relatively settled groups, respectively) have always had long established trading patterns with one another, which have created and re-created political alliances and cultural exchanges (art, sport, language, religion, war). People are sometimes more and sometimes less aware of these intercon-nections and how these influence their social relationships. This real historical variability means that humans "make their own history, but they do not make it just as they please; they do not make it under circumstances chosen by themselves, but under circumstances directly encountered, given, and transmitted from the past" (Marx 1978:595). Humans do not have unlimited choices and unlimited freedom to make them, but choices and freedom they do have. Over time, productive forces have transformed humans' capacities and needs. For instance, though it hasn't always been this way, literacy is increasingly a prerequisite for having a meaningful engagement in social life in more and more parts of the world. This is but one of the ways in which the dynamics between human experience and action are rooted in historical-materialist relationships.

Nomadic and feudal societies, in comparison to the present at least, were very slow to change. The experiences of the individual in both nomadic and feudal systems were shaped differently by the rate of social change in those societies in comparison to today's. When societal changes are slow and/or subtle, they are hardly noticed, and the facts of peoples' lives are often taken for granted. Thousands of years ago members of a nomadic tribe in the Kalahari Desert were likely to experience life very much in the same way as did their parents, their parents' parents, and their parents' parents' parents. When social change is rapid and dramatic, the tacit assumptions operative in everyday consciousness are shaken loose, providing the possibility of seeing previously hidden facets of social reality. Peasants in feudal Europe, reliant on agricultural-pastoralism, find themselves cut off from common lands by new legal powers. They can no longer afford to keep their herds up to an adequate level, and they are eventually uprooted from their homes and forced to migrate to the swelling cities of London, Paris, and Amsterdam. As this happened to more and more individuals, urban masses came into being. Such teeming masses, in the eyes of elites and traditional authority, were notoriously unchurched and disobedient toward traditional authority. Social change became a daily social fact for all social classes. Kingdoms fell. The world and the experiences of its people irrevocably changed.

The Individual in Capitalism

Life under capitalism has often been noted for the sense of individuality it produces, understood sociologically as **the abstract individual** (Marx 1845:145). This is the idea that modern life, in conjunction with other historical variables such as the belief in a soul, produces a sense of a universal individuality that each person experiences as an intimate "thing." A dialectical sensibility holds that the sense of individuality we experience today—including its fragmentary, isolated, and disconnected nature—is an outcome of the social relations that prevail in modern society. These social relations have the production and exchange of commodities as a foundation and these material conditions powerfully shape the fate of the individual (Lukacs 1971:91). Just as each commodity has specific qualities that are transformed into a universally calculable price, each person has unique traits that are interpreted as forms of a universal system of individuality. However, the structural-material sources of this sense of individuality are things we no longer control. We become ruled by the products of our labor, and the market brings us to treat each other in the same way we treat commodities, that is, as things (Marx 1867:77, 79). This state of existence is sometimes referred to as a state of **alienation**.

> The *alienation* of the worker in his product means not only that his labor becomes an object, an *external* existence, but that it exists *outside him*, independently, as something alien to him; and that it becomes a power on its own confronting him; it means that the life which he has conferred on the object confronts him as something hostile and alien. (Marx 1844:71-72)

Living as isolated individuals in a market that relates to them as it does to commodities, humans experience a sense of wonder and powerlessness in the face of the changes brought by capital. Capitalism involves a set of social relationships that produces externally coercive sociological laws that compel both workers and capitalists to behave in particular ways. As a system, "the laws, immanent in capitalist production, manifest themselves in the movements of individual masses of capital, where they assert themselves as coercive laws of competition" (Marx 1867:300). For the average capitalist, this means either expanding the value of his or her firm or going out of business. For the average worker, this means becoming the appendage of a machine, or going homeless and starving. The pace and quality of these laws and the changes they produce result in a sense of powerlessness where neither capitalists nor workers control the system.

> Constant revolutionizing of production, uninterrupted disturbance of all social conditions, everlasting uncertainty and agitation distinguish the bourgeois epoch from all earlier ones. All fixed, fast-frozen relations, with their train of ancient and venerable prejudices and opinions, are swept away, all new-formed ones become antiquated before they can

> ossify. All that is solid melts into air, all that is holy is profaned, and man
> is at last compelled to face with sober senses, his real conditions of life,
> and his relations with his kind. (Marx and Engels 1848:476)

Marx and Engels wrote this in the mid-1800s. They were trying to capture the central drama of modern life. Similar to the sorcerer's apprentice, they depict capitalism as a special material force that no one person or group can control. While its material imperatives account for a large measure of why capitalism has survived for about 500 years, the system also has so influenced the ideological sphere that it prevents people from seeing the system as it is. Marx believed that making people aware of the relationships between these social facts is the task of the scientific method and those who use it.

Ideology and the Camera Obscura

Marx and Engels both believed that ideas are most often rooted in material relationships and held that the ideas that rule in any one period tend to be the ideas of the **ruling class** (Marx and Engels 1846). Sociologically, the tendency is that when specifiable social groups are in a relationship of hierarchical domination with one another, forms of knowledge develop that strive to explain and justify why such relationships are right, acceptable, and legitimate. Marx and Engels refer to such forms of knowledge as **ideology**: "If in all ideology men and their relations appear upside-down as in a camera obscura, this phenomenon arises just as much from their historical life-process as the inversion of objects on the retina does from their physical life-process" (Marx and Engels1846:36). The camera obscura is a box-like device used in early photographic technology that reverses an image and projects it on a surface for viewing, in a way similar to a human eye. Marx and Engels assert that ideological discourse tends to gloss over important social facts by adjusting to and endorsing the central power relationships in a society. So, for example, the ideology of "Divine Right" of kings and queens was a belief fit for feudalism but not for capitalism, whose ideology is often described as a form of **meritocracy**. The belief that prevailed during feudalism was that the ruling class was put in place by God, an ideology that served to justify their domination of society. In capitalism, the ideology of meritocracy holds that the rich and the poor alike receive the social rewards they deserve because things like talent, intelligence, and hard work determine who advances to the highest levels of the social system. This belief overlooks and masks the fact that it is labor from working classes that creates fortunes for the privileged and most wealth in modern society is inherited wealth (i.e., great fortunes are rarely "earned" by the people possessing them).

It is a sociological commonplace that social systems develop forms of knowledge that interpret institutionalized social relationships as a product of human nature. Nothing has yet been discovered, however, that determines it as such that private property and money are products of human nature. In modern capitalist society, Adam Smith's (1776:13) world view—that there exists "a certain propensity in human nature; the propensity to truck, barter, and exchange one thing for another"—is very often accepted as an unquestionable fact. For a sociological thinker such as Marx (1973:83), "This illusion has been common to each new epoch to this day." Even more conservative sociological thinkers admit that patterns of human behavior as competitive animals are the result of socialization and training within specific material relationships (Parsons 1954:37). Competition between individuals and societies is not the result of biological causes that cannot be overcome, and the belief that the modern economic system is the product of the abstract individual who is inherently a competitive actor is a piece of modern ideological knowledge.

The people original to the Americas were always bewildered by European attitudes toward land and the physical products of human labor. Land could not be "owned" any more than money could be eaten. From their point of view, natural resources should be extracted only at a rate that matched social needs and nature's ability to absorb human impact. The capitalist system, which had propelled Europe outward and into an era of **colonialism**, is based, in part, on the private ownership of productive resources, including such things as land, minerals, natural products, and tools and technology. The birth of this central component of modern life lies in the death of European feudalism, a society that participated in a property system somewhat different from that of its capitalist successor. Under feudalism, land might have been "owned" by an estate or an elite family, but the commoners had **subsistence rights** to it for grazing, collecting wood, and hunting at certain times of the year. Historically speaking, land that began as belonging to no one particular group became a communally organized resource under nomadic and tribal society, developed into a class-structured resource in feudalist relations, and was transformed into an increasingly class-monopolized resource under capitalism (Piven and Cloward 1982). Violence by states against masses in the pursuit of land has been routine in human history. It is with some justification, then, that Pierre Proudhon (1890) declared property to be a form of theft. Capitalism's birth was so violent that Marx (1867:668-669), too, was driven to argue that

> In actual history it is notorious that conquest, enslavement, robbery, murder, briefly force, play the great part. . .As a matter of fact, the methods of primitive accumulation are anything but idyllic. . .The so-called primitive accumulation, therefore, is nothing else than the historical process of divorcing the producer from the means of production. . .And the history of this, their expropriation, is written in the annals of mankind in letters of blood and fire.

The wealth of those at the top of all class structures in history has been acquired less through work, labor, and initiative than through exploitation, swindle, and conquest. This is as true about capitalism's birth as it is about the history of slavery or feudalism.

Capitalism, as an expanding system of political and economic relationships, has created and integrated various nation-states. The **capitalist world-economy**, indeed, has become a globally integrated system that is increasingly sharing a common institutional structure across its various geographical regions (Wallerstein 1974a-b, 1979). This integration has created a semi-evolutionary pattern where global interconnections develop. As a result, through the influence of England and the United States as capitalist centers, much of the world today speaks English, enjoys soccer and basketball, and eats McDonald's hamburgers. Reciprocally, many of those in Europe and the United States today enjoy reggae music from Jamaica, eat sushi and drive cars from Japan, and drink vodka from Russia. More and more people in all these regions are buying their winter coats, athletic shoes, and blue jeans from companies using sweatshop and prison labor in Central

America, the Philippines, Mexico, and China. Slave labor in Western Africa, not abolished yet, provides the cocoa for much of the western world's chocolate.[5] An untold number of people wear diamonds that jewelers in South Africa have acquired from warring groups, some of whom have used amputation of children's limbs as a method of terrorizing people in their military campaigns, often paid for by these very same diamonds (Campbell 2002). Cars worldwide are fueled by gasoline whose cost we see at the pump does not reflect the price paid by the destruction and extermination of indigenous peoples in places such as East Timor (Barsamian and Briere 1992; Chomsky 1987; Jardine 1995, 1999; Udin 1996). Our immediate experiences of life, then, are interconnected with wider historical and structural events, whether or not we are conscious of this. Making us aware of such things is the sociologist's job, though this often makes them less than respected in their culture's eyes.

C.W. Mills and the Sociological Imagination

Sociology helps us see through the ideological structures that dominate our thinking. In advocating sociology, C. Wright Mills (1959:5) assured us that the "first fruit of this imagination—and the first lesson of the social science that embodies it—is the idea that the individual can understand his own experience and gauge his own fate only by locating himself within his period." The use of the sociological imagination provides individuals a chance to exercise their agency and develop themselves in a way that allows them more control over the manner in which external forces shape them. To be sure, they still are shaped by these forces and must confront them, but the sociological imagination provides a crucial tool in the pursuit of autonomous thought and collective action, two of the bulwarks of Enlightenment thought. Mills called this "the promise" of the field.

Putting the Sociological Imagination to Work: History, Social Structure, and the Rise of Racism

The previous chapter claimed that sociology often debunks truths that are widely accepted in popular knowledge. For example, the interpretation of human variation we call **race** is not a product of our bodies but rather a product of modern structural forces in the political-economic arena working in conjunction with various realms of historical knowledge (Bonilla-Silva 1996). Our knowledge of race, that is, as a biological characteristic, is a piece of fiction that modern forms of power—including economics, politics, and science—played a role in creating (Gould 1981; Graves 2001; Harding 1993). Race is not something that exists within us as a biological fact. Rather, it is a social fact. By extension, **xenophobia**—the fear of outsiders or strangers—is something other than that phenomenon in modern society we call **racism**. First, people suffering from racism are not strangers or outsiders to a society and its forms of knowledge but rather are insiders to it (Wallerstein 1983:77-79). Second, racism is something unique to modernity itself rather than a social universal. Third, contrary to popular conceptions, the racism we know in the modern world came into existence *after* slavery rather than before it. To assume that slavery was the result of Europeans' "racist" ideas is to assume it was racism that motivated slavers to venture to Africa, and then to the Americas, with the intent of subduing a people they hated and feared. This makes no sense. Why would wealthy investors and shippers risk life, limb, and personal fortune to sail to a little-known and much feared continent to enslave a people they both feared and hated? Why not leave them alone? Here, idealist explanations breakdown.

Racism did not cause slavery. In fact, it was slavery that caused racism. Using a controlled comparative method in analyzing history (McMichael 1990) helps explain how this happened. Slavery is a practice that has existed for a very long portion of human history. In Rome, the slave was seen more as a product of war, that is, as a captured soldier. In America, the slave was the product of commerce and a system of labor exploitation. In Roman slavery, the slave could work or buy his or her way out of servitude. In America, slavery was usually lifelong. In Roman slavery, the slave had certain political rights, such as the right to own property and to testify in court. In America, where early colonial powers concluded that importing slaves was necessary for early economic development, slaves were chattel: pieces of property with no formal rights. Modern Western slavery, unlike the slavery in Rome, was a profit-driven industry where an individual's body was transformed into a commodity to be bought and sold in a free market.

In both ancient and modern forms of slavery, skin color initially played no part whatsoever in determining who would be enslaved. In Africa and portions of the Middle East, slave trading existed prior to European expansion, and this provided the first slaves that were brought to the "New World" by the Spanish (to the Caribbean, Mexico, Central and South America), the Dutch (to South Africa and Indonesia), and the Portuguese (to Brazil and Indonesia). It was these groups, not the Americans or English, who were the first slavers in the New World. There were also attempts at enslaving local populations, which failed for several reasons: Local populations in colonial settings are familiar with the land; they are likely to have nearby allies to help them escape; and their languages are intact, which provides them the ability to communicate, an essential element in allowing them to resist. Further, British ruling classes had enslaved the Irish for a period and once considered enslaving their own working classes in England. In the U.S. colonies, the British initially used indentured servants as a primary workforce because importing slaves was not cost-effective. The slaves available to early colonists at the time were on labor-intensive plantations in Hispaniola and Cuba, essentially worked to death, and thus had too short a life span to make them a profitable investment. As the Spanish, Dutch and Portuguese pulled out of the slave trade, importation into places like the Caribbean and South America declined. Slave owners there thus had to reproduce their own workforces locally rather than rely on constant imports from Africa. Slaves were given better living and working conditions because plantation owners needed their slaves to live longer and to have more children. Extension of the average life span increased slaves' market value to colonial buyers. British shareholders in the colonies slowly changed from using indentured servants to slave labor as the former became less cost-effective (Cox 1976; Zinn 1980; Fredrickson 1981; Wood 1997). What we know today as racism was not a catalyst in this process.

European Christianity accepted the idea that Christians were not allowed to enslave Christians, but could enslave "heathens." Military law accepted the enslavement of captured soldiers, and Africans were legally seen as just that. Recognizing the loophole, many slaves began converting to Christianity. Colonial slave owners needed a way to keep them in servitude, so they found a legal stopgap. "Heathen ancestry" was hit upon as the criteria of enslavement, which did not require interrogation of a slave's mind ("Are you a Christian?") but rather only a visual inspection of his or her skin. Africans and other dark-skinned people were thus branded as uniquely suitable for enslavement (Fredrickson 1981). Law, education, science, and religion all were influenced by this racialized division (Gould 1981; Graves 2001; Harding 1993). The resulting cultural hostility, marginalization, violence, and exploitation we call *racism*, therefore, came after slavery, not before it (Wallerstein 1983). Once a "color line" was drawn, it worked its way into all manner of American institutions (Dubois 1903). Science, education, and law subsequently endorsed the idea of "race" as a reality, and a color line found its ideological justification. This review of the historical facts reveals that what we experience today as racism is not something found in human nature. Rather, racism is the result of historical-sociological processes. If racism came into existence because of social processes, it can be dismantled through them too. This realization is one of the "fruits" of the sociological imagination, a reflection of its debunking and relativizing motifs.

Berger and Luckmann: The Social Construction of Reality

Berger and Luckmann (1966) describe a set of dialectical relationships by which humans create a world and at the same time create a vision of that same world and thus re-create themselves in the process. As animals, humans do not live in a world ready-made for them and thus they must undertake **world-building** activities, such as building shelter, securing food, and learning to communicate. These things must be done within a set of social relationships. Berger and Luckmann (1966:52) use the term **externalization** to refer to the process by which humans create a world in the pursuit of solving the problems involved in surviving in nature. The methods that are developed become repeated, regularized, dispersed, and general in a culture, and this means that such methods take on a life of their own, a process Berger and Luckmann (1966:35, 47-128) call **objectivation**. Knowledge subsequently formed is taught at various locations, including the family, religion, school, lore, and sport. As the individual is born and ages, he or she **internalizes** this knowledge as his or her own (Berger and Luckmann 1966:61, 129-183). The more consistent and unchanging the content of this knowledge, the less incongruity is created for the individual's inner experience. Berger and Luckmann (1966:65) elaborate:

> The primary knowledge about the institutional order is knowledge on the pretheoretical level. It is the sum total of "what everybody knows" about a social world, values and beliefs, myths, and so forth, the theoretical integration of which requires considerable intellectual fortitude in itself, as the long line of heroic integrators from Homer to the latest sociological system-builders testifies. On the pretheoretical level, however, every institution has a body of transmitted recipe knowledge, that is, knowledge that supplies the institutionally appropriate rules of conduct.

This relationship between institutions and behavior is part of the "dialectic" between the individual and society. We become, in part, what our institutions make us.

The Social Construction of Gender:
Becoming Male and Female

A more complex and unequal gendered and class-based division of labor emerges as a result of the transformation of nomadic culture into small-scale agricultural-pastoral settlements and the production of surplus goods (Leaky and Lewin 1977; Lenski 1966, 1984). As nomadic systems become sedentary, a division of labor emerges whereby men become the primary hunters and women the primary childcare providers. The reasons appear obvious. Maternity, as opposed to paternity, is always known and women are uniquely equipped to feed infants. This is a parent-child relationship ill-suited for hunting of game. This, not men's supposed greater strength, is the source of men's role as principal hunters (though men as the solitary hunters is not universally true). Men's greater muscular strength is not enough to defeat most animals in battle nor is it so much greater than women's that women are prevented from using spears, bows, or slingshots. The allotment of surplus goods has often been given to the groups that are the best hunters, and thus, certain cliques of males attain a slightly higher status and their families more wealth. Hunters also begin to dominate the skills of weaponry and become the main mechanism of defense of the group. As males attain the main sources of meat and become the weapon specialists, they accumulate more wealth and power than females. Control of surplus goods and weapons brings in a new system of property and power relations, dissolving communal property and instituting the idea of personal, familial, or clan property, most often controlled by men. There grows an interest in keeping a tolerable amount of property within the family unit or even expanding it. Thus, handing family property on to the next generation of males is seen as important. This often has been the firstborn male, or at least the longest surviving eldest male, and this means that there is an interest in having male babies born before female babies. Thus, female infanticide becomes customary in relatively small sedentary groups. Because of the need to marry females off, they become bargaining chips in their parents' exchange negotiations with other parents. As a consequence of seeing virginity as a key to a female's exchange-value, there develops a need to control female sexuality, chaste females become highly prized, and single adult females are shunned. By arranging marriages, exchanging dowries, and controlling female sexuality (e.g., clitoridectomy), women become a part of the male property system. The few physical differences between men and women that do exist are used to justify the set of institutionalized practices that are differentially attached to the social roles of men and women. This social, economic, and sexual marginalization becomes embodied in norms, morals, myths, stories, codes, and rituals. Women and men are then produced as specific types of individuals through these relationships and cultural understandings (Chafetz 1984; Eder 1995; Haney 1996; Heng and Devan 1997; Henslin 2003; Kimmel and Messner 1989; Sanday 1981; Thorne and Luria 1986).

Figure 1. Structural Analysis of Women's Historical Marginalization

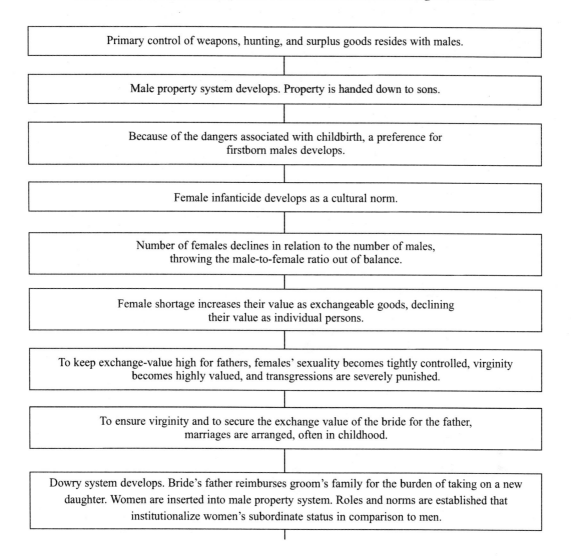

Primary control of weapons, hunting, and surplus goods resides with males.

Male property system develops. Property is handed down to sons.

Because of the dangers associated with childbirth, a preference for firstborn males develops.

Female infanticide develops as a cultural norm.

Number of females declines in relation to the number of males, throwing the male-to-female ratio out of balance.

Female shortage increases their value as exchangeable goods, declining their value as individual persons.

To keep exchange-value high for fathers, females' sexuality becomes tightly controlled, virginity becomes highly valued, and transgressions are severely punished.

To ensure virginity and to secure the exchange value of the bride for the father, marriages are arranged, often in childhood.

Dowry system develops. Bride's father reimburses groom's family for the burden of taking on a new daughter. Women are inserted into male property system. Roles and norms are established that institutionalize women's subordinate status in comparison to men.

Given that maternity is always known and women are equipped to feed infants, it would be surprising if a system of institutionalized male and female norms and roles *did not* develop. Norms "define. . .desirable. . .action in the form of goals and standards of behavior" (Parsons 1949:33). **Gender**, therefore, can be conceptualized as a symbolic role performance of normative expectations associated with one's sex within a cultural system (West and Zimmerman 1987). The particular features specific social systems designate as unique to men and women, that is, **masculinity** and **femininity**, are norms that differentiate the social meaning of being "male" or "female." These are primarily culturally constructed. However, once institutionalized, such norms come to dominate and shape individuals' behavior and judgments.

Ollman: The Dialectical Imagination

The sociological imagination must be able to understand the significance of history and social structure for the biography of the individual (Mills 1959). Bringing history and structure together into a unified analysis is the task of any dialectical investigation (Ollman 1993, 2003). Bringing this dialectical imagination to the reader is one of the sociologist's primary goals.

The Individual and the Levels of Historical Generality

Human realities exist at **multiple levels of generality**, ranging from the very broad across time and space, to the very specific and recent. These levels profoundly shape the human experience. Like **matter**, humans have weight and mass and can move at various rates of speed. Like other species, **humans as animals** grow hungry and reproduce through sexual unions. As a species, **humans as humans** are symbolic creatures as well as social ones and are aware of themselves as a unique and separate species (Ollman 1993:53-67). Symbols, words, and institutions must be socially created, something that has significant sociological implications. "Without speech we would have no political, economic, ecclesiastic, or military organization; no codes of etiquette or ethics; no laws; no science, theology, or literature; no games or music, except on an ape level. . .Indeed, without articulate speech we would be all but toolless" (White 1949:33-34). Though like them in many ways, what separates us from the rest of the animal kingdom, in part, is our capacity to create a symbolic universe. Without language, culture is not transmitted and a person "would be merely an animal, not a human being" (White 1949:33).

Social relationships, including **a social division of labor**, are the strategies evolutionary history "chose" for humans as their survival mechanism in their struggles in and against nature. Humans are dependent on shared social skills. Understood at the level of **society in general**, what we call **culture** emerges from institutionalized patterns of survival techniques that are often forgotten to be as such but rather are known as "chores," "art," "cuisine," "music," "style," "technology," "hobbies," "gardening." Such practices trace their historical-cultural lineages to methods of attaining human survival through manipulating the natural environment. However, if "society" as a concept is meant to capture the unique aspects of different social systems, then it is too broad a category to distinguish between different types of systems. There are relationships characteristic of

class societies, and these need to be specified and understood. All class systems share such things as ideologies, types of property and legal relations, and, of course, the various manifestations of the **class struggle** (Marx and Engels 1848). There are many types of class systems, however, and the "essential difference between [them] lies only in the mode in which . . . surplus-labour is in each case extracted from the actual producer, the labourer" (Marx 1867:209). Class systems in history have included slavery, Asiatic despotism, feudal-ism, and capitalism, the most recent and powerful form. For this reason, the characteristics of **capitalism in general** attract much attention from dialecticians (Ollman 1993, 2003).

Capitalism is a system marked by the private ownership of the means of produc-tion, the systematic production and exchange of commodities, and the constant thirst for the accumulation of capital. Historically, exchange developed as a way to broaden a group's access to material goods as they came in contact with other groups. Growing interdependence among social groups for goods and services broadened the division of labor and established external trading and political relationships. Money arose in different places and at different times as a way of producing a symbolic, universal-equivalent that would facilitate economic exchanges. Among the various types of production systems, capitalism is the one *based* on investing money in order to attract ever more money (Marx 1867). As a global-historical system, capitalism developed through establishing political-economic relationships between **core** sectors of the world economy (European society in the fifteenth century) and **peripheral** ones (regions of labor and resource extraction, e.g., Africa and Central and South America). This core-periphery relationship is as much a cen-tral feature of the capitalist world-economy as are money, commodities, and the multi-plicity of firms in various nation-states (Wallerstein 1974a-b). For example, once England became a *core* capitalist region, both Ireland and what would become the United States were established as colonies in *peripheral* areas. The logic of the system is that it experi-ences long waves of change and development (Mandel 1980), which brings different states to a dominant position in the core regions over time, usually after wars among them (Wallerstein 1983). As the United States expanded outward, for example, it fought suc-cessful wars with the British and the Spanish, and its position changed from periphery to semi-periphery, and later to core status during and after the period of World War I. During the same period, Spain declined as an early **hegemonic** (Gramsci 1971) power, that is, as the dominant state in the core regions of the world-economy, and receded into the **semi-periphery** (i.e., areas of processing of raw materials and their production into goods for sale). This suggests that the world-economy undergoes cycles of expansion and contrac-tion that create states and then periodically reshuffles the interrelationships these states have with one another. The world-system contains an **inter-state** system where strong states dominate the weak (Wallerstein 1974, 1983).

Life under capitalism is not experienced at a constant pitch. Capitalism is a dynamic system, and it undergoes changes in its institutional policies and geographical realities, while certain structures remain in place. For example, while the legality of debtors' prisons has changed, the penal-regulatory function of the state in capitalist society has not. Many of the relationships between institutional change amid structural stability account for life under **capitalism's recent history** (understood as life under this system within the last 20 to 50 years), as well as for specific events in **the here and now** (Ollman 1993:55). These two levels of generality focus on those current events and historical developments that have played a significant role in setting the boundaries of action for both the immediate past and the present. To grasp the relationship between social structures, history, and troubles of personal milieu, as Mills (1959) asks of us, one must understand the logic of the system, events in its recent history, and the structural location of one's own life. History intrudes on the present and continually shapes us. What those in power do today sets boundaries and creates possibilities for what can be done tomorrow. For example, if a student wants to understand why his or her costly student loans buy them an education with no guarantee of financial payoff, they might examine the policies of the federal government in the post-World War II period. These began to significantly shift during the Reagan Era and reduced the range of citizens eligible for student loans. This occurred while core regions experienced a significant number of jobs either "downsized" or transferred overseas (Greider 1997). This has had ripple affects over generations: "We suffer not only from the living, but from the dead" (Marx 1867:20). We shape our destiny as much as it shapes us, showing the dialectic between our freedom and the coercive power of social relationships.

The Dialectic of Levels of Historical Generality, Social Change, and Human Knowledge

There is a dialectic between social stability, social change, and the human experience. To the extent that a level of historical generality is shared across societies, humans living in those societies will share certain experiences: "If all hearts beat in unison, this is not as a consequence of a spontaneous, pre-established harmony; it is because one and the same force is propelling them in the same direction" (Durkheim 1982:56). Forms of production change over time, and the failure to grasp them as transitory translates into the inability to understand the historical nature of our social institutions and our relationship to them. The dialectical imagination, therefore, "regards every historically developed social form as in fluid movement, and therefore takes into account its transient nature not less than its momentary existence" (Marx 1873:29). Stability and change are both to be grasped in the dialectical imagination.

The most important thing that affects the content of human knowledge is social change. *Rapid* change thrusts practices into social life that often eventually become institutionalized into new social norms. *Structural* social change affects central social relationships and tends to ripple out to many other social institutions. If such changes are *long-term*, then the odds that they will become institutionalized increases. This process can make former norms increasingly abnormal and senseless. For example, the private ownership of productive resources has profoundly shaped all other social institutions of modernity. Practices formerly kept outside the market, such as medicine, sexuality, and spiritual life, have been transformed by market forces. Knowledge of abortifacients has been appropriated from working women's worlds and inserted into state and capitalist institutions dominated by men. These same interests fostered the industrial revolution, which changed the character of cities almost overnight through creating mass communication, transportation and sewage systems, ethnic neighborhoods, the influx of various religious congregations, the loosening of social bonds, and greater levels of social anonymity. Each of these had a powerful impact on how people experienced life. Free public education transformed the literacy levels and technological skills of the work-force, transformed the power relations between men and women within the gender system, and increasingly brought political discourse to greater numbers of people. We changed the world and it changed us.

The various levels of historical generality interact with one another in important ways, so much so that our human existence lies within the dialectical relationships between history and social structures. Easing the hunger pangs of our animal drive can be determined by modern advertising's manipulation of our appetites. How we subsequently act makes our muscles grow hard and strong or our middles grow soft and weak. Though most humans share a capacity to experience a range of similar emotions, through historical analysis, cross-cultural studies, and experimentation, sociologists conclude that the human capacity for a range of emotion is great indeed. Emotions can be cultivated or suppressed by larger social variables. Evidence suggests some might even disappear if the social conditions upon which they are built fall by the wayside (Lutz and White 1986; Simons and Hughes 1985). Our animal sex drives, too, are shaped by the imagery of sexual indulgence found in contemporary discourse, only to be confronted by the rem-nants of Judeo-Christian morality, which are rooted in the beliefs of past class structures (e.g. agrarian-pastoral desert cultures of the (now) Middle East, the Roman Empire, and feudal Europe). How we make use of our sex is constructed for us as a peculiar moral problem. For example, the Western experience of sexuality is commonly seen as some-thing with moral implications if done outside of marriage. While this is shared with other societies, it certainly is not a universal code to which all humans in all societies are subject. The sexual universe of the typical American is filled with signals to engage in it recklessly, to assume it can be guilt free, all the while holding up monogamy as an ideal. A sort of schizophrenic, hypocritical, and frantic sexuality emerges (Foucault 1978). The world shapes and produces us in more ways than we even imagine.

Foucault: The Production of Individuality in Modern Society

Individuality and the Division of Labor

A dialectical imagination comprehends an internal relationship between the increasing historical complexity of social structures and the emergence of individuality in society. Sociologists thus speak of the "interpenetration between social systems and personalties" whereby social roles "are both institutionalized in the social system and internalized in individual personalities" (Parsons 1977:171). Greater varieties of individ-uals evolve out of and with changes in the division of labor in society. To greater or less-er degrees, all human beings possess the universal traits of persons in general: humor, kindness, abstract thinking, pleasure, jealousy, hate, mischievousness. However, certain traits are cultivated to greater or lesser degrees in different institutional configurations. In smaller, nomadic societies, there are lower levels of technological complexity and thus the number and quality of skills across the society as a whole are less developed. Rome was a warrior society, and the Arawaks were relatively peaceful. Both possessed belief systems in line with their social practices. Nomadic-communal societies believe human nature to be cooperative just in the same way as people in capitalist societies are conditioned to see human nature as competitive. Capitalist society has more characters and types of individuals than did feudalism, and feudalism had more characters and types than do nomadic peoples. Over the long course of history, the number of outlets available for expressing human traits and the division of labor that molds bodies and minds have increased innumber, in complexity, and in scope. This translates into an increase in the types of individuality expressed in society (Durkheim 1984; Marx 1973; Seve 1978). Such insights make it very difficult to settle on an answer to the question, *What is human nature?* Rather than human nature being an abstract state that must be discovered through thought or research, a dialectical-sociological imagination understands that we are what we can become. Only history will solve the riddle of human nature.

By grasping the internal relationship between individuals and changing material conditions across history, a dialectical approach to sociology allows "for a theory of the historical forms of human individuality" (Seve 1978:93). The rise of market society produced a variety of individuals acquiring new skills while at the same time the bureaucra-tization of industry and the state pushed toward the standardization of these same individu-als. The ways in which human traits are manifested "become institution-alized in terms of abstract stereotyped expectations" and this fact "tends to take on a meaning and stability apart from the specific tasks which happen at the time to be performed in its name. The front becomes a 'collective representation' and a fact in its own right" (Goffman 1959:27). While slyness, wit, and insight might be universal capacities, the modern world finds these traits expressed as the spy, the scam artist, the wheeler-dealer, the fast-talker, the slick politician, the player, the jester, the comedian, the wiseacre, and the humorist. These collective representations are not universal in the traditional sense, but rather are the manifestations of broader human traits shaped by roles found in social systems. Who we are is always something filtered through the lens of culture.

The Production of Individuals in Modern Systems of Power and Knowledge

After the mid-twentieth century, social theorists started asking questions about how relations of domination are maintained through forms of social **discourse** that function to shape scientific thinking and institutionalize behavior at the same time (Foucault 1972). The guiding thread of this research dealt with the relationships between systems of domination, the relationship between power and knowledge, and how these forces are related to the individual (Foucault 1980). The official version of science assumes that knowledge of humans has been objectively and dispassionately collected. Not only did Foucault's studies (1965) lead him to conclude that power and violence have played as much a role in the development of the sciences as did the experimental method, they also led him to conclude that these forms of power-knowledge played a part in pro-ducing the behaviors that science was claiming to simply observe (Foucault 1977, 1978). Broader structures of power simultaneously shaped both human behaviors and the scientific disciplines studying these behaviors, which in turn reciprocally shaped each other. In such instances, scientists might assume they have discovered a natural human law that has in fact been produced by forms of cultural knowledge and social institutionalization. Foucault thus hypothesized the existence of **productive power**, whereby forms of discourse—including legal, scientific, economic, religious, educational—functioned to shape institutions and the behavior of individuals, literally producing individuals as particular types of subjects (Foucault 1982). For example, new scholarship about the history of human sexual behavior has challenged dominant and accepted versions of it (Foucault 1978; Jagose 1996; Kirsch 2000; Murray 2000). There seems no one pattern of sexual behavior that societies have settled on and shared cross-culturally. Whether it be adult-child strictures, rules about first sexual experience, mores on extra-marital sex, or prohibitions against or acceptance of same-sex behaviors and unions, what is considered "acceptable" sexual behavior is as variable across the history of societies as what is considered "food" (Tannahill 1980).

The Production of Sexuality

Modern society, and by extension modern individuality, did not emerge fully formed. As Europe entered the contemporary era, many social practices from the feudal past remained. New people and new social institutions were built. A **micro-physics of power** emerged whereby institutions such as the prison, the hospital, the school, and the factory adopted rules of organization such as surveillance, testing, examining, and training. These shaped individuals into specific kinds of subjects like delinquents, patients, students, or workers (Foucault 1977). Previous experiences of bodily pleasure were transformed by modern forms of power and knowledge into what we now call **sexuality**, a sort of inner-psychic being with its own wants and desires that everyone supposedly possesses as a thing. In the Victorian period, the use of sex, like criminality and insanity, became a central concern of powerful institutions, such as the state, the church, and medical establishment (Foucault 1978). This created new **relationships of domination** between the state, the division of labor, and the status of the individual. Old forms of behavior became prohibited and subjugated and others were institutionalized (Foucault 1980). For example, midwifery and the keeping of folk-medicines were stolen from women and inserted into the rising field of medicine. Catholicism directed attention to "the soul" and used the "confession" to encourage the individual to "tell everything." Trespasses changed from being simply a mark against rules of social intercourse to a violation of spiritual laws. Sins thus marked one's inner-identity. State governments became concerned over the use individuals made of sex and developed both racist eugenics campaigns and policies that viewed married heterosexual unions as the performance of normal human sexuality (Foucault 1978). As with the racialization of the sciences, knowledge of sex in the medical establishment included applying taxonomic categories to human variations. Just in the same way the human sciences exhibited shifting definitions of racial categories over time, so did they shift in their categorization of sexual behavior (Sullivan 2003; Somerville 1997). Soon, a new human reality emerged—that is, the view that we possess inner-beings containing a "sexuality" that can be scientifically categorized (Storr 1998). With such knowledge the discursive basis for the modern "homosexual" was born (Foucault 1978; Greenberg 1997).

Contemporary society's knowledge of sexuality was reduced to a polarized model—that is, homosexual to heterosexual (Kinsey, Pomeroy, and Martin 1948, Kinsey 1953). The roots of this model can be traced to this same Victorian period (Foucault 1978). However, these categories *do not* fit well in observation of both history and cross-cultural comparison, but they *do play* a role in productive power. In modernity, people are produced as and thus become "heterosexuals" and "homosexuals." Today, these categories exist prior to the individual and contemporary discourse tells individuals that their sex-desires correspond with an inner-being, one that can be scientifically categorized. In acting on their sexual impulses, modern individuals come to see themselves as possessing a categorical identity and the forces of social discourse fill this identity with traits. For example, modernity's popular knowledge assumes that a tendency exists for homosexually inclined individuals to often possess cross-over traits in the gender system; homosexual men being somewhat effeminate and homosexual women being somewhat masculine (Lofstrom 1997). Individuals who engage in same-sex/opposite-sex behavior become the homosexuals/heterosexuals their cultural knowledge posits to exist as natural categories. Individuals socialize themselves, to a certain extent, to adopt and maintain the values, tastes, and behaviors of those who stand as both significant and generalized others for them (Mead 1934). Once internalized, individuals enact the standards of a group's norms for the outward presentation of self (Goffman 1959). When certain behaviors are defined as "homosexual," sufficient cues exist in a society as to what other behaviors should accompany that identity. Of course, "masculinity" and "femininity" are not written in stone, are not universally defined, and are not necessarily cross-reproduced in the sex-gender system when it comes to the homosexual category (or the heterosexual category, for that matter). To assume, for example, that men who engage in same-sex relations are universally read as also courting a feminine role is to misread how this behavior has been interpreted in societies over time. In some ways, the effeminate male homosexual is a new experience. Some cultures have social roles that accept males who do not feel their society's sex-gender system fits them. For example, India has a community of individuals known as "Hijras" that are ostensibly men living as women. They are often present at births of children, and if any genital deformity exists, they will adopt the children into their community. Usually composed of castrated males, the Hijras are considered good luck at weddings and perform other social functions. They are also known for ecstatic group-sex festivals. In this way, knowledge about sexuality, sex, and gender can function as a social force or power that produces forms of sexuality as an element of personality.

Knowledge that places humans on a polarized continuum of "heterosexual" to "homosexual" is a relatively recent social fact and fits poorly with the actual variations of practice (Gregersen 1994). An inner-inclination toward same-sex or opposite-sex desire has not always been assumed in different human cultures. Historically speaking, a wide variety of social roles has existed that has institutionalized the meaning and the license of sex acts between various sexes and genders. These roles are sometimes ceremonial, sometimes involve adult-children interaction, and sometimes are centered around inserter-insertee distinctions (Murray 2000). In modern society, same-sex behavior most often is a product of some mix of personal motivation, whether it be by choice or disposition, social conditions, or the expectations that accompany social roles. However, dialectical and sociological reasoning holds that same-sex behaviors are always filtered through social structures. So, for example, in terms of cross-cultural history, in different societies same-sex sexual behavior has been structured into the rituals of the warrior class, into gender-crossing relationships in kinship and social roles, into institutionalized forms of pederasty, and is correlated with forms of radical gender stratification. Such institutionalized same-sex relations are correlated with rules of inheritance, relationships involved in subsistence activities, a sexual division of labor, lack of male sexual access to females, adolescent male isolation and genital mutilation, class structures and urbanization (Murray 2000). Historically and cross-culturally, what is found is that same-sex behavior has been associated with structural variables and has been institutionalized within social roles, two things that occur prior to and outside of the choices and predilections of individuals.

Modern society tends toward the fragmentation of experience (Orbell, Zeng, and Mulford 1995). As various processes broke apart the village-community life, mobile work forces were created, followed by a rapid rise in urban metropolitan living. As the traditional bonds that anchored individuality to narrow, socially prescribed roles began to lose their sway, individuals could exercise more choice and free will in their living arrangements. As compulsory marriage and child-rearing became easier to avoid, people began organizing their social lives around new values and goals—for example, consumption, leisure, and sex. It became possible to live as a "homo"-sexual (D'Emilio 1997; Lofstrom 1997). This created a new community that forms of social, political, and scientific discourse could now target, utilize, and discuss. "Homosexuality" was suddenly "discovered." As legal, religious, and medical authorities directed their gaze toward the communities practicing non-standard sexualities, these groups emerged as political forces, demanding rights and constitutional protections (Lauristen and Thorstad 1974). Homosexuals have become a community, something that required a series of historical events. "Sexuality" was not always something in existence and it is not something that was simply discovered. Today, an individual learns that his or her use of sex corresponds to science's sexual categories and society's sex theories. Sexuality, like race, was invented and invested in the human body (Somerville 1997). Like race relations, struggles over rights to practice sex had their political flashpoints, such as the riots at Stonewall and contemporary debates over gay marriage. Regardless of how these debates get settled, "sexuality" is now a modern category of political, scientific, and experiential practice and struggle.

Conclusion

The history of human life demonstrates a remarkable range of variation and change, and this makes acquisition of the sociological imagination crucial. Understanding how human life unfolds is not beyond our grasp. The sociological imagination, especially when used dialectically, provides a significant advance in the scientific attempt to study the drama of our existence. Used wisely and toward its highest ideal, the sociological imagination reveals to us the reasons for our experiences and how we came to be who we are, both as individual persons and as individuals who are members of social groups. This revelation becomes increasingly important because human society produces not just types of individuality, but individuals whose existence places them in categories of inequality. These relationships of inequality have a profound affect on both the quality of an individual's life, and the length of life itself. Societies over history have been marked by inequalities in power, wealth, health, autonomy, general well-being, freedom of thought, and access to goods and education. These inequalities are more than sociological questions, but instead play a major role in determining who gets to live and die in modern life. This makes the sociological imagination and dialectical thought issues of importance for everyone.

Notes

1.
See:
http://www.alabev.com/history.htm
http://www.alabev.com/history.htm
http://www.sallys-place.com/beverages/beer/history_brewing.htm

2.
See:
http://law.indiana.edu/fclj/pubs/v55/no3/Rosenbloom.pdf

3.
See: Adams 1988:27.

4.
See:
http://memory.loc.gov/ammem/lohtml/lohome.html

5.
See:
http://gbgm-umc.org/umw/action_ivorycoast.html
http://www.stopchildlabor.org/internationalchildlabor/chocolate.htm
http:// news.bbc.co.uk/1/hi/business/1575258.stm
http://www.vanilla.com/html/aware-ivory.html
http://cbsnews.com/stories/2002/05/31/world/main510654.shtml

6.
See:
http://www.straightdope.com/classics.a4_212.html

References

Adams, Cecil. 1988. *More of The Straight Dope*, edited by Ed Zotti. New York: Ballantine.

Anderson, Will. 1987. *From Beer to Eternity: Everything You Always Wanted to Know about Beer*. Lexington, MA: The Stephen Green Press.

Barsamian, David and Elaine Briere. 1992. "East Timor: The Tragedy Continues." *Z Magazine* 7/8:33-40.

Becker, Howard. 1982. "Culture: A Sociological View." *The Yale Review* 71:513-527.

Berger, Peter and Thomas Luckmann. 1966. *The Social Construction of Reality.* Garden City, New York: Anchor Books / Doubleday & Company.

Bonilla-Silva, Eduardo. 1996. "Rethinking Racism: Toward a Structural Interpretation." *American Sociological Review* 62:465-480.

Campbell, Greg. 2002. *Blood Diamonds: Tracing the Path of the World's Most Precious Stones.* Boulder, CO: Westview Press.

Chafetz, Janet Saltzman. 1984. *Sex and Advantage: A Comparative, Macro-Structural Theory of Sex Stratification.* Totowa, NJ: Rowman & Allanheld.

Chomsky, Noam. 1987 (1985). "East Timor." Pp. 303-311 in *The Chomsky Reader.* New York: Pantheon.

Cooley, Charles Horton. 1964. *Human Nature and the Social Order.* New York: Schocken Books.

Cox, Oliver. 1976. *Race Relations: Elements and Social Dynamics.* Detroit: Wayne State University Press.

D'Emilio, John. 1997. "Capitalism and Gay Identity." Pp. 169-178 in *The Gender / Sexuality Reader: Culture, History, Political Economy*, edited by Roger N. Lancaster and Micaela di Leonardo. New York: Routledge.

Dubois, W.E.B. 1903. (1996). *Souls of Black Folk.* New York: Modern Library.

Durkheim, Emile. 1982. *Rules of the Sociological Method*, edited by Steven Lukes. Translated by W.D. Halls. New York: Free Press.

_____. 1984. *The Division of Labor in Society.* New York: Free Press.

Eder, Donna. 1995. *School Talk: Gender and Adolescent Culture.* New Brunswick, NJ: Rutgers University Press.

Foster, John Bellamy. 1995. "Global Ecology and the Common Good." *Monthly Review* 46 (9):1-10.

_____. 2002. *Ecology Against Capitalism.* New York: Monthly Review Press.

Foucault, Michel. 1965. *Madness and Civilization: A History of Insanity in the Age of Reason.* New York: Vintage.

_____. 1972. *The Archaeology of Knowledge.* New York: Pantheon Books.

_____. 1977. *Discipline and Punish: The Birth of the Prison.* New York: Vintage.

_____. 1978 (1980). *The History of Sexuality, Volume I.* New York: Vintage.

_____. 1980. *Power/Knowledge: Selected Interviews and Other Writings.* Colin Gordon, editor. New York: Pantheon.

_____. 1983 (1982). "Afterword: The Subject and Power." Pp. 208-226 in *Michel Foucault: Beyond Structuralism and Hermeneutics*, edited by Hubert Dreyfus and Paul Rabinow. New York: Harvester-Wheatsheaf.

Fredrickson, George. 1981. *White Supremacy: A Comparative Study in American and South African History.* New York: Oxford University Press.

Fried, Martha Nemes and Morton H. Fried. 1980. *Transitions: Four Rituals in Eight Cultures.* New York: W. W. Norton & Company.

Friedlander, Paul. 1996. *Rock and Roll: A Social History*. Boulder, CO: Westview Press.

Gerbner, George. 1995. "Television Violence: The Power and the Peril." Pp. 547-557 in *Gender, Race, and Class in Media: A Text-Reader*, edited by Gail Dines and Jean M. Humez. Thousand Oaks, CA: Sage Publications.

Goffman, Erving. 1959. *The Presentation of Self in Everyday Life*. New York: Anchor / Doubleday.

Gould, Carol C. 1978. *Marx's Social Ontology: Individuality and Community in Marx's Theory of Social Reality*. Cambridge, MA: MIT Press.

Gould, Stephen Jay. 1981. *The Mismeasure of Man*. New York: Horton.

Gramsci, Antonio. 1971. *Selections from the Prison Notebooks*. New York: International.

Graves, Joseph. 2001. *The Emperor's New Clothes: Biological Theories of Race at the Millennium*. New Brunswick, NJ: Rutgers University Press.

Greenberg, David F. 1997. "Transformation of Homosexuality-Based Classifications." Pp. 179-193 in *Gender, Race, and Class in Media: A Text-Reader*, edited by Gail Dines and Jean M. Humez. Thousand Oaks, CA: Sage Publications.

Gregersen, Edgar. 1994. *The World of Human Sexuality: Behaviors, Customs and Beliefs*. New York: Irvington.

Greider, William. 1997. *One World, Reader or Not: The Manic Logic of Global Capitalism*. New York: Simon & Schuster.

Haney, Lynne. 1996. "Homeboys, Babies, Men in Suits: The State and the Reproduction of Male Dominance." *American Sociological Review* 61:759-778.

Harding, Sandra, editor. 1993. *The "Racial" Economy of Science*. Bloomington, IN: Indiana University Press.

Harris, Marvin. 1974. *Cows, Pigs, Wars & Witches: The Riddles of Culture*. New York: Random House.

Heng, Geraldine and Janadas Devan. 1997. "State Parenthood: The Politics of Nationalism, Sexuality, and Race in Singapore." Pp. 107-121 in *The Gender / Sexuality Reader: Culture, History, Political Economy*, edited by Roger N. Lancaster and Micaela di Leonardo. New York: Routledge.

Henslin, James. 2003. "On Becoming Male: Reflections of a Sociologist on Childhood and Early Socialization." Pp. 143-154 in *Down to Earth Sociology*, edited by James Henslin. New York: The Free Press.

Jagose, Annamarie. 1996. *Queer Theory: An Introduction*. New York: New York University Press.

Jardine, Matthew. 1995. "APEC, The United States & East Timor." *Z Magazine* 1:34-39.

_____. 1999. *East Timor: Genocide In Paradise*. Monroe, ME: Odonian Press / Common Courage Press.

Kimmel, Michael S. and Michael Messner. 1989. *Men's Lives*. New York: Macmillan Publishing.

Kinsey, Alfred, Wardell B. Pomeroy, and Clyde E. Martin. 1948. *Sexual Behavior in the Human Male*. Philadelphia: W. B. Saunders Co.

Kinsey, Alfred. 1953. *Sexual Behavior in the Human Female.* Philadelphia: W. B. Saunders Co.

Kirsch, Max. 2000. *Queer Theory and Social Change.* New York: Routledge.

Lauristen, John and David Thorstad. 1974. *The Early Homosexual Rights Movement.* New York: Times Change Press.

Leaky, Richard and Roger Lewin. 1977. *Origins.* New York: Dutton.

Lenski, Gerhard. 1966. *Power and Privilege.* New York: McGraw-Hill.

_____. 1984. *Power and Privilege: A Theory of Social Stratification.* Chapel Hill, NC: University of North Carolina Press.

Lofstrom, Jan. 1997. "The Birth of the Queen/the Modern Homosexual: Historical Explanations Revisited." *The Sociological Review* 45 (1):24-41.

Lukacs, Georg. 1971. *History and Class Consciousness.* Cambridge, MA: The MIT Press.

Lutz, Catherine A. and Geoffrey M. White. 1986. "The Anthropology of Emotions." *Annual Review of Anthropology* 15:405-436.

Mandel, Ernest. 1980. *Long Waves of Capitalist Development.* New York: Cambridge University Press.

Marx, Karl. 1844 (1988). *The Economic and Philosophic Manuscripts of 1844.* New York: Prometheus.

_____. 1845 (1978). "Theses on Freuerbach." Pp.143-145 in *The Marx-Engels Reader*, second edition, edited by Robert C. Tucker. New York: W.W. Norton & Company.

_____. 1859 (1978). "Preface to *A Contribution to the Critique of Political Economy.*" Pp. 3-6 in *The Marx-Engels Reader*, second edition, edited by Robert Tucker. New York: W.W. Norton & Company.

_____.1867 (1992). *Capital, Vol.I: A Critical Analysis of Capitalist Production.* New York: International.

_____. 1873 (1992). "Afterward to the Second German Edition." Pp. 22-29 in *Capital, Vol.I: A Critical Analysis of Capitalist Production.* New York: International.

_____. 1973. *The Grundrisse.* New York: Vintage.

_____. 1978. "The Eighteenth Brumaire of Louis Bonaparte." Pp. 594-617 in *The Marx-Engels Reader*, second edition, edited by Robert C. Tucker. New York: W.W. Norton & Company.

Marx, Karl and Frederick Engels. 1846 (1976). *The German Ideology—Karl Marx and Frederick Engels—Collected Works*, Moscow/New York: International Publishers.

_____. 1848. "Manifesto of the Communist Party." Pp. 469-500 in *The Marx and Engels Reader*, second edition, edited by Robert Tucker. New York: W.W. Norton & Company.

McLellan, David. 1973. *Karl Marx: His Life and Thought.* New York: Harper & Row Publishers.

McMichael, Philip. 1990. "Incorporating Comparison Within A World-Historical Perspective: An Alternative Comparative Method." *American Sociological Review* 55 (6):385-397.

Mead, George H. 1934 (1967). *Mind, Self, and Society; From the Standpoint of a Social Behaviorist*, edited by Charles W. Morris. Chicago: University of Chicago Press.

Mills, C. Wright. 1959 (1975). *The Sociological Imagination*. New York: Oxford University Press.

Murray, Stephen O. 2000. *Homosexualties*. Chicago: University of Chicago Press.

Ollman, Bertell.1971 (1976). *Alienation: Marx's Conception of Man in Capitalist Society*. New York: Cambridge University Press.

_____.1993. *Dialectical Investigations*. New York: Routledge.

_____. 2003. *The Dance of the Dialectic: Further Essays on Marx's Method*. University of Illinois Press.

Orbell, John, Langche Zeng, and Matthew Mulford. 1996. "Individual Experience and the Fragmentation of Societies." *American Sociological Review* 61:1018-1032.

Padover, Saul K. 1979. *The Letters of Karl Marx*. Englewood Cliffs, NJ: Prentice-Hall.

Papazian, Charlie. 1991. *The New Complete Joy of Home Brewing*. New York: Avon Books.

Parsons, Talcott. 1949. *Essays in Sociological Theory: Pure and Applied*. Glencoe, IL: The Free Press.

_____, editor. 1954. *Essays in Sociological Theory*. Glencoe, Illinois: The Free Press.

_____. 1977. *Social Systems and the Evolution of Action Theory*. New York: The Free Press.

Piven, Frances Fox and Richard Cloward. 1982. *The New Class War: Reagan's Attack on the Welfare State and Its Consequences*. New York: Pantheon Books.

Podell, Janet, editor. 1987. *Rock Music In America*. New York: The H.W. Wilson Company.

Proudhon, Pierre-Joseph. 1890. *What is Property? An Inquiry into the Principle of Right and Government*. New York: The Humboldt Publishing Company.

Rhodes, Christine P., editor. 1995. *Encyclopedia of Beer*. New York: Henry Holt and Company.

Sanday, Peggy. 1981. *Female Power and Male Dominance: On the Origins of Sexual Inequality*. New York: Cambridge University Press.

Seve, Lucien. 1978. *Man in Marxist Theory and the Psychology of Personality*. Atlantic Highlands, NJ: Humanities Press.

Simons, Ronald C. and Charles C. Hughes. 1985. *The Culture Bound Syndromes: Folk Illnesses of Psychiatric and Anthropological Interest*. Boston, MA: D. Reidel Publishing Company.

Smith, Adam. 1776 (1937). *The Wealth of Nations*, edited by Edwin Cannan. New York: Modern Library.

Somerville, Siobahn. 1997. "Scientific Racism and the Invention of the Homosexual Body." Pp. 37-52 in *Gender/Sexuality Reader*, edited by Lancaster, Roger N. and Micaela di Leonardo. New York: Routledge.

Storr, Merl. 1998. "Transformations: Subjects, Categories, and Cures in Kraft-Ebing's Sexology." Pp. 11-26 in *Sexology in Culture: Labeling Bodies and Desires*, edited by Lucy Bland and Laura Doan. Chicago, IL: University of Chicago Press.

Sullivan, Nikki. 2003. *A Critical Introduction to Queer Theory*. Washington Square, New York: New York University Press.

Tannahill, Reay. 1980. *Sex in History*. New York: Stein and Day.

Thorne, Barrie and Zella Luria. 1986. "Sexuality and Gender in Children's Daily Worlds." *Social Problems* 33:176-190.

Thomas, W.I. 1966. *On Social Organization and Social Personality: Selected Papers*, edited by Morris Janowitz. Chicago, IL: University of Chicago Press.

Udin, Jeffery. 1996. "The Profits of Genocide." *Z Magazine* 5:19-25.

Wallerstein, Immanuel. 1974a. *The Modern World-System*. New York: Academic Press.

_____. 1974b. "The Rise and Future Demise of the World Capitalist System: Concepts for Comparative Analysis." *Comparative Studies in Society and History* 16:4:387-415.

_____. 1979. *The Capitalist World-Economy*. New York: Cambridge University Press.

_____. 1983. *Historical Capitalism*. New York: Verso.

_____. 2000. "From Sociology to Historical Social Science: Prospects and Obstacles." *British Journal of Sociology* 51:25-35.

West, Candace and Don Zimmerman. 1987. "Doing Gender." *Gender and Society* 1:125-151.

White, Leslie. 1949 (1969). "The Symbol: the Origin and Basis of Human Behavior." Pp. 22-39 in *The Science of Culture*. New York: Farrar, Straus and Giroux.

Wood, Betty. 1997. *The Origins of American Slavery: Freedom and Bondage in the English Colonies*. New York: Hill and Wang.

Zinn, Howard. 1980. *A People's History of the United States*. New York: Harper and Row.

Chapter Three: Macro-Micro Connections:

Humans in Societies and Societies in Humans

Groups, Societies, and Institutions

Why Groups?

Societies and Institutions

Social Dilemmas, Altruism, and Social Support

The Cultural Context

Cultural Relativity

Culture and Social Facts

Contextualizing Human Nature

Nature and Nurture

Nature, Nurture, and Gender Anomalies

Socialization and the Sociological Imagination

Homo symbolicus

Language and the Categorical Attitude

Inner Experience and Human Connections

Selective Perception and Cognitive Development

The Social Organization of Emotional Experience

Subjective Memories and Human Relationships

Conclusion

Notes

References

Chapter Three
Macro-Micro Connections:
Humans in Societies and Societies in Humans

Our humanness and our social relationships are woven tightly together. "Human nature" really has no meaning apart from our participation in societies, groups, institutions, and cultures. "*Homo sapiens* is always, and in the same measure, *homo socius*," write Berger and Luckmann (1966:51). What is so distinctive about humans is not that they possess some universal, uniform nature. Rather, what is so distinctive is that they work together to an exceptional degree to make a world in which to live. Humans have put whatever natural predispositions and potentialities they may have to a wide range of activities, purposes, functions, and relationships. Human nature is *social* and *historical*, and this means that humans are characterized by **world-openness** (Berger and Luckmann 1966:47). They demonstrate a remarkable adaptability and flexibility to a wide range of geographical circumstances and social conditions. Humans are found in practically every region on earth. They can be practically anything that the situation demands: sons or daughters; mothers or fathers; husbands or wives; nomadic gatherers or industrialists; and so on. The relationship between human beings and their environment is a dialectical one, but things are weighted much heavier on the side of environment than on "human nature." Berger and Luckmann (1966) call for a genuinely "dialectical social psychology," based on Mead's social psychology, but also drawn from other strains of social scientific thought. A dialectical social psychology would show just how much "human nature" is a product of social relationships.

One notable work in a dialectical psychology is the work by Lucien Seve (1978). Based on a materialist analysis, this approach argues that "Every development of the productive forces is at the same time the development of human capacities" (Seve 1978:91). If true, this means that the potentialities contained in the human mind change with the historical development of human society. Seve (1978:93) explains that a materialist approach allows "*for a theory of the historical forms of human individuality*. Its principle is that the individual, in the developed social sense of the term, is a product of history: 'human beings become individuals only through the process of history'." (Seve acknowledges Marx's influence; see Marx 1973:496). In a historical materialist and thus dialectical approach to human psychology, "forms of social unconsciousness . . . go with [various] types of relations," such as wanders in nomadic societies, the hoarder in medieval society, and the capitalist and/or the proletarian in modern society (Seve 1978:93). As humans produce their means of subsistence, they produce themselves. While some of their needs may be biologically based, as new forces and/or modes of production develop, new needs and capacities develop, too. "More generally, *everything* which is *specifically human*, in the developed social sense of the term, is a product of history and not a natural given" (Marx, in Seve 1978:102).

Social context and opportunity structures must be understood in order to make sense of the behavioral characteristics and subjective experiences of human individuals (Maccoby 1998:9). What humans are or do is only partially determined or shaped by biological predispositions or by any factors that might be called human nature. It is sociocultural learning and social constructions—not some inherited human nature—that must be understood and placed at the forefront of our explanations of human acts and interpersonal relationships. At some time in the past, human evolution reached the point where a fixed, biologically determined sexual division of labor was replaced by a division of labor based on learning, understanding, and intent. This made it possible for men and women to swap roles when the need arose (Taylor 1996:50). For example, *both* females and males can till soil, gather water, swing hammers, smoke cigars, wear dresses, or urinate sitting down. Some of these, however, are more likely for one sex than the other because of group-context factors. A woman might enjoy smoking cigars in private, but she avoids this in public because it just doesn't seem appropriate given the sociocultural understandings about gender roles (Neilsen 2000). Individual predispositions and proclivities have a lot more to do with socialization within institutions and exposure to cultural expectations than they do with biological heritage (Kimmel 2000:106-7). In countless ways, society controls our thoughts, emotions, and remembrances, as well as our acts and interactions. Society penetrates us as much as it envelops us (Berger 1963:121). It is for such reasons that sociologists reject reductionist arguments that try to explain problems of social structure as a result of the universal characteristics of the human individual.

Groups, Societies, and Institutions
Why Groups?

Not all human collectivities qualify as groups (Merton 1968:353). A **group** exists if two or more people interact regularly, taking account of one another and letting that accounting direct the course of their relationship. Usually group members identify themselves as belonging to a group, and they are identified that way by others. A family is a group and so are fraternities and sororities, athletic teams, and book clubs. Groups create shared ideas and develop rituals that strengthen their sense of purpose and establish their boundaries (Smith-Lovin 1999:8). This means that a group is more than the sum of its members. Members of a group may come and go without destroying it, and this **boundary maintenance** provides groups their sustaining power. Groups retain a memory and forms of knowledge that are deposited in no one person but, rather, are collectively shared. Humans could not survive as a species if it were not for living in groups.

Evolution of the human species is intricately connected with our collective experience. The groupings of our early human ancestors were, in all probability, loose-knit and fluid, tending toward low-density networks, low sociality, and strong individualism (Maryanski and Turner 1992:13). For the millions of years during which we developed to our current state in terms of brain size, methods of locomotion (bipedal), systems of communication (symbolic), and methods of reproduction (sexual), groups were an essential part of the process. Groups are crucial for human development and so much a part of all that we are it seems impossible to imagine how we could ever have been without them. No one learns to talk or communicate, and therefore think, without living with others in social groups.

Even though group living produces some costs for individuals such as increased competition for resources (e.g., food, water, territory, mates) and an increased likelihood of disease and transmission of germs and parasites (Alexander 1979:59), the costs are outweighed by the benefits. Groups make it easier for their members to find and obtain both food and water, and such necessary reproductive functions are best achieved by humans within and through social relationships. This was especially operative when humans lived in primarily **nomadic** (or wandering) societies, which comprises the vast majority of human history. Other species have discovered the benefits of groups, too. Wolves, for example, learned to hunt in packs because it allows them to bring down larger game than would be possible if each hunted alone. Human hunter-gatherers have extensive relationships, and they do practically everything together, having a clear sense of group purpose and shared identity. What they catch or grow is shared among members of the group, often according to elaborate rules of relationships within a complex network of mutual obligation and reciprocity (Wood and Hill 2000). Groups offer excellent protection for their members, because a potential predator can be met with an aggressive group defense (Alexander 1979:64). Groups maintain a society's cultural knowledge without depositing it in one person or place, providing a greater chance for that knowledge's survival. Groups provide meanings of the world by socializing children so that they learn to use a language and follow cultural norms. Groups provide access to sexual mates and marriage partners, which increases the odds that a society's daily activities will produce a new generation without too much effort. Groups allow for a complex division of labor, and this increases a society's odds of surviving as its members struggle with nature. Group living is not a deliberate choice that humans made but rather a strategy for survival that was influenced by evolutionary pressures.

Societies and Institutions

Society is a name for a particular type of collectivity, one that is large, inclusive, and enduring. Human societies have both an **ideational component** and a **relational component**. The ideational refers to an individual's personal identification with a particular group or category. The relational component refers to the actual connections between group members (Moody and White 2003:104). Members of a society share knowledge and develop and adopt customary ways of acting, thinking, and feeling. They occupy the same general territory, and they pay allegiance to the same political authority. Let's think about it this way. The people who work at the local hospital are not a society even though they, too, share knowledge, do things together, and occupy the same general area. However, take those same people and transport them to some deserted island or to some cave in the rain forests of the Philippines and that would all change. These same people would start living together as a society, and they would worry about their society's survival and well-being. They would form families, find ways to obtain food, and come up with ways to meet and deal with the problems they face as a society. At some place and time, the number of people in a society may be quite small, while at some other place and time, a society may number in the millions. It may even be appropriate to speak of an emerging global society as the social networks connecting people all across the world become more extensive (Wellman 1999:36).

Societies contain more than just groups. They also contain institutions, which have a direct and powerful impact on human experience (Nee 1998:1). **Social institutions** (see Chapter One) are recurrent or repetitive ways of acting and interacting, organized around important or even essential tasks in a society like raising children or finding (or producing) food. Institutions channel human relationships in some directions rather than in others (Berger and Luckmann 1966:55). Children must be born and then taught the essentials of life, so families develop in ways to make it happen. Likewise, individuals must be educated, so schools are created to transmit knowledge from generation to generation. Other institutions—economy, political, religious—organize human behavior around other important tasks to help societies and the people in them survive or even flourish. In regard to love, marriage, childrearing, work, education, recreation, and so on, a wide range of activities is possible. If not for institutions, humans would have to invent procedures anew in every situation in which they find themselves. What instincts do for nonhumans—preorganize and predetermine their activities in important areas of life— institutions do for us. Not all societies will have every possible institution, but each society will have at least some institutions; the more complex the society, the greater the number it will have.

Social Dilemmas, Altruism, and Social Support

Some individuals refuse to exhibit much loyalty to groups. They look out for themselves rather than doing what their culture deems morally right or politically just (Balkin 1998:104; Sumner 1994:134). When groups break into mutually antagonistic factions or self-centered individuals, we have a **social dilemma**. Each individual in a group pursues only his or her own interest, which undermines or destroys collective rewards and makes cooperation nearly impossible (Yamagishi and Cook 1993:236). Social dilemmas are found everywhere: in small and large groups, as well as in formal and informal organizations (Liebrand and Messick 1996:1). A social dilemma creates a situation in which all members will eventually suffer (Yamagishi 1995). If conflicts in a group are extensive enough, the group members will eventually become so fractious that the collectivity can simply disappear. One classic instance of this is called the "tragedy of the commons" (Hardin 1968). In feudal Europe, peasants had access to a common land for feeding their flocks. If individuals who used these lands moderated what their livestock ate, then the land would recover enough for others to use it and everyone benefitted. However, if herders got greedy and allowed their animals to eat too much, then the plants available for grazing would be consumed at too great a pace for the land to recover, destroying the commons for everyone. As feudalism was transformed into modern capitalism, more and more land was monopolized by landowners, and the amount of land available as commons became scarce. Farmers, struggling for survival, eventually were too numerous for the available land, and it was over-grazed, destroying the livelihoods of many. As their economic conditions declined, mass migrations to cities ensued. A rural agrarian population was transformed into an urban working class, forever changing both worlds.

Most social relationships contain an element of reciprocity or exchange. They also contain elements of empathy and altruism (Hunt 1990:24; Lieberman 1991:166). Altruism—true altruism—is a unique behavior. First named by Auguste Comte in 1851 (Hunt 1990:26; Heckert:2000:33), **altruism** is behavior that benefits another at some cost to the benefactor, and it is done without the anticipation of rewards from some outside source (Hunt 1990:21). Curiously, acts of altruism elicit not only admiration but also incomprehension or even suspicion. Why would one individual help someone else when it brings the donor no clear advantage? One way to explain this is to insist that, despite all appearances, the benefactor actually *is* getting some reward. In **generalized exchange**, an individual donates something in what seems to be an act of pure charity, but the donor eventually is rewarded, just not from the person to whom the donation was made (Takahashi 2000:1107). An example of generalized exchange is the donation of blood to a blood bank during a blood drive. You may not receive an immediate reward from your contribution, but at some future time you will if you ever need a transfusion. What looks like altruism may simply be a form of generalized exchange (Takagi 1996:313-7). A more charitable view of altruism is that self-sacrifice and concern for others are central to social life. Even infants show some **empathic arousal**, and they become unhappy when they see suffering in others (Hunt 1990). Reflexive? Perhaps. But even if so, an emotive reaction to the suffering of others is important in developing a child's concern for others.

Frances Cullen (1994), in his Presidential Address to the Academy of Criminal Justice Sciences on March 9, 1994, presented his views of a "social support paradigm." While Americans as individuals are generous in donating time and money to charitable organizations, U.S. society is not organized structurally or culturally to encourage high levels of social support (Cullen 1994:531). Because of the mobility, heterogeneity, and anonymity of urban life, individuals are inclined to put self-interest above the common good. Social bonds—family, community, neighborhood—have deteriorated over time, and this has produced real costs for us all (Putnam 2000:402). While social support cannot eliminate all the conflicts in a society—they are ubiquitous and often lead to beneficial outcomes—it can have great value for a society. It can help to reduce levels of crime, delinquency, stress, greed, and self-interest, making more formal methods of control less necessary (Cullen 1994:551). People who support or help others can also gain self-esteem, a new sense of purpose, and new friendships from the experience (Coles 1993; Hunt 1990:143). Rewards *can* come from altruism.

The Cultural Context
Cultural Relativity

The anthropologist Edward Tylor coined the word culture, and he used it to refer to all the material, spiritual, and behavioral products of social life (Mintz 1982:499). **Culture** refers to a historically derived system of designs for living that one generation passes on to the next (Kluckhohn 1949). It includes shared objects that are regularly used in interaction like books, chairs, frying pans, rubber bands, or eyeglasses (called **material culture**) and more abstract forms of shared knowledge like ideas, values, norms, symbols, ideologies, or technologies (called **nonmaterial culture**). Culture, a synthesis of both the material and the nonmaterial, is a systematized strategy for survival that is learned, shared, and symbolic.

The concept of culture received an important elaboration in the work of anthropologist Franz Boas. He avoided the inclination among most of his contemporaries to demean or devalue cultures no matter how "primitive" they might appear to outsiders. For him, the first task of anthropology was to carefully describe and understand the cultures of as many different societies as possible, not to rank them from good to bad (Mintz 1982:501). **Ethnocentrism**—the practice of condemning one culture by using standards from some other culture that are totally inappropriate—is something that Boas believed all responsible social scientists should avoid. Students of his, especially Benedict and Herskovits, carried on his legacy, particularly his commitment to **cultural relativity**. They believed that cultures were—or at least could be considered—equivalent and that cultural differences should be accepted and tolerated no matter how extreme they were (Hatch 1997:371). Cultural relativity has been an important principle for more than fifty years in anthropology, and it was formalized and instituted for both practical and humanitarian reasons. It was developed to defend indigenous people against threats to their collective and individual well-being, as well as to generate respect for cultural variability and diversity (Nagengast and Turner 1997:270). Recall from Chapter One that a "relativizing motif" is an essential part of sociological consciousness. This is the recognition that both social identities and cultural knowledge are a reflection of specific social locations (Berger 1963:52). For example, what it means to be a "citizen," a "female," or a "soldier" has changed over time, and it will probably change again in the future.

Culture and Social Facts

Culture is actually a process. Broadly speaking, culture is the socially learned ways of living that are found in all human societies, which includes both thought and action (Harris 1999:19). The fact that societies have cultures shows us in yet another way that individuals never act alone nor can they be understood in a social vacuum. Cultural explanations of human experience nurture the sociological imagination by showing us how history and biography work together to produce action in a society. Decisions are made about the proper and improper ways of acting, thinking, feeling, and remembering by people in some other place or time or in *this* place at some other point in time. These decisions are incorporated in culture, and they are handed on so that they are right here and right now, directing and channeling practically all that we do and experience. What humans are—the totality of the experience of being human—is a result of learning and the accumulation of human social experiences, incorporated in culture. We take account of others and construct our action based on the anticipated consequences of their action and our own, using shared knowledge and meaningful objects that we (or people like us) have created. **Cultural alternatives** exist that provide options for individuals as they construct their relationships with others. While these may be equivalent, they are not identical. For example, the shoes one wears might range from the comfortable, inexpensive and unfashionable to the uncomfortable, costly, and stylish. At meal time, some Americans eat fried fish, baked fish, or raw fish (sushi). Young people are taught to use "darn," "shoot," and "jeez" instead of more profane words that they may use as adults. Individuals do not "read" culture in the same way, nor do they enact it in the same way, either. People in similar situations may do things differently, and they may mean very different things by what they do (Mintz 1982:509). Because humans have a variety of cross-allegiances, one individual's stake in conformity may differ from that of others. He or she may even be misinformed or indifferent to cultural expectations. Cultures develop over time, and they are created as they are experienced by people acting together.

Culture is used by sociologists to explain relationships, activities, or experiences that are made possible partly because humans acting together share understandings or ideas (Becker 1982). This approach makes "culture" subservient to "relationships." When humans are committed to acting collectively and adjusting to one another to get some task accomplished—dates, marriages, work assignments, child care—in the most direct way, culture is a valuable resource to have. With a minimum of thought and effort, even strangers can fit their lines of behavior together and act in concert if they wish (Becker 1982:515). All that is really required is that interactants know—or think they do—what everyone else is likely to do in a particular situation. When people share some of the same general understandings or definitions of situations and are willing to act on shared knowledge, then joint acts will be smooth and orderly (Becker 1982:518). The participants will look like they know what they are doing. In terms of cultural contexts, sociologists want to understand how interpersonal relationships create cultural understandings and how cultural understandings influence social relationships and individual experiences. What matters more than culture—or at least no less—is **teamwork** (Goffman 1959:77-80). Like members of a team, members of a group must be willing to carry out the group's purpose and to support one another in what they are trying to do. Without adequate levels of teamwork, culture would matter little.

The potential for people to understand things differently is great, so cultural life is a dynamic, often indeterminate, affair. Some cultural processes are harmonious and stable, but others are filled with conflict and change. At times, what sociologists call **anomie**—or normlessness—exists. People are uncertain or unclear about how they should act or what is expected from them. For example, during a riot, ordinarily law-abiding citizens might steal a television set from a store, or during a sexual revolution, men and women might be confused about how to relate to one another. Normlessness eventually disappears as individuals come up with certain ways of acting, thinking, feeling, and remembering and make them customary. This is how cultural norms form by humans acting together (Becker 1982:522). When institutionalized customs are repeated, other ways to achieve the same outcome are far less likely to be adopted (Becker 1982:524; Berger and Luckmann 1966:53-58). Prejudices against these alternative customs might even form.

Culture is an excellent example of a social fact. A **social fact** (Durkheim 1938:13) is anything that is created by people but that then seems to have a life of its own and serves to constrain or regulate collective and individual action. A social fact that most of us have familiarity with is a crosswalk. These lines crossing physical space on the pavement have no inherent power to keep a car from running over someone who is crossing a street. They do, however, have a great deal of *social* power to regulate the activities of both the pedestrians who seek them out and the motorists who bring their vehicles to a complete stop to allow pedestrians to cross in front of them. Shared understandings guide behavior and shape our inner human experience (like feelings, thoughts, or remembrances), but cultural scripts in return are transformed in the process. "Clearly, behavior and ideas must be seen as elements in a feedback relationship. In the short run, ideas do guide behavior; but in the long run, behavior guides and shapes ideas" (Harris 1999:28). Cultural understandings that "work" are likely to continue. Parents will correct their children the way that they themselves were corrected when they were children, and schools will educate students pretty much as they always have, year in and year out. However, we must not lose sight of the fact that each and every component of each and every culture is a human construction. Culture is not something that automatically coordinates all members of a group into some integrated whole. No cultural script will offer perfect solutions for the multitude of problems individuals face on a daily basis (Becker 1982:521).

Different social worlds exist, and these are identifiable as distinctive subcultures of practice, discourse, and understanding. A **subculture** is a culture within a culture, having certain similarities with the dominant or host culture, but still being unique. Bikers are a subculture, as are UFO enthusiasts, joggers, golfers, circus clowns, skateboarders, and carnival workers. Subcultures have both temporal and territorial dimensions. A subculture that exists today may not exist tomorrow, and a subculture that is very important in one place may be nonexistent in some other place. What is true of cultures is also true of subcultures. Subcultures change over time, and they regulate how members of them act, think, feel, and remember. People may move from culture/subculture to culture/subculture on a continual basis, which invites the possibility of **culture shock** (Berger 1963). This is the feeling of disorientation or uneasiness that comes from moving from one culture (or subculture) to another that has a very different system of shared knowledge or designs for living. The revulsion you experience upon learning that what you thought was chicken was really freshly killed rattlesnake is culture shock. You, unlike whoever served the snake, are unaccustomed to eating reptiles. Culture wars develop, and members of different cultures or subcultures may display increased hostility toward one another; even in the absence of an actual difference in behaviors or ideas, conflicts can erupt because a *perception* of incompatibility exists (Miller and Hoffmann 1999:723). In the United States, the Republicans and the Democrats agree on many issues. However, when election time comes they elevate cultural clashes to a higher level of significance, which can polarize the population. For example, the amount of time spent debating marijuana use, gay marriages, and abortion rights detracts from what are arguably more important debates over economic insecurity, global conflicts, environmental destruction, and a crumbling physical infrastructure.

Contextualizing Human Nature
Nature and Nurture

Does a uniform, universal human nature exist, separate and separable from outside influences? Is anatomy destiny? The growing influence of Darwin's ideas about evolution meant that humans could no longer be viewed as entirely separate and independent from other animals.

> Every part of Darwin's thesis is open to test. The clues—from fossils, genes or geography—differ in each case, but from all of them comes the conclusion that the whole of life is kin. This is no mere assertion, but a chain of deduction with every link complete. (Jones 2000:3)

Sociobiology, the field that studies the biological basis of social behavior in both nonhumans and humans, has certainly forced social scientists to seriously consider that some relationship exists between human and nonhuman animals (Wilson 1975:547-575). **Nature** (innate or inborn) and **nurture** (learned or environmental) work together in all kinds of ways to make a creature what it is. What is found in the members of one species has some connection with the evolutionary changes and modifications in other species from which they may be descended (Lindesmith, Strauss, and Denzin 1999:37). It is no coincidence that humans are more like chimpanzees than they are like bullfrogs or that deers are more closely related to whales than they are to pigs (Jones 2000:19). Evolution is at work. **Continuity** (similarities *between* species) exists and it is important.

However, another important aspect of evolution also exists. It is called **emergence** or, more technically, "the theory of punctuated equilibria" (Lieberman 1991:6). This reminds us that evolutionary changes are not—and do not have to be—gradual and continuous. Levels exist, and it is possible for new processes and capacities to emerge in a species that make its members distinctive and unique from all other species around it (Lindesmith, Strauss, and Denzin 1999:37). "A series of small, gradual *structural* changes can lead to an abrupt change in behavior that opens up a new set of selective forces" (Lieberman 1991:8). Although members of different species move toward some of the same general end-states like food-gathering, reproduction, and protection, the *way* these ends are achieved can vary from species to species. Food-gathering activities in one species may be primarily under the control of innate factors but entirely learned and directed by culture in some other species. The instinctual food-gathering of a robin to feed its brood is substantially different from a night out at a local eatery by a human family.

While some resistance to Darwin's views of natural selection did exist in early U.S. sociology, especially his implication that humans were biologically determined, evolution was too powerful an idea for sociologists to abandon (Hinkle and Hinkle 1954:9).[1] While Darwin himself clearly did recognize the intricate (and dialectical) relationship between nature and nurture, his ideas were misconstrued as proving that nature was the bedrock on which nurture was built. The pendulum shifted too far in the direction of nature. In the social sciences, instinct and biological determinism overshadowed—at least for a while—explanations of human experience in terms of environmental and group factors. The fact is, however, that human beings are socially constructed in so many ways that it is impossible to separate any human abilities, traits, or temperaments that might actually be universal and natural from those that are acquired or historically and socially constructed (Petersen 1998:67-68).

A volume by the British psychologist William McDougall was the first authoritative book to explore the question of human instincts (Hinkle and Hinkle 1954). His view was that if you wanted to explain human behavior, you had to start with the innate package of determining forces that a human creature inherited from its ancestors. The relevance of instincts for an understanding of human behavior—especially at the social level—was ultimately challenged because the **instinct doctrine** left too little room for the impact of environment and learning on human social relationships. No simple, elegant, and convincing way could be found to separate behaviors that might be instinctual from those that were caused by things such as reflexes, drives, simple conditioning, cultural learning, or even just plain choice. Was sex or aggression an instinct or was it produced by learning? What percentage of behavior was nature and what percentage was nurture? Were certain responses instinctual in some species but entirely learned in others? No clear answers to these questions were forthcoming.

Bernard's critique of the instinct doctrine was simple and powerful: too many instincts were being blamed for just too many things (Hinkle and Hinkle 1954:29). After examining the work of a large number of writers, Bernard was able to identify 15,789 separate instincts that these writers used to explain behavior, divisible into 6,131 different types. Anytime something needed explaining, an instinct was called into service to do it. Had supporters of the instinct doctrine only used instinct to explain a few types of behavior among a limited number of species, they might have been more successful in spreading their views. However, as it was, they killed the goose that laid the golden eggs.

Bernard did not totally abandon instinct as a cause of human behavior, but he did show how little room the instinct doctrine left for learning and choice in human affairs.

The two terms "nature" and "nurture" are actually inseparable (Lewontin, Rose, and Kamin 1984:34). Humans are neither robots whose actions and inner experiences are determined by genes, nor are they clean slates upon which "society" writes whatever it wants (Steen 1996:21). Some of what a human does—some of the social differentiation between individuals and groups of individuals—has to do with chromosomes, genes, body chemicals, and brain structure. That evolution exists in some form or another, and that humans have evolved in some way or another from lower life forms, seems beyond dispute (Udry 1995:1269). However, no instinctual or innate human characteristics—even if they were to exist—can account for the arrangements of a society. What genes determine, if they determine anything at all, is a *range* of likely or possible responses of a particular organism to a constantly changing environment (Lewontin 2000:68). This means that a dialectical relationship exists between individuals and society, each being a condition of the other's existence and progression (Berger and Luckmann 1966:61; Lewontin, Rose, and Kamin 1984:257).

The belief in the ideology of biological determinism, instinct doctrine, and the search for universal, uniform human nature is closely affiliated with what anatomists call "organizational theory." According to this theory, organs of the body are organized in such a way that different parts have clear and consistent functions (Wijngaard 1997:27-30). Depending on the kind of prenatal hormones to which a developing human is exposed, the individual becomes either male/masculine or female/feminine unless something unusual happens. The dualistic view of sex differences and the belief that androgens (male hormones) invariably make a brain masculine and their absence invariably makes a brain feminine is too simple to do us much good. In this contested terrain, new understandings develop all the time. Neither hormones nor behaviors—or even human bodies—fit neatly into a masculine-feminine dualism (Wijngaard 1997:83-96). The concepts of "male," "female," "masculine," "feminine," and "sexuality" are neither defined nor definable by any one universal biological characteristic. None of these has cross-cultural or trans-historical significance; they all derive from their social positioning in a system of social difference and domination (Petersen 1998:6). The ancient Greeks recognized differences between the sexes, but they usually considered them a matter of degree, not kind. This mode of perceiving sexual differences had disappeared by the end of the eighteenth century. The development of a two-sex, two-gender model of human identity was founded on a faith in the existence of immutable, natural, universal, essential differences between males and females (Petersen 1998:43-4). Simply, males and females were viewed as naturally and qualitatively different—in terms of flesh, bone, and brain—and therefore inclined to be better at different things. Women were defined as being naturally better at raising children and doing domestic chores—the private realm—and men were defined as being naturally better at performing activities in the public realm of business and politics (Oliker 1998). The danger of dualistic thought, especially when differences are defined as innate, immutable, or natural, is that one half of the duality may be assigned an inferior significance (Wijngaard 1997:109). The relegation of women to the private sphere went hand in hand with their typification as inherently inferior to men (Oliker 1998:21-26).

Since the mid-1970s, it has practically been an article of faith in neuroendocrinology and related fields that biological masculinity is caused by prenatal exposure to androgens (especially testosterone) and femininity by prenatal exposure to estrogens (Wijngaard 1997:43). This view may be incorrect because it assumes that each chemical has its own distinctive function. Biomedical researchers now acknowledge that prenatal androgens must be converted into estrogens before they become functional in brain development (Wijngaard 1997:105). Because a male body contains *both* masculinizing and feminizing hormones, as does a female body, it is therefore *not* true that androgens are the sole agent responsible for producing masculinity and suppressing femininity (Wijngaard 1997:36-37). At the human level, hormones seem neither to create masculine or feminine brains nor to force males into some activities and females into different ones (Wijngaard 1997:73).

Human experience and individual identity cannot be divorced entirely from our biological heritage, but they are not determined by it either (Lewontin, Rose, and Kamin 1984:10). Wijngaard (1997:115) calls for a **transformative model** to clarify the relationship between nature and nurture. This model is based on the idea that no feature of human experience is a result of biology *only* or a result of environment *only* (Wijngaard 1997:115). Behavior plays an important role. A transformative model allows us to understand our biological characteristics themselves, in part, as an element in a network of interactive operations. "Gender identity is no longer a static attribute of individuals. Gender undergoes a lifetime of reconstruction to reflect social and biological events, such as menstruation, sexual activity, childbirth, and parenthood, or the absence of any of these experiences. Gender reconstruction among individuals eventually changes the meanings of social and biological experiences" (Wijngaard 1997:117). Neither biology nor environment, all by itself, determines our behavior, skills, temperament, or outlooks.

Nature, Nurture, and Gender Anomalies

The role of nature in relationship to nurture is continually debated. According to Money and Tucker (1975:89), what makes it possible for an individual to define himself as a male or herself as a female is the interaction between an inborn disposition for gender and the gender signals that a child learns in the first few years of life. Humans are wired but not programmed for gender in the same way that they are wired but not programmed for language. Innate factors and learning work together. Although gender identity cannot be modified once it has crystallized, Money and Tucker's (1975:90) theory holds that a **gender identity gate** is wide open in the early days of life and stays open for some time thereafter. They relate the case of twin boys, one of whom experienced a bizarre event, to demonstrate the malleability of gender.

A young farm couple took their sturdy, normal, identical twin boys to a physician in a nearby hospital to be circumcised when the boys were seven months old. The physician elected to use an electric cauterizing needle instead of a scalpel to remove the foreskin of the twin who chanced to be brought into the operating room first. When this baby's foreskin didn't give on the first try, or on the second, the doctor stepped up the current. On the third try, the surge of heat from the electricity literally cooked the baby's penis. Unable to heal, the penis dried up, and in a few days sloughed off completely, like the stub of an umbilical cord. (Money and Tucker 1975:91-2)

Colapinto (2000) gives a more detailed account of the botched circumcision and the twins' experience. About the age of seven months, the twins developed a condition diagnosed as phimosis. The boys' foreskins were constricting the opening of the penis and making urination difficult. The condition could be fixed by a circumcision. The boys' regular physician was unavailable, so Dr. Jean-Marie Huot, a forty-six-year-old general practitioner, did the operation. The child picked to go first, named Bruce, was anesthetized, a clamp was placed on his penis, and the foreskin was stretched to make it easier to cut the skin. Huot elected to use a Bovie cautery machine to do the circumcision instead of a scalpel. The machine was set at low current and it failed to cut the skin. The current was increased. On the second try, the current was still not high enough. On the third try, with the current even higher, the child's penis was severely burned when the needle touched him. In fact, a puff of smoke rose from his groin. The child was taken immediately to the burn ward, and his parents were summoned. When they arrived, Dr. Huot told them about the "accident," a rather charitable and self-serving way to describe what he had done to their child. When Ron and Janet were allowed to see their son, what they saw was unforgettable. The child's penis was blackened like a piece of charcoal. Over the next few days, the penis dried up and then broke away in pieces. It was not long before nothing remained of the organ. The parents were almost as shocked as was their hapless child. What could be done?

The Reimers experienced a glimmer of hope after seeing a television interview with Dr. John Money of Johns Hopkins, one of the country's leading sexologists. The Reimers first met with Dr. Money early in 1967. Money was very interested in the case, perhaps because he cared about the Reimers and was alarmed over the tragedy that had befallen their son. He also saw it as a potential test of his theories of sex, gender, and gender reassignment. Here was an individual with an identical twin brother (to serve as a comparison), who was normal at birth in terms of genitals and probably hormones and nervous system, but who had been irreparably damaged through physician error and general stupidity. The patients that Money usually dealt with had been born with ambiguous genitals. As adults they elected to have surgery to synchronize their genitals with their gender of identification. Money's career could benefit enormously from his involvement with a case like the Reimer's. He laid out the options for the parents but nudged them toward the view that it would be best to try to change their "son-without-a-penis" into their "daughter-with-a-vagina." Money assured the parents that Bruce's young age meant that he would accept the new gender and pattern erotic interests and activities accordingly. However, he instructed that if they chose gender reassignment for their son, it would work best if it were started as soon as possible.

Ron and Janet Reimer decided to follow the advice from the expert at Johns Hopkins as they understood it. Shortly after their return from Baltimore to their home in Winnipeg, Canada, they came up with a new name for the child—Brenda Lee Reimer—and they started treating Brenda like a girl and as if she had always been one. Her hair was allowed to grow long, she was given clothing meant for girls to wear, and she was encouraged to act in "girlish" ways. At twenty-two months, she was returned to Johns Hopkins (on Monday, July 3, 1967) where she was surgically castrated. Both of the testicles were removed (bilateral orchidectomy)—this time with a scalpel—the ducts that would have carried sperm to the urethra were tied off, and the scrotal tissue was used to make external genital structures. More extensive surgery was needed to construct a vaginal opening and the vaginal channel. Hormone treatments would promote breast development, a widening of the pelvis, and suppress both hair growth and a masculine voice. Intensive therapy sessions by trained professionals would add to the efforts of parents, the child's brother, and other family members to erase any memories of the child's previous life and to get her to live as a female and identify with her new sex. For the next several years, socialization would have to take its course until hormone treatments would be initiated to continue the feminization process, and additional surgical reconstruction to enhance her feminine appearance would be done. No one could know, of course, how things would turn out for this family and the boy who would be raised as a girl. Certainly, any predictions should have been guarded precisely because the case was so unique.

Money and Tucker (1975:97-8) reported that as a result of the treatments received by the girl child from all interested parties, she eventually did become a little lady, though tomboyish. By age five, they claimed, the child liked to stay neat, to dress in pretty clothes, to experiment with different hair styles, to play with dolls and doll carriages, and to help her mother in the kitchen. They used this case to demonstrate the power of learning to make gender reassignment successful and that the gender identity gate is open at birth for a normal child and stays open for years thereafter. Money and Tucker were being less than honest, however, and in actuality the child strenuously resisted the reassignment. From their analysis, Diamond and Sigmundson (1997) reached conclusions very different from those offered by Money and Tucker. Diamond and Sigmundson (1997) think that gender identity is innate and caused by prenatal hormones and other genetic factors that differentiate the nervous system and brain while a child is still in the womb. "The evidence seems overwhelming that normal humans are not psychosexually neutral at birth but are, in keeping with their mammalian heritage, predisposed and biased to interact with environmental, familial, and social forces in either a male or female mode" (Diamond and Sigmundson 1997:303). Thus, they conclude gender flexibility (in children with normal chromosomes and nervous systems) is significantly limited by prenatal factors.

The saga of the Reimers, what happened to them and the eventual outcomes, has been more thoroughly chronicled by Colapinto (2000) in his book, *As Nature Made Him: The Boy Who Was Raised As a Girl*. This case's details are at the heart of a discussion of human nature, nature and nurture, genetics and environment, and biology and rearing. Though a sample of just one, this case seems to refute strongly Money and Tucker's idea of the gender identity gate. The girl child never really adjusted to her assigned gender, had always been stubbornly tomboyish, hated frilly dresses, preferred playing with boys and boy toys, and considered herself an outsider from the beginning of her reassignment. She never felt that she was the girl that everyone assured her she was.

Brenda Lee Reimer, according to photographs, certainly looked the part of a pretty, brown-eyed, brown-haired, little girl. However, according to reports of those who knew her, that was as far as her femininity went. When she walked the walk and talked the talk, she did it as a boy. The toys that she preferred were the toys of her brother, and she used her girl toys to play "boy's" games. She used her jump rope to tie up people or to whip them; the sewing machine that she was given was totally ignored. Brenda even insisted on standing to urinate, a position that meant the urine would shoot directly out and end up all over the toilet seat (Colapinto 2000:61). She would even sneak out to an alley to urinate (Colapinto 2000:166). This case, presented by Money and others at Johns Hopkins as a fine example of a successful gender reassignment, just wasn't going according to the way their theories predicted. Despite the intensive efforts, Brenda never felt that she was a girl. Even the regular visits with John Money at Johns Hopkins, trips that her parents had to force her to make, did little to change her mind. She was not a girl and never would be, no matter what anyone said. However, the combined forces of her parents, physicians, and Dr. Money eventually had a cumulative effect. They were just too much for her to resist, and on the eve of her twelfth birthday, at their request, she started taking a feminizing drug (estrogen). In the beginning, she only pretended to take the medication, throwing it in the toilet. Her parents got wise and began to watch her while she swallowed the daily dose of medicine. Breasts did develop on Brenda, along with an accumulation of fat on her hips and waist. These physical changes were most embarrassing, and she gained weight to make them easier to hide. When her voice got huskier and more masculine, she was baffled. Her mother told her that many girls have deep voices. It was becoming increasingly clear to practically everyone that the feminization process was not working.

On the afternoon of March 14, 1980, her father picked her up from school. They went for ice cream, and then headed for home. In the family's driveway, Ron told her the details of the botched circumcision. While Brenda remained impassive throughout, her father was brought to the point of tears while relating the tale. Brenda's principal feeling after hearing what her father had to say was one of relief. She finally understood why she felt the way that she did. She wasn't nuts or some kind of oddball (Colapinto 2000:180). Brenda decided that she would no longer live as a female. First on the agenda was the selection of a new name. Brenda didn't want to return to her birth name, Bruce, because she thought it was a name for "geeks and nerds" (Colapinto 2000:182). She came up with two possibilities, Joe or David, and let her parents make the final decision. "Brenda" became "David." Second on the agenda was to go public with the big news. In August, a week after he turned fifteen, David told his extended family that he was no longer Brenda (and never had been). Next, he had to get his female form changed. After receiving injections of testosterone, he sported peach fuzz on his face, a few hairs over an inch. He later had a painful double mastectomy (Colapinto 2000:183). A month before his sixteenth birthday (July 2, 1981), David had surgery to construct male genitals. A penis was crafted from tissue and muscles on the inside of his thighs, and artificial urethra and testicles were fashioned out of plastic and placed in his reconstructed scrotum (Colapinto 2000:190). David was very pleased with the results. In 1988, his brother introduced David to Jane Fontane, a divorced woman and mother of three. The two hit it off and they started to date regularly. On September 22, 1990, approximately two years after they were introduced, David and Jane were married at Regents Park United Church in the city of Winnipeg. David continued to struggle—unsuccessfully as it turned out—with his experience. He suffered from depression, and had many personal and professional problems. His twin brother killed himself in 2002. David lost his job and separated from his wife. He lost most of his life savings in a questionable golf shop investment. After three unsuccessful attempts at suicide, David Reimer finally accomplished it. On May 4, 2004, at the age of 38, David Reimer sat alone in a car and shot himself in the head.

The penile ablation that David suffered as a child, his reassignment as a girl, all the accompanying difficulties experienced by him and his family, and his physical change back to male allow us a unique opportunity to think about the relationship between nature and nurture, between the group and personal identity. Does this story prove—as it seems to—that nature is more important than nurture? It is quite clear that David was unhappy as Brenda, markedly so. It is also quite clear that he was happier as David, although the suicide complicates *any* interpretation. However, the fact that he was unhappy as a girl doesn't mean that gender is programmed in us by our prenatal environment and present at birth. So many factors are operating in this particular case that it's impossible to know what to make of Bruce's change to Brenda and then to David. First, and most important, this is a sample of one, hardly enough on which to base any generalizations about human nature. Second, this case is unique. How many times will identical twin boys be circumcised electrically by an incompetent physician, who manages to burn off the penis of one of the children? What this case shows is that when unexpected events happen, the outcome will always be a product of a complex interplay between biology, behavior, roles, expectations, relationships, and environmental contingencies. To reduce the final outcome to some unfolding of an inexorable biological process is, of course, to miss important points.

It is clear that Dr. Money and those who followed his lead were patently wrong in their assessment of this case. While Money (and his supporters) can't be blamed for believing that gender is flexible, he certainly *can* be blamed for the cavalier way he tried to get Brenda Lee Reimer to feel right about being a girl. It was clear, and Money should have known, that Brenda was not adjusting at all to the sex reassignment; he should have had the professional detachment and integrity to admit it. By failing to do so, he not only did a disservice to this child and the child's family but to the entire scientific enterprise. Even if Money is right that gender is flexible, he certainly was wrong in this case about what exactly that point is. The Reimer case gives us no reason to be optimistic that even children who are two-and-a-half to three-years old can be switched successfully from one gender to the other. It might, however, be possible if a child is much younger; clearly, if reassignment is to have any chance of success, it must occur as early in life as possible.

David was more than a boy interrupted in his development. He became a test case for the nature-nurture controversy, a role, of course, that he never coveted. Much of the interpretation of this case, and therefore much of what happened, has to be understood in the context of a socially constructed binary world in which the only possibilities are boy *or* girl, male *or* female, or masculine *or* feminine. The answer to the question, "Why am I not happy as a girl?" can only be found in David's case with the answer, "Because I'm really a boy." Other people, who may be no happier, will find the answer to this question along very different lines. Several societies have social roles for the sexually ambiguous, who are often seen as one among many different possible human varieties. India has its "hijras" (castrated males), Oman has its "xaniths," and Native Americans have their "berdaches." Each one is a case where a male plays a role that is neither entirely male nor female.

David's conviction that he was a male all along, despite all that was done to convince him otherwise, does not prove that it is natural for boys to urinate standing up or that girls naturally like dolls better than trucks. It does not prove that maleness/masculinity is natural. Kessler's (1998) study of the **intersexed**, that is, people who are born with genital, gonadal, or chromosomal characteristics that are neither all female nor all male, shows that some of David's experiences are shared with others. Kessler shows the "power of the penis" in determining how decisions are made about sex assignment and surgical reconstruction. She notes that a small penis almost always means a child will be reassigned as a girl. The prevailing belief among most sexologists and medical personnel is that gender is biologically determined and that a lack of male genitals means that an individual will be better off being raised as a female.

While David defined his happiness in terms of returning to his "natural" sex, the intersexed examined by Kessler were more critical of the separation of the world into two mutually exclusive, non-overlapping categories of male/female or masculine/feminine. They defined *their* happiness in terms of an increased societal acceptance and tolerance of genital variation and of the intersexed (Kessler 1998:105). The intersexed must continually grapple with the confusing and contradictory messages that swirl around them in regard to what they "really" are. Kessler's respondents and "the boy who was raised as a girl" all would probably agree that far too much attention is directed to the size and shape of the genitals in making crucial decisions about sexual identity, self-concept, happiness, well-being, and personal adjustment. Kessler's subjects as well as David Reimer had their sex defined exclusively in terms of the *absence* of a body organ. "All humans without penises are females" is the prevailing view, which is like saying, "All pets that are not dogs are cats." This formula obviously fails the rules of logic.

Our thoughts, actions, and feelings are products of a complex interplay between happenings in our brains and bodies and happenings in our society and groups. Our identity is a reflection of membership in social groups, traits we show, traits that others think we show, and traits that we think we show. Becoming a person cannot be separated from the people, historical events, and social circumstances that surround us all. Our personal identities are embedded in a network of complex, interactive processes. All human events are both social and biological, just as they are both chemical and physical (Lewontin, Rose, and Kamin 1984:282).

> The properties of individual human beings do not exist in isolation but arise as a consequence of social life, yet the nature of that social life is a consequence of our being human and not, say, plants. It follows, then, that a dialectical explanation contrasts with cultural or dualistic modes of explanation that separate the world into different types of phenomena—culture and biology, mind and body—which are to be explained in quite different and nonoverlapping ways. (Lewontin, Rose, and Kamin 1984:11)

A constant and active interpenetration exists between an organism and its environment. Organisms do not passively respond to an environment; they actively seek out options and alternatives or work to change the world in which they live (Lewontin, Rose, and Kamin 1984:12). Life is a kaleidoscope of perceptions, thoughts, feelings, remembrances, and relationships. To the extent we believe that human experience is encoded in the genetic instruction book, to that extent it is more difficult to see just how much our lives are shaped and reshaped by our dialectical relationships with other people.

Socialization and the Sociological Imagination

The human brain increases in size for about eighteen months after birth inside a skull that allows it room to grow, as the cranial sutures do not fuse for months after birth (Taylor 1996:46-7). Humans may have the most voluminous brain in proportion to their body size of any large animal species that has ever lived (Wilson 1998:105). This is great for us because a close association exists between cognitive ability and the size of the brain compared to body size (Page 1999:166). Considering the amazing complexity of the human brain and its connections, it is likely that no two people organize their experiences and memories of the same event in the same way, and an individual may remember and respond differently to identical stimuli on different days of the week (Lewontin 2000:67). A human baby's dependency on others for its survival, its immaturity, and its helplessness at birth, make social interaction an important and necessary process in the making of the human. Human development is channeled or even constituted by socially determined interferences from others. For simplicity's sake, we can say that humans have a "nature," but it is far more correct to say that humans produce themselves (Berger and Luckmann 1966:49).

Socialization refers to the lifelong process of acquiring the social heritage, during which humans learn what society expects from them and they develop a self. **Self** is the process of viewing oneself as an object and then using those understandings or meanings of self to construct further action. Socialization is the process of social interaction within which an individual learns about society and develops an identity. Socialization is concerned with what is learned and how, when, and why this happens. While an understanding of socialization does start with an assumption that a newborn is relatively helpless and dependent, this view of the newborn as passive is an inadequate view of the nature of things (Danziger 1971:14). Newborns are quite active, and they have a great impact on others even on the day of their birth and, in the usual case, for evermore. Infants cannot correctly be viewed as blank slates, and certainly not for long. Parents will testify to the unique dispositions of their different children, even from the moment of their births. Some infants are docile, and others are active. The prevailing view of socialization is that the developing child both influences and is influenced by others in a lifelong process of learning (Corsaro and Eder 1995:428). If it is true that the world a child enters into is strange and confusing to him or her, it is also true that the world becomes increasingly familiar as the developing child overcomes his or her **egocentricity** and learns adult ways of acting, thinking, feeling, and remembering.

Homo symbolicus

Approximately sixty-five million years ago, primate sensory abilities changed dramatically, because a **neocortex** developed on top of older brain structures. The expanding neocortex, especially the visual cortex, is an important characteristic of the primate brain (Maryanski and Turner 1992:44). This new structure allowed primates to monitor subtle changes in the outside world in a quick and efficient way.

> . . . this primate adaptation involved a neocortical expansion that allowed
> for rapid adaptation to new situations and avoided the problem of devel-
> oping a highly specialized body form. This elaboration of the new cortex
> also created connections within, and among, the tactile, auditory, and
> visual sensory paths. (Maryanski and Turner 1992:43)

The neocortex made it easier for creatures to perform complicated motor tasks, to have improved sensitivity to sensory data, and to integrate perception, thought, and action in highly efficient ways. It is the part of the brain that is the most closely associated with thinking and being able to respond to an ever-changing environment with precise and effective responses (Lieberman 1991:21). The visual system became the primates' principal sense perception (Maryanski and Turner 1992:49). Visually guided behavior allowed more purposeful, intentional responses to the outside world, while making it possible to create mental representations of it. In a very dialectical fashion, a reciprocal and interactive relationship developed between natural forces and the developing individual.

> This dramatic change in the nature of sensory input made the primates a cortical step removed from most other mammals. What began as an increasing dominance of the visual organ over the olfactory in information processing was to culminate in the capacity to represent the world symbolically and use language. (Maryanski and Turner 1992:47)

These early creatures had the ability to monitor visually their world, which, in turn, enhanced the brain structures of the cortex. These changes in the brain led to a greater reliance on learning and memory, which eventually led to more flexible and intentional behavioral responses (Maryanski and Turner 1992:50). Humans and their world changed each other.

A crucial leap in the size of the human brain occurred between 2.5 million and 1.6 million years ago, a factor that probably gave our human ancestors an edge over close rivals. Reasons may have included the demands of a more complex social division of labor and its relational requirements, the advantage of being able to plan ahead or to integrate sensory data more effectively, and the increasing size of human culture (Taylor 1996:49). However, the principal and most fundamental event responsible for human brains, and thus for much of human progress, is the human capacity for rapid, precise, vocal communication (Lieberman 1991:9). Specialized brain structures and other features of human anatomy make it possible for us to make speech sounds, as well as to decode them effectively (Lieberman 1991:38). Language and culture select for bigger brains, it is true, but they also select for a different *kind* of brain (Hockett and Ascher 1964:146). Pathways and connections that are used frequently become stronger, while those that are not used either disappear or start performing other functions. Humans have highly evolved vocal structures that make it possible for them to speak, and humans have brain structures that allow them to engage in rule-governed movement of lungs, tongue, and lips to make human speech possible (Lieberman 1991:1). Our closest nonhuman relatives, as intelligent and humanlike as they are, lack both the kind of brain and the kind of vocal structures to make anything close to human speech possible at all.

Maryanski and Turner (1992) identify two crucial sets of environmental pressures that encouraged the development of speech. First, on the open plains of the savanna (the birthplace of the human line), where sound travels easily and little protection exists, random sounds and emotional outbursts would scare potential prey away and draw the attention of hungry predators (Maryanski and Turner 1992:60-1). Silence—or at least the ability to remain silent when the situation demanded—was golden. Selection pressures must have made it more likely that the individuals who would survive would be able to suppress random vocalizations even when they were excited or upset (Maryanski and Turner 1992:61). It is a short leap to the purposeful control of vocal sounds. Although we might utter involuntary sounds (e.g., when we hit our thumb with a hammer), or say things that we regret, the essence of human speech is that we can consciously construct complex thoughts and then verbalize them to others (or even aloud to ourselves) in order to produce a particular outcome. Second, the advantages of group living and social relationships make human speech more likely. Because human social bonds are not genetically programmed, they had to be built through symbolic communication (Maryanski and Turner 1992:67). Symbolic speech provides a common universe of discourse, and this can generate feelings of cohesion and solidarity. When the auditory-vocal channel became the principal medium of communication, it led to further changes in the brain that set the foundation for the development of symbolic interaction through logically based speech (Maryanski and Turner 1992:66). Symbolic speech allowed the effective transmission of cultural and technical knowledge such as how to start a fire, when to plant the crops, how to build a wheel, or how to stay dry in a heavy rain.

Recall from Chapter One that a symbol is a vocal or physical gesture that stands for or represents something else because of group agreement. For different communities of language users, the word "rabbit" might represent a cute, furry creature to be adored or it might mean the main prey on a hunt to be chased and killed. The "okay" symbol in the United States takes on different meanings elsewhere, just as moving the forefinger across the throat can mean "stop it," "knock it off," or "your days are numbered." Sign language used by the deaf is another example of symbolic gestures. When you know what a physical or vocal gesture means, you can use it to interact with others. Symbols are more than just conventional, however; they are elastic and versatile. Anything can be a symbol, and symbols can refer to anything if members of a group use them in the same way. Symbols allow humans who use them to share attitudes or outlooks in the context of a social or collective act. By recognition of this shared reality, "We are calling out in the other person something we are calling out in ourselves, so that unconsciously we take over these attitudes" (Mead 1934:68-9). It is the vocal gesture that is especially powerful for creating a shared tendency to respond. As individuals utter words, the meanings of which are shared with others, this shared meaning maximizes the possibility for a shared or joint act (Mead 1934). Symbols are the basis of language, and human society requires the development of language for its organization (Mead 1934:235). The ability to create, use, and respond to symbols is a distinctly human enterprise, and it is at the heart of understanding all that we are.

> Language is, first of all, a form of behavior. It is not merely a system of symbols, but the activity of using and interpreting symbols. Speech is often said to be the most primitive form of language behavior, but speech is meaningless unless it is addressed to an understanding listener. Hence conversation is the essential and original form of language; language behavior not only originates in cooperative social action, it is such action. (Lindesmith, Strauss, and Denzin 1999:82)

Self and the transmission of culture take place in and through symbolic interaction.

Children acquire meanings by learning what particular sounds, words, or physical gestures will do in terms of how others respond (Rose 1962:15). Eventually, sounds, words, or physical gestures come to evoke in children the same response that they have evoked in others. A child can complete an act or predict what is likely to happen in his or her mind because he or she has learned what effect it has on others. At the heart of symbolic learning, then, is the ability to take the role of others and look at the world—and one's own self—through their eyes. Role-taking is a process that was explored in great depth by Mead, and it may, in fact, be his most original and useful term. When you **role-take** you mentally project yourself into the position of another and look at the world (and yourself) from that other position. "Language in its significant sense is that vocal gesture which tends to arouse in the individual the attitude which it arouses in others, and it is this perfecting of the self by the gesture which mediates the social activities that gives rise to the process of taking the role of the other" (Mead 1934:160-1). As a child matures and becomes both more social and more socialized, he or she continues to get better and better at taking the role of the other. The beginning days of one's life are characterized by an egocentricity in which little or no role-taking exists. However, day by day, a child gets better at projecting himself or herself mentally into the position of others. Eventually, the child internalizes these views and uses them, sometimes for its entire life. We eat food made from recipes of our parents and grandparents, and we often adopt their religion as our own. As children mature and get more proficient with symbols, they are able to learn with greater speed and ability. Symbolic representations of people, places, objects, and experiences can become harder and firmer with the passage of time (Berger and Luckmann 1966).

Language allows a flexible and innovative response to a constantly changing world of people, places, and things. Talk is flexible (Goffman 1981:52). Language and symbols allow precise responses to new situations and happenings.

> As many scholars have noted, human language is creative; its rule-governed syntax and morphology allow us to express "new" sentences that describe novel situations or convey novel thoughts. (Lieberman 1991:81)

Written language has a remarkable structure. Alphabets are finite lists of characters or "letters." Letters in an alphabet do not contain inherent meaning. They can be listed in any order. However, abbreviated strings of letters, ordered in a particular way, create "words." An almost infinite number of words can be created out of a finite number of letters. Words by themselves contain some content, but their meaning remains very limited. A "grammar" is a system of rules with formal properties but no inherent meaning of its own. If words are strung together within the rules of a grammar, however, then "sentences" can be made. Sentences strung together create things like prose, personal letters, short stories, books, and so on. The number of possible ideas, sentences, and books is virtually unlimited.

Our symbolic system is the lens through which we interpret the world and with which we relate to others or even to ourselves. Symbols are not simply attached to things that need to be named. Symbols provide a script or text for viewing the world. We think of things and evaluate them as "good" or "bad," "right" or "wrong," "just" or "unjust." The world is not simply expressed and described with language; it is, in large part, constituted by language. Language determines consciousness in so many ways that our perception and understanding of the world are inextricably tied to our symbolic representations of it (Sapir 1949; Whorf 1956). According to the **Sapir-Whorf hypothesis**, language constructs reality, and to possess a language is to have a narrative to make sense of the world. Words are not simply neutral descriptors but linguistic devices that create the world within which humans live. What we perceive, know, feel, and remember, then, are not simply expressed or described by language; they are actually created in many ways by how they are symbolically described. Language precedes thought, not the other way around, and material relationships often precede both. The difference in experiencing "love" versus "lust" is constituted in part by having two different words, along with their distinctive definitions and accompanying feelings, that make it possible for humans to experience sexually related emotions differently.

Language and the Categorical Attitude

The evolution of symbolic interaction for the species *homo sapiens* has a direct and immediate impact on each and every member of the human race. The distinctively human ability to communicate with symbols impacts both our relationships to others and our own inner experience. We would not get very far in our social development if we did not learn to understand and use language and the symbols on which it is based. Lindesmith, Strauss, and Denzin (1999:73-4) describe this ability as the **categorical attitude**. It has two principal parts. The first is the realization that things can be named. Humans attach names such as "mother," "father," "home," "school," "chair," or "bed" to people, places, and things. The second part of the categorical attitude is the realization that named objects can be placed into larger and more inclusive categories like "animal" or "plant."

The categorical attitude in its naming phase is the first point in a child's life in which he or she uses a symbol. Prior to this point, whatever words the child uses were said because of imitation or simple conditioning. With the categorical attitude, however, the child realizes that *this* particular sound, gesture, or word stands for something else because he or she consciously understands the relationship between symbols and whatever is symbolized. A child "agrees" to use the word "water" to refer to that cool stuff in the glass because that's what other people do. The child learns that words exist and that words can be used to refer to objects, people, situations, and experiences in his or her life. Categorical thinking allows us to group things together that we want to group, to distinguish one category from all others, and to relate to the world as if it is orderly.

> Hierarchical categorization systems implicitly code knowledge. When someone tells you that the item on the counter is a fruit, you immediately know a great deal about it. You know that it is a plant, that it can be eaten, and that it probably tastes sweet. (Lieberman 1991:144)

Categorical thinking helps to reduce a great deal of the confusion and chaos of the world. Money may come and money may go, but the *category* of money has a certain permanence and stability to it. The arrival of the second part of the categorical attitude represents a "cognitive milestone" in the learning process and usually occurs sometime during the second year of life (around fourteen to eighteen months) (Lieberman 1991:145). Once we have mastered higher-order concepts like number, weight, length, and color, we can use them to think about anything we like, from bed knobs to broomsticks. Without categories we would be unable to think in an advanced or sophisticated way (Lindesmith, Strauss, and Denzin 1999:75).

It seems that youngsters can understand talk before they can enter into conversation themselves (Hauser 1997:338). When newborns do start making sounds, they are not words. Infants cry, grunt, shriek, squeal, squeak, and coo. As with all forms of human communication, an early stage exists. In the evolution of an individual's speech, sounds are at first reflexive and meaningless; the child emits them because the child can. However, at some later point in time, the child uses the same (or comparable) sounds and vocalizations voluntarily with purpose and intent. Even cries seem to have this potential.

> The earliest cries appear to be completely involuntary, driven by the limbic system. As cortical structures mature, however, cries can be voluntarily produced and used to manipulate the behavior of potential caretakers. (Hauser 1997:327-8)

Babbling (e.g., "mamamama" or "dadadada") is an important form of communication for the newborn, and of all a baby's noises, it is the one that most clearly qualifies as a precursor to speech. Hearing oneself babble helps a child acquire speech by letting him or her realize that he or she has the capacity to vocalize (Hauser 1997:331). Babbling also gives other members of a group an opportunity to reward and echo back the child's sounds in a way that promotes the child's acquisition of language. Not much interaction can take place around the child's utterance of a grunt or a coo. However, when a child babbles "mama," or "dada," a whole series of responses—most highly pleasurable from the standpoint of the child—are directed at him or her. This reinforcement may be all the more reason for the child to continue to babble in more purposeful ways on future occasions.

Children's first words almost always refer to concrete and immediate objects or to specific individuals, and youngsters learn words through a direct process of association and deduction.

> Young children clearly do not run off to consult a dictionary every time they encounter a new word—for one thing, they cannot read at first. Nor do they continually ask their caretakers for formal definitions of new words. Children listen and observe; they make use of the real-world context and of words and syntactic rules that they have previously acquired to learn the meanings of new words. (Lieberman 1991:123)

By eighteen months, children usually stop using single words and start speaking in more complicated ways, using simple sentences. While it will take a long time before a child develops an extensive vocabulary, the syntactic rules of language are mastered early in life and without too much effort (Deacon 1997:113). The human child has an inborn capacity for learning language. One reason for this is because we can recognize and learn quite early in life the logic behind symbolic reference (Deacon 1997:141). Children's learning limitations with regard to most things might actually be an advantage when it comes to learning the fundamentals of a language. After a certain age, it may be practically impossible to learn a new language and use it as well as do native speakers (Lieberman 1991:137).

Symbols move language users away from the concrete world of sights, sounds, tastes, touches, and smells, while it nudges them even further away from their egocentricity. Once symbolic interaction is possible, we no longer—and never will again—respond to the world directly; we respond to our symbolic representations of it. Responses can be quite varied. Flag burning for one person is a political statement against a country or regime, while for another it is the greatest of insults and can elicit a violent response. When humans start using symbols to communicate with others, it makes it much easier for them to project themselves into the position of others (and correctly figure out others' intended plans of action). This mental projection into the position of another makes it possible for the developing child to become aware of the existence of multiple perspectives. In time, children internalize some of these views and start using them in their relationships with others. They also use these views to judge and direct their own self-development. Symbols and role-taking are remarkable abilities, abilities that are correlated with other things that make humans so distinct.

Human mind or mental activity is closely associated with our language abilities. **Mind** exists when an individual is making indications to himself or herself in some meaningful way. Thinking is an inner conversation or the organization of brain processes through language. It is an internalized conversation of meaningful gestures (Mead 1934:156). It takes place when an individual is using a symbol privately that calls out a response in some other that it calls out in one's self (Mead 1934:146-7). If language is essential for thinking, it is also necessary for the development of self (Mead 1934:135). We may be born with a body, but the self is something that emerges later in the process of symbolic interaction (Mead 1934:136). A creature can act intelligently and consciously without acting in a self-consciously or reflexively intelligent manner, that is, without reference to self. When a human acquires a sense of self, it means that he or she has a self-definition and can imagine what that image is and evaluate it from situation to situation. While we may be tempted to think of the self as something tangible and concrete, self-development is a *process*. Self is continually created and re-created during interaction in the many situations in which humans find themselves (Carver and Scheier 1998; Cooley 1902; Hewitt 1997:51), and held together by the thread of memory (Berger 1963:106).

The social construction of self involves the participation of many different people in interaction. In their mutual, tacit understandings about their social situation, actors must take into account one another's claims about personal character (Goffman 1959). People are constantly in the process of constructing and reconstructing their own biographies and presenting them to others (Goffman 1959). Individuals must pick and choose as they construct their performance of their roles, because humans don't always receive or give off consistent messages. They must learn to reconcile incompatible expectations of others.

> A child who cries at home gets—if he's lucky—attention and sympathy. In nursery school, a child who cries too much is avoided by his peers; in grade school he is jeered at. A child who acts cute and babyish for her daddy evokes a different reaction from her classmates. Children who get laughs for their clever remarks at home wind up in the principal's office if they don't learn to hold their tongue in school. At home the squeaky wheel gets the grease; outside, the nail that sticks up gets hammered down. (Harris 1998:58)

Play represents a transitional stage between childhood and what comes after, because it frees the child from total reliance on the concrete, immediate world and all its situational constraints (Vygotsky 1978:99). It helps the child learn that differences exist between the ordinary world and the world of imagination and pretense (Vygotsky 1978:93). Children eventually reach a point where the responses that they call out in themselves are similar to the responses that they have called out in others (Mead 1934:150).

With more experience, maturation, and practice, we reach the point where we are able to take the role of a **generalized other**. The generalized other is the view or perspective of the entire society or community, internalized in the self. Once this occurs, the individual really is a society in miniature. While he or she may still take on the role of some specific other, the individual can also take the role of a wider population or perspective and use this viewpoint to judge and evaluate his or her conduct. Individuals often adopt tastes from peer groups at school or work, they participate in the sports offered by their church leagues, and they hold political opinions pushed by already established political parties in their states or nations. The emergence of the generalized other means that the individual has figured out the views of a large number of individuals, integrated them into some coherent whole, and internalized this viewpoint (Mead 1934:151). We continually take account of many other individuals and, at least partially, internalize their views. We must do this if we are ever to develop proper social relationships and to reach a point where we can interact with others with any proficiency (Mead 1934:154-5).

Inner Experience and Human Connections
Selective Perception and Cognitive Development

Social environment plays a crucial role in what we perceive and interpret. The way we mentally process what we perceive through our senses is to a great extent socially mediated. Perception is irreducibly social, and what we see, smell, hear, taste, and touch is almost always filtered through social lenses that make it possible for us to differentiate and respond to some things instead of others. For example, Americans perceive fewer races in the world than do Brazilians. Social perception is dependent on two basic processes: (1) lumping and (2) splitting (Zerubavel 1991:21). **Lumping** occurs when people, objects, situations, and experiences that are believed to be alike in some way are placed in a single perceptual cluster. Red roses, yellow daisies, and pink tulips are all lumped together in a cluster called "flowers," even though they are of different sizes, colors, and shapes, just as Saint Bernards and Chihuahuas are both called "dogs," even though they look very different in many ways. **Splitting** occurs when perceptual clusters are separated from each other. For example, poodles can be separated from both terriers and beagles. It is easy to miss the arbitrary and conventional nature of lumping and splitting, especially if we had no personal hand in the construction of the categories used in the lumping and splitting process. These perceptual clusters seem to be natural facts that we can neither ignore nor wish away, but they can be *un*made just as easily as they were made (Zerubavel 1991:74). This conclusion reflects the relativizing motif of the sociological imagination.

> Being a member of society entails "seeing" the world through special mental lenses. It is these lenses, which we acquire only through socialization, that allow us to perceive "things." The proverbial Martian cannot see the mental partitions separating Catholics from Protestants, classical from popular music, or the funny from the crude. Like the contours of constellations, we "see" such fine lines only when we learn that we should expect them there. As real as they may feel to us, boundaries are mere figments of our minds. Only the socialized can "see" them. To all cultural outsiders they are totally invisible. (Zerubavel 1991:80)

While a few universal or natural laws of perception and attention do exist because we are human beings (and not reptiles or amphibians), for the most part, our experience of perception and attention is best viewed as a fluid, dynamic, socially constructed process. "It is our social environment that normally determines what we attend to but then ignore. In helping set the horizons of our attention and concern, it is often society that defines what we consider relevant" (Zerubavel 1997:42). We think about and know the world as husbands, wives, grandparents, teenagers, students, teachers, liberals, conservatives, fundamentalists, atheists, athletes, vegetarians, stamp collectors, magicians, and so on. Americans, unlike ancient Romans, would probably not find it particularly attractive to witness an execution of real-life convicts on stage during a theatrical performance (Zerubavel 1997:61).

Children go through stages of cognitive development (Piaget 1954; Piaget and Inhelder 1969). **Primary cognitive socialization** is the process of learning the basic fundamentals of thinking or knowing that allow us to survive as members of the human race and as members of a particular society. **Secondary cognitive socialization** is the process of learning the more specialized knowledge and skills of some particular group (Zerubavel 1997:18-9). In the United States, learning to speak, read, and write is part of primary cognitive socialization; learning to fly a kite or swim laps at the local pool is part of secondary cognitive socialization. The more elaborate or involved a culture is, the greater its cognitive demands. Secondary cognitive socialization will take on special importance in any society in which a profusion of competing groups and subcultures exists. Individuals will find increasingly that what they learned during primary cognitive socialization is insufficient for all the demands placed upon them as they mature. They will have to continuously learn new things to be able to function in all the different groups and organizations they will encounter.

The Social Organization of Emotional Experience

A crucial part of human experience is emotion or feeling. Because emotions sometimes seem to erupt from nowhere, they may seem to be more asocial and idiosyncratic than are other parts of inner experience. While an emotional response may involve physical responses that cognitive response does not—for example, changes in breathing, skin temperature, blood pressure, and heart rate—our experience of emotion is still heavily influenced by sociocultural processes. Lupton (1998:167) argues that "the experience of emotion involves the interpretation of physical sensations mediated through a body image that is culturally contingent." Emotions can change other bodily states such as memory, inference, and decision-making (Howard 1995:101). When we are feeling good we attend to different cues inside our bodies and in the outer world—and we remember different things about what we attend to—than when we are feeling bad. Good moods lead people to rate practically everything else as better and to make judgments more quickly (Howard 1995:101). An irony of human existence is that our emotions are never as subjective as they feel.

Writers like Freud or Darwin believed that emotions were part of biological heritage: all animals had emotions, and the range and complexity of emotions were determined by brain and body. Certain stimuli produce certain definite emotions—period. However, in all actuality, emotions are situational and cannot be reduced to the workings of biology. While nonhuman animals seem to experience certain emotions like anger or fear—the so-called primary emotions—it is most unlikely that these are comparable to human emotional experience. Without a self and reflexive intelligence, it is impossible to experience secondary or higher-level emotions like embarrassment or empathy (Lewis, Sullivan, Stanger, and Weiss 1998). Even so basic and primary an emotion as fear cannot be divorced entirely from our relationships to others or our sense of self (Glassner 1999). Humans can become terrified at the prospect of developing cancer, losing a job, or being deserted by a loved one (Tomkins 1998:210). Fears change over a lifetime, from fear of staying home the night of the big dance, to fear of being unable to provide enough security for one's family or to take care of one's ailing parents. Human emotions arise in response to the meaning structures of given situations. Fridja (1998:271) reminds us of the "law of situational meaning." Positive emotions are produced by events that are defined by individuals as satisfying their goals, and negative emotions are produced by events that are defined by individuals as harmful or threatening to the achievement of their goals. Emotions change when meanings change, and meanings are always embedded in social relationships and therefore are always socially constructed.

Emotional experiences always involve a complex interaction between physiological happenings of our bodies and external events; the way we label, interpret, and assess an emotion is a central part of what that emotion is and how it unfolds. An emotion always signals us about states of our body *and* of the nature and quality of our relationships (Hochschild 1983:28; Scheff 1990; Smith-Lovin 1995:121). "You are starting to make me mad" is a statement about emotions and relationships, and it conveys a world of meaning to anyone who hears it. No human experience can be only emotional, and no emotional experience can be purely physiological (Lindesmith, Strauss, and Denzin 1999:132). Emotions have a strong foundation in neurophysiological processes—some people are depressed by rain—but they are still flexible and responsive to cultural norms and values, as well as to the behavior of others (Elster 1999:205; Illouz 1997). Emotions reflect the historical, social, political, and economic contexts within which they are created and expressed (Lupton 1998:16). What triggers our emotions, how they are expressed, and even what qualifies as an emotional response in the first place are all powerfully influenced by social context. All emotions are interpreted by the self at some level of awareness (Lindesmith, Strauss, and Denzin 1999:135; Stinchcombe and Heimer 2000:313). Certain emotions may be aroused more frequently in one society or group than in another, and the way emotions are expressed can vary, not only from person to person, but also from status to status.

Emotions are vocabularies used by each of us to make sense of our own inner experiences and our relationships to others. "I did it all for love" is a powerful claim that will produce a constellation of subsequent feelings and thoughts in others, as well as in the self, that other emotional claims would not (e.g., "I did it all for lust"). The process of naming feelings is part of how those feelings are experienced and expressed. Our definitions of situations are a central part of what we experience and can perceive, and so they are an important part of what we feel (Hochschild 1983:221). Emotions reflect particular features of a relationship we choose to contemplate. The same person, the same relationship, or the same event almost always produces a range of emotions like love, joy, hate, anger, pity, disappointment, guilt, and so on. It is not possible to experience all these different feelings all at once. We experience **compound emotions**. Sometimes, all we seem to be able to remember are the bad feelings, while at other times, it is the good feelings that predominate. What happens is that from moment to moment we focus on different features of the situation (Hochschild 1983:224), or we reevaluate or recategorize what we are feeling in new ways.

Subjective Memories and Human Relationships

Every collectivity—nation, community, corporation, school, family—has things it wishes to remember and other things it wishes to forget. Because groups and social relationships influence our thoughts and emotions, they also influence how and what we remember or don't remember (Howard 1995:95). The past, as a socially constructed reality, impacts all those who share in its terrain. "These environments (which include, for example, the family, the workplace, the profession, the fan club, the ethnic group, the religious community, and the nation) are all larger than the individual yet at the same time considerably smaller than the entire human race" (Zerubavel 1997:81). Most of our important memories are memories of things that happened with, around, or because of others: first dates, marriages, divorces, first jobs, birthdays, vacations, important books, an act of kindness (or meanness), the death of a loved one, dissolution of a relationship, a favorite movie, a summer romance, and the like. Of equal importance is the fact that much of what we remember is shared with other people. These relationships or connections constitute the lens through which memories are constructed, recalled, and renewed. Hollywood directors revere the names of Orson Wells, Alfred Hitchcock, and Francis Ford Coppola, but other people may not even know who they are. Young women who are considering a career in professional soccer know the names Mia Hamm and Brandi Chastain, but most other people do not. Memories and recollections pool in groups and maintain significant meanings for them. Phrases or slogans such as "Hell no, we won't go!" "Kent State," " Less Filling, Tastes great." or "9-11" will evoke different memories for people at different times and places. Individuals in society often negotiate exactly what happened (and why), and these social constructions pass into the collective memory. These memories—distorted or not—come to be "what really happened," and they may become harder and firmer with the passage of time as they are told and retold.

We do not remember in a social vacuum. The social world plays a big part in determining what we should remember and what we can, or ought to, forget (Zerubavel 1997:84). The social control of collective memory is not absolute, and unpopular or despised recollections may surface time and time again; children may learn things about the family that their parents would just as soon have kept from them. Many battles are fought over how we should remember the past, who should be given central roles in it, where a given history should start and end, when particular events and happenings should be remembered and celebrated, and whose version of history is most correct. In cultural conflicts that go on over generations, such as the Israeli/Palestinian conflict, who "fired the first shot" is either lost, contested, or misrepresented. One group's "first shot" is another's "self-defense"; one group's "forced expulsion" is another group's "abandonment of lands." Group memories are almost always contested memories, and they are continually constructed, deconstructed, and reconstructed (Irwin-Zarecka 1994; Zerubavel 1997:12). In a real sense, we are what we remember (Lembcke 1998).

Conclusion

By occupying social positions, humans are placed at the juncture of a multitude of social forces. As a result of these pressures and forces of social control, humans come to be what they *must* be from the standpoint of a society. Society determines not only what we do but also what we are. Identity is socially created and socially transformed, and the limits of human nature are shockingly broad (Mills 1959:6). Society gets inside of each of us as it constrains us. In the intersection of history and individual biography, it is societies, groups, institutions, and cultures that play a principal role in making us what we are.

Darwin's ideas about evolution and survival of the fittest had a powerful impact on explanations of human experience. His work was interpreted as saying that nature was more important than nurture, meaning that instincts and biology were more important than learning and environment. Continuity in species development does exist, but so does emergence of new traits in response to environmental stimuli. Sociologists believe that the instinct doctrine leaves too little room for intention and deliberation in human affairs, while missing the role of groups and interpersonal relationships. Human beings are socially constructed in a multitude of ways, and it is impossible to separate learned traits from those that might actually be universal and natural. Nature and nurture act together, and a dialectical relationship exists between biology and society, each being a condition of the other's existence.

Socialization is the lifelong process during which individuals learn the way of life of their society, internalize its culture, and develop both mind and self. Fundamental to this process is the existence of symbolic interaction and the acquisition and use of language. The ability to use language requires a specific type of brain and vocal structures. These are products of human evolution. The emergence of language was encouraged by environmental changes, as well as by the demands of our emergent patterns of interaction. Language makes it possible for humans to exhibit a flexible, innovative response to a changing environment. It also encourages the development of role-taking, mind, and a sense of self. Children acquire language through watching others, though their brains are designed to be ready to develop this ability. They go through stages in language development. They first realize that things can be named and then they discover that named people, objects, situations, or experiences can be placed into categories. Rapid, precise vocal communication played an interactive and reciprocal role in making the human brain what it is now.

Because social environment plays a powerful role in making us what we are, it directly influences the nature of our perceptions, thoughts, emotions, and remembrances. Perception is based on the processes of lumping and splitting. It is a fluid, dynamic, socially constructed experience. When we think, we do it as members of thought communities or cognitive subcultures. We think not only as human beings but also as members of groups, categories, or cultures/subcultures. Our emotions, too, are heavily influenced by group-context factors. Emotion always involves the interpretation of physical sensations that are viewed and understood through a body image that is culturally contingent. Emotional experiences always involve a complex interaction between physiological happenings of our bodies and external events. The way an emotion unfolds has much to do with how it is labeled, interpreted, and assessed. Our remembrances reflect our relationships to others: most of our important memories are of things that happened with people, and we share these memories with others and often construct them together. "What really happened" is often a product of negotiation and compromise. Rules of remembrance exist that tell members of groups what they should remember and what they should forget. Our inner lives, therefore, are intimately tied up with our relationships to others.

Notes

[1]The opposite could also be held to be true. Darwin borrowed the phrase "survival of the fittest" from an early sociologist, Herbert Spencer.

See: http://www2.truman.edu/~rgraber/cultev/spencer.html

References

Alexander, Richard. 1979. *Darwinism and Human Affairs*. Seattle, WA: University of Washington Press.

Balkin, J.M. 1998. *Cultural Software: A Theory of Ideology*. New Haven, CT: Yale University Press.

Becker, Howard. 1982. "Culture: A Sociological View." *The Yale Review* 71:513-27.

Berger, Peter. 1963. *Invitation to Sociology: A Humanist Perspective*. Garden City, NY: Anchor Books / Doubleday Company.

Berger, Peter and Thomas Luckmann. 1966. *The Social Construction of Reality*. Garden City, NY: Doubleday.

Carver, Charles and Michael Scheier. 1998. *On the Self-Regulation of Behavior*. Cambridge, UK: Cambridge University Press.

Colapinto, John. 2000. *As Nature Made Him: The Boy Who Was Raised As a Girl*. New York: HarperCollins.

Coles, R. 1993. *The Call of Service: A Witness to Idealism*. New York: Houghton Mifflin.

Cooley, Charles Horton. 1902. *Human Nature and the Social Order*. New York: Scribner's.

Corsaro, William and Donna Eder. 1995. "Development and Socialization of Children and Adolescents." Pp. 421-51 in *Sociological Perspectives on Social Psychology*, edited by Karen Cook, Gary Alan Fine, and James House. Boston: Allyn and Bacon.

Cullen, Francis. 1994. "Social Support As an Organizing Concept for Criminology: Presidential Address to the Academy of Criminal Justice Sciences." *Justice Quarterly* 11:527-59.

Danziger, Kurt. 1971. *Socialization*. Baltimore, MD: Penguin.

Deacon, Terrence. 1997. *The Symbolic Species: The Co-Evolution of Language and the Brain*. New York: W.W. Norton and Company.

Diamond, Milton and Keith Sigmundson. 1997. "Sex Reassignment at Birth: Long-term Review and Clinical Implications." *Archives of Pediatrics and Adolescent Medicine* 151:298-304.

Durkheim, Emile. 1938. *The Rules of Sociological Method*, 8th edition, translated by Sarah Solovay and John Mueller and edited by George Catlin. New York: Free Press.

Elster, Jon. 1999. *Strong Feelings: Emotion, Addiction, and Human Behavior*. Cambridge, MA: MIT Press.

Frijda, N.H. 1998. "The Laws of Emotion." Pp. 270-87 in *Human Emotions: A Reader*, edited by Jennifer Jenkins, Keith Oatley, and Nancy Stein. Malden, MA: Blackwell.

Glassner, Barry. 1999. *The Culture of Fear: Why Americans Are Afraid of the Wrong Things*. New York: Basic Books.

Goffman, Erving. 1959. *The Presentation of Self in Everyday Life*. Garden City, NY: Doubleday Anchor.

_____. 1981. *Forms of Talk*. Philadelphia, PA: University of Pennsylvania Press.

Hardin, Garrett. 1968. "The Tragedy of the Commons." *Science* 162:1243-48.

Harris, Judith Rich. 1998. *The Nurture Assumption: Why Children Turn Out the Way They Do*. New York: Free Press.

Harris, Marvin. 1999. *Theories of Culture in Postmodern Times*. Walnut Creek, CA: AltaMira Press.

Hatch, Elvin. 1997. "The Good Side of Relativism." *Journal of Anthropological Research* 53:371-81.

Hauser, Marc. 1997. *The Evolution of Communication*. Cambridge, MA: MIT Press.

Heckert, Druann Maria. 2000. "Positive Deviance." Pp. 29-41 in *Constructions of Deviance: Social Power, Context, and Interaction*, 3rd edition, edited by P. Adler and P. Adler. Belmont, CA: Wadsworth.

Hewitt, John. 1997. *Self and Society: A Symbolic Interactionist Social Psychology*, seventh edition. Boston: Allyn and Bacon.

Hinkle, Jr., Roscoe and Gisela Hinkle. 1954. *The Development of Modern Sociology: Its Nature and Growth in the United States*. New York: Random House.

Hochschild, Arlie Russell. 1983. *The Managed Heart: Commercialization of Human Feeling*. Berkeley, CA: Univeristy of California Press.

Hockett, Charles and Robert Ascher. 1964. "The Human Revolution." *Current Anthropology* 5:135-68.

Howard, Judith. 1995. "Social Cognition." Pp. 90-117 in *Sociological Perspectives on Social Psychology*, edited by Karen Cook, Gary Alan Fine, and James House. Boston: Allyn and Bacon.

Hunt, Morton. 1990. *The Compassionate Beast: What Science is Discovering About the Humane Side of Humankind*. New York: William Morrow and Company.

Illouz, Eva. 1997. *Consuming the Romantic Utopia: Love and the Cultural Contradictions of Capitalism*. Berkeley, CA: University of California Press.

Irwin-Zarecka, Iwona. 1994. *Frames of Remembering: The Dynamics of Collective Memory*. New Brunswick, NJ: Transaction.

Jones, Steve. 2000. *Darwin's Ghost: The Origin of Species Updated*. New York: Random House.

Kessler, Suzanne. 1998. *Lessons from the Intersexed*. New Brunswick, NJ: Rutgers University Press.

Kimmel, Michael. 2000. *The Gendered Society*. New York: Oxford University Press.

Kluckhohn, Clyde. 1949. *Mirror for Man: The Relation of Anthropology to Modern Life*. New York: Whittlesey House, a division of McGraw-Hill.

Lembcke, Jerry. 1998. *The Spitting Image: Myth, Memory, and the Legacy of Vietnam*. New York: New York University Press.

Lewis, M., M.W. Sullivan, C. Stanger, and M. Weiss. 1998. "Self Development and Self-conscious Emotions." Pp. 158-67 in *Human Emotions: A Reader*, edited by Jennifer Jenkins, Keith Oatley, and Nancy Stein. Malden, MA: Blackwell.

Lewontin, Richard. 2000. *It Ain't Necessarily So: The Dream of the Human Genome and Other Illusions*. New York: The New York Review Books.

Lewontin, Richard, Steven Rose, and Leon Kamin. 1984. *Not in Our Genes: Biology, Ideology, and Human Nature*. New York: Pantheon.

Lieberman, Philip. 1991. *Uniquely Human: The Evolution of Speech, Thought, and Selfless Behavior*. Cambridge, MA: Harvard University Press.

Liebrand, Wim B.G. and David Messick. 1996. "Social Dilemmas: Individual, Collective, and Dynamic Perspectives." Pp. 1-9 in *Frontiers in Social Dilemmas Research*, edited by Wim Liebrand and David Messick. Berlin, Germany: Springer-Verlag.

Lindesmith, Alfred, Anselm Strauss, and Norman Denzin. 1999. *Social Psychology*, 8th edition. Thousand Oaks, CA: Sage.

Lupton, Deborah. 1998. *The Emotional Self: A Sociocultural Exploration*. London: Sage.

Maccoby, Eleanor. 1998. *The Two Sexes: Growing Up Apart, Coming Together*. Cambridge, MA: Belknap Press of Harvard University Press.

Marx, Karl. 1973. *Grundrisse*. New York: Vintage.

Maryanski, Alexandra and Jonathan Turner. 1992. *The Social Cage: Human Nature and the Evolution of Society*. Stanford, CA: Stanford University Press.

Mead, George H. 1934. *Mind, Self, and Society: From the Standpoint of a Social Behaviorist*. Chicago: University of Chicago Press.

Merton, Robert K. 1968. *Social Theory and Social Structure*, enlarged edition. New York: Free Press.

Miller, Alan and John Hoffman. 1999. "The Growing Divisiveness: Culture Wars or a War of Words?" *Social Forces* 78:721-52.

Mills, C. Wright. 1959. *The Sociological Imagination*. New York: Oxford University Press.

Mintz, Sidney. 1982. "Culture: An Anthropological View." *The Yale Review* 71:499-12.

Money, John and Patricia Tucker. 1975. *Sexual Signatures: On Being a Man or a Woman*. Boston: Little, Brown and Company.

Moody, James and Douglas White. 2003. "Structural Cohesion and Embeddedness: A Hierarchical Concept of Social Groups." *American Sociological Review* 68:103-27.

Nagengast, Carole and Terence Turner. 1997. "Introduction: Universal Human Rights Versus Cultural Relativity." *Journal of Anthropological Research* 53:269-72.

Nee, Victor. 1998. "Sources of the New Institutionalism." Pp. 1-16 in *The New Institutionalism in Sociology*, edited by Mary Brinton and Victor Nee. New York: Russell Sage Foundation.

Neilsen, Joyce. 2000. "Gendered Heteronormativity: Empirical Illustrations in Everyday Life." *Sociological Quarterly* 41:283-97.

Oliker, Stacey. 1998. "The Modernisation of Friendship: Individualism, Intimacy, and Gender in Nineteenth Century." Pp. 18-42 in *Placing Friendship in Context*, edited by Rebecca Adams and Graham Allan. Cambridge, UK: Cambridge University Press.

Page, George. 1999. *Inside the Animal Mind*. New York: Doubleday.

Petersen, Alan. 1998. *Unmasking the Masculine: 'Men' and 'Identity' in a Sceptical Age*. London: Sage.

Piaget, Jean. 1954. *The Construction of Reality in the Child*. Translated by Margaret Cook. New York: Basic Books.

Piaget, Jean and Barbel Inhelder. 1969. *The Psychology of the Child*. Translated by Helen Weaver. New York: Basic Books.

Putnam, Robert. 2000. *Bowling Alone: The Collapse and Revival of American Community*. New York: Simon and Schuster.

Rose, Arnold. 1962. "A Systematic Summary of Symbolic Interaction Theory." Pp. 3-19 in *Human Behavior and Social Processes: An Interactionist Approach*, edited by Arnold Rose. Boston: Houghton Mifflin.

Sapir, Edward. 1949. *Selected Writings of Edward Sapir in Language, Culture, and Personality*, edited by David Mandelbaum. Berkeley, CA: University of California Press.

Scheff, Thomas. 1990. *Microsociology: Discourse, Emotion, and Social Structure*.

Chicago: University of Chicago Press.

Seve, Lucien. 1978. *Man in Marx's Theory and the Psychology of Personality*. Atlantic Highlands, NJ: Humanities Press.

Smith-Lovin, Lynn. 1995. "The Sociology of Affect and Emotion." Pp. 118-48 in *Sociological Perspectives on Social Psychology*, edited by Karen Cook, Gary Alan Fine, and James House. Boston: Allyn and Bacon.

_____. 1999. "Core Concepts and Common Ground: The Relational Basis of Our Discipline," presidential address given April 9, 1999, at the Southern Sociological Society Meetings in Nashville, Tennessee. *Social Forces* 78:1-23.

Steen, R. Grant. 1996. *DNA and Human Destiny: Nature and Nurture in Human Behavior*. New York: Plenum.

Stinchcombe, Arthur and Carol Heimer. 2000. "Retooling for the Next Century: Sober Methods for Studying the Subconscious." *Contemporary Sociology* 29:309-19.

Sumner, Colin. 1994. *The Sociology of Deviance: An Obituary*. New York: Continuum.

Takagi, Eiji. 1996. "The Generalized Exchange Perspective on the Evolution of Altruism." Pp. 311-36 in *Frontiers in Social Dilemmas Research*, edited by Wim B.G. Liebrand and David Messick. Berlin, Germany: Springer-Verlag.

Takahashi, Nobuyuki. 2000. "The Emergence of Generalized Exchange." *American Journal of Sociology* 105:1105-34.

Taylor, Timothy. 1996. *The Prehistory of Sex: Four Million Years of Human Sexual Culture*. New York: Bantam.

Tomkins, S. S. 1998. "Script Theory: Differential Magnification of Affects." Pp. 209-18 in *Human Emotions: A Reader*, edited by Jennifer Jenkins, Keith Oatley, and Nancy Stein. Malden, MA: Blackwell.

Udry, J. Richard. 1995. "Sociology and Biology: What Biology Do Sociologists Need to Know?" *Social Forces* 73:1267-78.

Vygotsky, Lev. 1978. *Mind in Society: The Development of Higher Psychological Processes*, edited by Michael Cole, Vera John-Steiner, Sylvia Scribner, and Ellen Souberman. Cambridge, MA: Harvard University Press.

Wellman, Barry. 1999. "The Network Community: An Introduction." Pp. 1-47 in *Networks in the Global Village: Life in Contemporary Communities*, edited by Barry Wellman. Boulder, CO: Westview Press.

Whorf, Benjamin. 1956. *Language, Thought, and Reality*, edited by J.B. Carroll. Cambridge, MA: MIT Press.

Wijngaard, Marianne Van Den. 1997. *Reinventing the Sexes: The Biomedical Construction of Femininity and Maculinity*. Blommington, IN: Indiana University Press.

Wilson, Edward. 1975. *Sociobiology: The New Synthesis*. Cambridge, MA: Belknap Press.

_____. 1998. *Consilience: The Unity of Knowledge*. New York: Alfred A. Knopf.

Wood, Brian and Kim Hill. 2000. "A Test of the 'Showing-Off' Hypothesis with Ache Hunters." *Current Anthropology* 41:124-5.

Yamagishi, Toshio. 1995. "Social Dilemmas." Pp. 311-35 in *Sociological Perspectives on Social Psychology*, edited by Karen Cook, Gary Alan Fine, and James House. Boston: Allyn and Bacon.

Yamagishi, Toshio and Karen Cook. 1993. "Generalized Exchange and Social Dilemmas." *Social Psychology Quarterly* 56:235-48.

Zerubavel, Eviatar. 1991. *The Fine Line: Making Distinctions in Everyday Life*. New York: Free Press.

_____. 1997. *Social Mindscapes: An Invitation to Cognitive Sociology*. Cambridge, MA: Harvard University Press.

Chapter Four: Social Inequality: Difference, Dominance, and Deviance

Chapter Four: Social Inequality:
Difference, Dominance, and Deviance
Understanding Inequality
What is Social Inequality?

An individual's identity contains two separable parts, social identity and personal identity (Goffman 1971:189). **Social identity** consists of those categories to which one belongs like sex, race, class, community, and country—all those statuses through which one is perceived and known. **Personal identity** is more idiosyncratic and requires first-hand knowledge of an individual. It includes an individual's name and appearance, as well as distinctive attributes, traits, or marks. These two identities, of course, complement one another, and social identity is always "fleshed out" by personal characteristics. Being a "mother" is part of social identity, but each mother has unique characteristics that make up her personal identity (e.g., *this* mom likes to mow the lawn and jog five miles a day). Some relationships are "pegged" or "anchored," and interactants know one another personally and know that they are known in both their social and personal identities. Other relationships, however, are "anonymous" and interactants know one another only as possessors of a social identity (Goffman 1971:189).

One of the most consequential features of human experience is that our social relationships are characterized by a great deal of stratification or inequality. **Social stratification** refers to the hierarchical arrangement of a society in which positions at the top are highly rewarded and those at the bottom are poorly rewarded. We rarely relate to one another as whole persons, certainly not in our public relationships, and elements of social identity can be more prominent and important than elements of personal identity. Others may zero in on our sex, gender, skin color, religion, social class, ethnicity, and the like, and treat us exclusively in terms of one of these traits. The rewards that we receive and the quality of the life that we enjoy may be largely determined by what these statuses mean to others or our socioeconomic status.

> Human inequality in general consists of the uneven distribution of attributes among a set of social units such as individuals, categories, groups, or regions. Social scientists properly concern themselves especially with the uneven distribution of costs and benefits—that is, *goods*, broadly defined. Relevant goods include not only wealth and income but also such various benefits and costs as control of land, exposure to illness, respect from other people, liability to military service, risk of homicide, possession of tools, and availability of sexual partners. (Tilly 1998:25)

Groups of people must perceive or recognize certain traits, categorize them, evaluate them, construct rewards and attach high rewards to some statuses but not to others, and pass on to others a belief system that justifies and perpetuates the system of inequality.

Social stratification is based on two universal human inclinations. The first inclination is for humans to differentiate among themselves, establishing both individual and group differences. Some of these differences are **ascribed,** being related to physical characteristics like sex, skin color, age, body build, eye color, hair texture, hand preference (right-handed, left-handed, or ambidextrous), and so on. Even when biological markers are used as the principal cue (e.g., sex or skin color), these cues still depend heavily on social organization and shared beliefs (Tilly 1998:7); a system of stratification or inequality is irreducibly social and relational (Koggel 1998:10). At other times, the differences are **achieved,** being based on acquired or learned characteristics like gender, personality, language abilities, religion, occupation, hobbies and habits, body adornments (e.g., tattoos), or years of schooling. A second inclination is for humans to evaluate and rank social differences, placing them into a hierarchy. For example, we may recognize that left- and right-handed people exist and then decide that right-handed people are *better* than left-handed ones (or vice versa).

> Social and economic inequalities regularly accompany—and are interwoven with—categorical differences among people. Wherever people differ on nominal characteristics (e.g., race, gender), they also possess different amounts of the things societies value. As an example, members of ethnic group A get more or less education, more or less income than those in group B. (Walker, Moen, and Dempster- McClain 1999:2)

An individual has many different traits and occupies many different statuses (e.g., sex, gender, race, ethnicity, social class), and traits and statuses work together to influence how an individual is ranked by others (Cotter, Hermsen, and Vanneman 1999).

Constructing Status

How do we get from difference to inequality? How do **nominal descriptors** or social differentiators like sex or race become the basis for categorical or positional evaluation and ranking? In principal—in fact, it happens all the time—it is possible to have difference without inequality or stratification. For example, at one time being left-handed was a highly stigmatizing trait. People who were left-handed wished they weren't, and they found life more difficult because of their left-handedness. This is less true now. Generally, left-handed people no longer feel particularly embarrassed by their use of the left hand, although they still realize they are in the minority. As sex, gender, skin color, ethnicity, and sexual orientation go through a similar process, U.S. society's system of stratification will also change. People will experience no more prejudice and discrimination toward their sex, gender, race, ethnicity, or sexual orientation than they do now toward their hand use.

The status construction process is complicated but some of the major elements can be identified. First, the nominal descriptors that play an important role for the status construction process are usually the ones that are the most visible. Sex and skin color, for example, are important descriptors, and they are both more visible than, say, sexual orientation. This is just part of the story, however, because some traits that are visible (e.g., hair color) are not nearly as important in assigning status as less visible traits (e.g., sexual orientation). Second, a nominal descriptor must become associated with some "exchangeable resource" (Webster and Hysom 1998:356). An exchangeable resource is any source of wealth or value in a particular society or group that can be transferred, earned, or used up. Money certainly qualifies but so do other things. In a slave-owning society, an important exchangeable resource would be how many slaves one has, and in a maritime society, an important exchangeable resource would be how many boats and fish-ing nets an individual owns. Third, nominal descriptors and exchangeable resources get institutionalized into **doubly dissimilar** encounters (Ridgeway et al. 1998:334). These are goal-oriented encounters between individuals who differ both on some nominal category (e.g., sex, gender, occupation, race) and on some scarce resource (e.g., money or power). Males may come to be seen as "better" than females because males make more money, or judges may come to be seen as better than police officers because judges have more power. As ideas and practices spread throughout a society, in time, *everyone* may admit that one category is better or more socially worthy than all others (Webster and Hysom 1998:357). Members of *both* disadvantaged and advantaged groups come to believe as a matter of course—and are certain that most people agree—that the advantaged are more worthy and competent than everyone else (Ridgeway et al. 1998:332). Small differences in attractiveness, talent, or other nominal differences can be amplified into large status differences between, for example, "stars" and everyone else (Gould 2002:1167-68).

Exploitation and Opportunity Hoarding

Why would some categories receive more exchangeable resources than other categories? Why, for example, would men have more exchangeable resources than women, or whites more than blacks? The categorical inequalities that are found in human societies can be traced to two important social processes or causal mechanisms. First is **exploitation**. It exists when powerful individuals control resources that they have received from manipulating others, who are denied the full value of what their labor produces (Tilly 1998:10). Exploitation exists in direct proportion to the degree to which individuals are kept from earning what they're worth. Let's assume that Individual X is paid five dollars an hour but provides services that allow his or her boss to charge customers twenty-five dollars an hour. Individual X, then, is exploited because he or she does not receive the full value of what he or she produces. The second causal mechanism in the creation of social inequality is **opportunity hoarding**. This exists when individuals—advantaged or disadvantaged—get, or try to get, access to a resource that is valuable, renewable, and supportive of their activities; the resource is then stockpiled at every opportunity (Tilly 1998:10). Groups use their resources to get more resources if they can.

> . . . the American people are both diverse *and* divided. They differ along common divisions such as race, ethnic heritage, religion, and gender. They differ as well on dimensions that have always existed but have only recently entered the public discourse, dimensions such as sexual orientation and patterns of family life. Many of these categorical differences are linked to durable social and economic inequalities, thus fostering divisiveness. Groups of Americans who have less of some socially valued good than their fellows—whether income or respect—express discontent with their position and, increasingly, disaffection with the American ideal. (Walker, Moen, Dempster-McClain 1999:3)

Inequality is divisive and, for many individuals, destructive (Feagin and McKinney 2003).

Durable Inequalities

A principal feature of social stratification is that systems of social differentiation and evaluation persist over time and show remarkable degrees of firmness. People at the top of the hierarchy in any society do what they can to maintain their advantaged positions, while those nearer the bottom try to move closer to the top if they can (Reskin 2003:7-14). However, the deck is stacked, and the game is really not fair. Access to scarce resources allows the advantaged to get even more scarce resources (opportunity hoarding), making it that much harder for individuals lower in the stratification system to improve their lot in life. With a little effort, wealth and power can be used to get more wealth and power. This is a state of affairs that favors the privileged and powerful in any group and the principal reason that inequalities are so enduring (Scott 2001). Inequalities that endure over whole careers, lifetimes, or organizational histories are the ones that really do make a difference in people's lives.

Various methods exist to place, position, or reward individuals, groups, communities, or societies. In an elementary school, the youngsters might be rewarded with extra helpings at lunch or extra minutes at recess, while in a boot camp, recruits might be rewarded with a weekend pass or a more desirable assignment. Sociologists divide social rewards into three categories: privilege, power, and prestige. **Privilege** refers to money, land, or other valuables in a society. An individual's income is part of privilege, as is the value of his or her total assets (called wealth). In an agrarian society, privilege might mean the number of plows or cows a farmer owns. Sociological studies have made it abundantly clear that an unequal distribution of both wealth and income exists in the United States, with wealth inequality being the most striking (Braun 1997:23). **Power** refers to the ability or capacity to do what one wants when one wants, despite opposition or interference (Weber 1968). A police officer can give a motorist a speeding ticket, but the motorist cannot give one to the officer. **Prestige** refers to the degree of respect or status that occupants of a position enjoy. Physicians have greater prestige than social workers even though they both help people in need. While these social resources or rewards are valuable and pleasurable in their own right—privilege, power, and prestige can produce all kinds of psychological gratification for those who have them—they are also the means for getting *more* privilege, power, and prestige. Hunters may be able to capitalize on their abilities to find and catch food and increase both their power and prestige. They might reach the point where they have a say in almost every decision that affects the life of the group. If they can pass their hunting abilities on to their offspring, then hunters as a group will experience a much better quality of life from generation to generation than will nonhunters.

Elites in societies use language, symbols, and ideologies—the entire range of symbolic paraphernalia—to maintain their positions and, more important, their control of people and situations (Art and Murphy 2000). Members of subordinate classes regularly accommodate to the whims and wants of the advantaged because the content of language imposes a sense of order and legitimacy on human affairs and social arrangements (Bourdieu 1991). By using their power to shape symbolic meanings of norms (e.g., laws), moral proscriptions and prescriptions, and social values, elites use language to justify inequalities in a society. They create **ideologies** to benefit themselves. Subordinates reach the point where they internalize these ideologies and they want to do—or at least are willing to do—what is best for elites. During the Middle Ages, a power was exercised forcefully but silently through the symbolic construct known as the "divine right of kings."

Distilled, it was little more than the general belief that rulers received their instructions and authority directly from God. It made rulers and their rules, and, more important, rulers' advantages seem to be sanctioned by a supernatural power. This discouraged peasants from complaining about the misery of their own lives and the prosperity of their rulers. It made it even more unlikely that peasants would rebel against an unfair and unequal society. Who would want to risk eternal damnation along with whatever penalties the rulers dispensed?

Human Capital, Social Capital, and Social Mobility

Class background and social position affect how parents raise their children, as well as how parents view both parenting and childhood. Middle-class parents employ childrearing practices that have been called **concerted cultivation** (Lareau 2002:748). They engage their children in activities that they hope will encourage their youngsters' cognitive and emotional growth so that they develop self-reliance and language skills. Middle-class parents refrain from using corporal punishment because they think that verbal instruction will better teach their children what they need to know. After their school day ends, middle-class children are shuttled from one age-specific, organized activity to another so that they will learn how to interact with other children and develop valuable life skills. This means that parents must be willing and able to maintain a rapid pace, too. Working-class and poor parents, however, are inclined to use a different approach to childrearing. They emphasize the importance of **natural growth** (Lareau 2002:748-9). They believe that their children will develop nicely if only they are given love, nourishment, and security. These children are *not* encouraged to participate in a large number of organized activities, and the pace of family life is less hectic than is found in the typical middle-class home. They spend more time with family members and less time in age-specific, organized activities. These parents are more likely than are middle-class parents to use physical discipline to correct their children.

Children from different class backgrounds reflect their differential treatment. Concerted cultivation nudges middle-class youngsters in the direction of developing a sense of entitlement and self-reliance. They fully expect to do well in life, and they achieve a maturity that allows them to interact in effective and assertive—but polite—ways with adults (e.g., teachers). As a childrearing strategy, natural growth has different effects. Instead of self-expression and independence, these children develop a sense of containment and self-control. They are inclined to act in respectful ways toward authority figures, but they hold inner feelings of resentment or suspicion toward them (Lareau 2002:748-9). Children from higher classes reach early adulthood with a stronger sense of entrepreneurial ability and a greater willingness to take risks than those from disadvantaged backgrounds, something that increases their chances of success (Halaby 2003). Privileged social background makes it possible for offspring of the advantaged to one day obtain advantaged positions of their own (Lucas 2001). In these ways (and many others), families reproduce class privileges for their members.

Social mobility, movement upward or downward in a socioeconomic system, is influenced by both human capital and social capital. **Human capital** refers to an individual's ability to produce goods and supply services, which can vary because of differences in innate ability, education, experience, and many other intangibles (Thurow 1970:15).

Human capital is not a fixed entity, because it can be increased by things like additional years of schooling or greater training and experience. Human capital is different from social capital. **Social capital** refers to the connections among individuals and the social networks and norms of reciprocity that exist (Putnam 2000:19). Social capital can offer both a private and a public good (Putnam 2000:20). If you need to borrow sugar for a meal you're making, find someone to watch your children while you're at a job interview, or locate a neighbor to mow your lawn while you're on vacation, strong community ties make any of these—and countless other things—much easier to accomplish. A well-connected individual in a poorly connected community fares worse than does a well-connected individual in a well-connected community (Putnam 2000:20). In fact, an increase in social capital makes it easier for democracy itself to flourish, which feeds back and strengthens social capital itself (Paxton 2002:263-72). Because individuals share a stronger sense of commitment and community, they will be more likely to express their views and participate in the decision-making process.

Certain attitudes, skills, and temperaments may make success and upward mobility more likely for an individual, and their absence may increase the likelihood of failure and restricted social mobility. In a society where knowledge is power and computer skills are in high demand, individuals who are highly educated and can use computers skillfully increase their chances of success. Likewise, in a society where strength is highly valued, Conan the Barbarian will do better than a highly educated computer analyst who has little muscle mass. It never hurts to be strong in a society where strength matters or smart in a society where smarts are valued. However, because of the operation of ascriptive forces and the existence of *positional* inequality, no one trait will guarantee upward mobility.

> Where one ends up in the income distribution reflects, after all, where one began, who one's parents were, what kind of education one received, race and gender, and a host of other factors—including just plain luck. (McMurrer and Sawhill 1998:1)

Family background affects one's status as an adult (McMurrer and Sawhill 1998:46-7). This is because family background has such a powerful influence on members' educational achievements and cognitive abilities (Mayer 2001:11-21; Warren, Hauser, and Sheridan 2002:445-48). The effects of socialization and social structure are powerful, and an understanding of social capital is crucial for understanding why some individuals are more successful than others (Knapp et al. 1997). No scrutiny of human capital—no matter how extensive—will help us understand why professional basketball players earn more than presidents of countries, college professors, police officers, firefighters, physicians, nurses, teachers, dentists, or social workers.

Dual Labor Markets

Inequality in the United States can be understood in large part by remembering that the economy is divided or split into sectors, and some sectors are more highly valued and rewarded than are other sectors (Grodsky and Pager 2001:544). The **primary labor market** contains those jobs characterized by high pay, pleasant working conditions, upward mobility, job security, and interesting and important work. The **secondary labor**

market contains those jobs characterized by low pay, little mobility, poor working conditions, rapid turnover, and few benefits. More and more, the secondary labor market is dominated by temporary workers, many of whom are females (Rogers 2000). While the flexibility of temporary work is presented as one of its advantages—women can stay on the "fusion track," allowing an integration of both employment and family life (Adams and Tancred 2000)—it actually may be one of its disadvantages. Employers use flexibility to exploit their temporary workers. It is used to justify low pay and lack of benefits that "temps" receive (Rogers 2000). Mobility, lifestyle, and quality of life for workers are directly dependent on their positions in the labor market, and a direct relationship exists between the characteristics of workers in terms of age, race, ethnicity, and sex and whether they work in the primary or secondary labor market (Hodson and Kaufman 1982). In other words, the labor market is segregated along the dimensions of race, ethnicity, class, sex, and gender.

The advantage of the dual-labor market view, as opposed to those that focus on human capital, is that it forces us to pay attention to the effects of the structure of society as a whole on the patterns of social inequality and how they persist over time. Individual traits and skills—the whole range of human capital—are not irrelevant. In *some* ways, individuals are the masters of their own destinies. Certain choices and decisions will predictably lead to certain outcomes, while other choices and decisions will predictably lead to different ones. Characteristics of an individual—intelligence, academic performance, drive, ambition—do play a role in his or her successes (Sewell, Haller, and Ohlendorf 1970). However, we must give social relationships and social context their due (Tilly 1998:24). No matter how brilliant, hard working, or talented individuals are, only nine of them will become U.S. Supreme Court Judges, because nine are all there are. It would be possible to create additional social mobility by expanding the number from nine to, say, twelve, but this will have a negligible impact on the well-being and quality of life of most people. An individual's intellectual ability or commitment to work is insufficient to explain why economic inequality takes the form it does (Arrow, Bowles, and Durlauf 2000). No individual trait by itself—no particular feature of human capital—guarantees upward mobility for a person. Many people work hard, having admirable qualities and a multitude of skills, but they still face restricted upward mobility (Collins and Yeskel 2000:7), because social rewards do not correspond closely with individual differences in skill, hard work, and determination (Schwarz 1997).

The Cult of Individualism

The Western heritage has always exaggerated the role of individual determination and self-reliance in accounting for patterns of social mobility. Large groups and social organizations were viewed with suspicion by the average nineteenth-century American, and men and women were held responsible for the decisions that they made and the consequences of those decisions. Social problems were almost always blamed on defects in individuals, as were social inequalities. However, to understand social problems and social inequalities, we must understand our lives and the progression of our society as a collective journey.

> Our national myths often exaggerate the role of individual heroes and understate the importance of collective effort. Historian David Hackett Fischer's gripping account of opening night in the American Revolution, for example reminds us that Paul Revere's alarum was successful only because of networks of civic engagement in the Middlesex villages. Towns without well-organized local militia, no matter how patriotic their inhabitants, were AWOL from Lexington and Concord. Nevertheless, the myth of rugged individualism continues to strike a powerful inner chord in the American psyche. (Putnam 2000:24)

The "rugged individualism" that is so much a part of our culture's sentimental journey is more a result of an idealization of our history than it is an accurate reflection of it (Vela-McConnell 1999:226). The West was tamed by people working together, not some lone gunslinger, town sheriff, or high-kicking Texas Ranger (Charbeneau 1992:132). The ethos of competitive individualism, whatever good it produces, has allowed the relative few to succeed at the expense of the many, while it has undermined community organization and social solidarity.

Relational elements have much to do with social inequality. "Social structure affects who interacts with whom, and as people interact they share, create, and forget information, which affects future probabilities of interaction" (Mark 1998:317). Even minor differences in social capital can permutate and evolve over time in ways that will produce a multitude of differences that are no longer traceable to what caused them in the first place. The contributions that others make to an individual's successes and/or failures are sometimes difficult to fully appreciate, but they are there and important.

> In most job settings, for example, any individual's performance—indeed, any individual's apparent skill—depends subtly on communication and collaboration with co-workers, including supervisors. Great dancers need supportive partners; great journalists lean on skilled editors. (Tilly 1998:101)

Even a great basketball player or highly acclaimed opera star would not have gone very far without a supportive team or adoring public. Nobody can win basketball games alone, and if audiences did not find opera pleasant enough to hear, opera singers would be unemployed. What is highly valued in one place and time is not necessarily valued in some other place and time. In 1920s United States, typing was something that was in demand, and employers were willing to pay for it; in the twenty-first century, however, this is no longer true. Computer skills are now what employers want and reward in their employees.

Imaginary Prosperity

Capitalist societies are characterized by two central contradictions (Wallerstein 2001:24). First, capitalists find that one of the best ways for them to increase their profits is to get workers to do more and more for less and less. Fire or lay off workers, decrease their wages, or replace them with machines are some of the ways that capitalists can extract more and more value from the production process. The process of cheapening or displacing workers, and the inequalities that this produces, is an inherent feature of capi talist accumulation (Zeitlin and Weyher 2001:430-31). When workers are paid less and less so that capitalists can have more and more, it means the economy will regularly run up against a stagnating (or nonexistent) demand (Burris 2001). Workers just don't have enough money to cover even the basic necessities of food, shelter, and health care. The second contradiction is that capitalists tend to think that what is good for them is good for everyone else and the nation as a whole. They think, incorrectly, that prosperity is identical to merit and that wealth is the same thing as worth. This attitude produces a **social dilemma** in which wealthy individuals put their own interests far ahead of the interests of the society, community, or group (Wallerstein 2001:24). These contradictions make capitalism a fundamentally unstable, conflictual, and alienating social system.

In the closing decades of the twentieth century, Blau (1999:3) tells us, we in the United States embarked on a great experiment. Both at work and in the national economy, U.S. workers re-embraced the market as the key to improving their standard of living. Now that the twenty-first century is upon us, we can assess the consequences of this for workers and their families. U.S. businesses have prospered, but U.S. workers and their families have not (Blau 1999:3). Despite the creation of millions of new jobs and rising incomes, the standard of living of U.S. workers and their families did not improve. Income and wealth inequality increased, and living standards for most Americans deteriorated. Highly skilled, experienced, and educated workers made real wage gains and those without skills, experience, and education suffered real wage losses (McCall 2000). The demand for low-skilled, poorly educated workers decreased, hurting those who were already in a precarious market position even more (Fernandez 2001:275-79). Increases in global competition, the decreasing influence of unions, and the use of temporary workers played an important role in the declining wages of workers at the low end of the income distribution. The market catered more and more to the needs and interests of the most advantaged, while most others suffered by comparison. The losses are not measured only in dollars but in deteriorating health, well-being, security, in fact, in the very fabric of social life (Blau 1999:4).

U.S. workers, faced with few alternatives, were forced to turn to the market at a point in time when the market itself was creating the very problems that workers were trying to solve in the first place. They asked their bosses for secure jobs and decent wages, but they got deteriorating wages, layoffs, and the flight of capital to other countries (Blau 1999:6). The turn to the market brought prosperity to the advantaged, but it did not bring much to anyone else (Blau 1999:20). Corporate boosters claimed that it was only good business for them to go wherever profits were the highest. Capitalist ventures follow a pattern that repeats itself with boring regularity. Economic markets start to weaken as consumer demand for goods and/or services plummets, workers complain more because they become increasingly unhappy with tedious work for low pay, and other communities (either at home or abroad) make offers to businesses that are too good to refuse (Cowie 1999). A company then moves to a new place and stays there until the pattern repeats itself. The bottom line is that U.S. workers are in effect powerless to affect the economic forces that impact them. They have very little leverage (Blau 1999:201).

Global Village or Global Pillage?
The World-System

If it is true that people in a society are interdependent in many ways, it is equally true that societies are interdependent, too. It would be stretching a point to claim that humans live together in a global village, but it certainly is true that what happens in one part of the world can have effects—sometimes profound ones—for people in other parts of the world (Weiss 1998). Economic relationships among the countries of the world are becoming more extensive and integrated (Bradshaw and Wallace 1996:26), even though regional alliances (e.g., OPEC or NAFTA) are constantly being formed and re-formed. The language of money is becoming a universal language (Bradshaw and Wallace 1996:26). Unlike economic relationships, political structures continue to become more and more fragmented, and multiculturalism and ethnic identity are likely to continue to grow in importance throughout the world. The global movement is toward ethnic and racial separation and increasing levels of conflict between ethnic and racial groups in the world (Bradshaw and Wallace 1996:35-6). Citizens of the world fight among themselves, mobilizing the color of their skin and/or the content of their cultures as the justification for the conflicts. The reasons for social conflicts continue to change. For example, it is likely that as the twenty-first century unfolds, religion will supplant race and ethnicity as the major source of intergroup conflict (Frederickson 2002:150).

Inequality and World Processes

A world system is a social unit with a single division of labor but containing multiple cultural systems (Wallerstein 2000:75). The development of individual societies, as well as the institutions, groups, and individuals in them, cannot be understood separate from the world system of which they are a part (Wallerstein 2001:77). Members of the world system are interdependent and operate on the assumption that the totality of their needs (sustenance, protection, pleasure) will be met by a combination of their own productive activities and the exchange of goods and services with other nations (Wallerstein 2000:82).

> The functioning then of a capitalist world-economy requires that groups pursue their economic interests within a single world market while seeking to distort this market for their benefit by organizing to exert influence on states, some of which are far more powerful than others but none of which controls the world-market in its entirety. (Wallerstein 2000:92)

World-system theorists believe that the lesson of history is that if nobody is at the bottom, then nobody is at the top. Modern, rich, developed countries like the United States, Japan, or the United Kingdom—called **core** countries—have prospered because they have exploited and used unmercifully all that poorer countries in the **periphery** and **semiperiphery**—mostly in Latin America and Africa—and their peoples have to offer (Beckfield 2003:418; Wallerstein 1974). Core nations have gone into periphery nations in search of raw materials, a cheap and docile labor force, land, a stable political system, tax breaks, interest-free loans, and an unregulated market system. World-system theorists insist that international capitalism, the profit motive, and a nation's position in the global pecking order (whether core, semiperiphery, or periphery) are responsible for the state of global inequality. They make a powerful and influential case.

Capital has the whole world within which to operate. It can follow the path of least resistance or, more correctly, least cost in ways that workers cannot. Once a company gets large enough (i.e., once an "economy of scale" is achieved), it can migrate pretty much at will to any place where the labor is cheap, the resources are abundant, and the profits are great. Labor, however, is far more restricted. Workers still do maintain a sense of loyalty and commitment to their families, communities, and nations. The flight of capital and the nationalism of workers combine to weaken laborers and strengthen their bosses (Blau 1999:215). If workers demand salary increases or improved working conditions, capital can move (or threaten to), leaving employees with no job at all. As wages deteriorate, consumption does too. The flight of capital eventually hurts not just U.S. workers and their families but the entire fabric of U.S. society. Workers are forced to accept half a loaf only because it is preferable to no loaf at all. Eventually, they may find that they are crawling for crumbs.

Inequality in the world is impacted both by differences *between* nations and differences *within* them at any point in time. At the beginning of the nineteenth century, income inequality in the world was caused principally by within-nation differences. The gap between the well-paid and everyone else *within* societies was the major source of stratification; *between-nation* differences in average annual incomes were relatively small. However, during the 1800s and 1900s, between-nation levels of inequality increased enormously so that by the middle of the 1900s, income inequality between nations had become the principal source of world income inequality. For example, at the beginning of the nineteenth century, the difference in average income between rich and poor nations was on the magnitude of four to one; at the end of the twentieth century, the difference was closer to thirty to one (Firebaugh 1999:1597).

> Thus, over a period of 150 years, the defining attribute of world income inequality switched from income differences within nations to income differences between them. (Goesling 2001:745).

By the middle of the twentieth century, between-nation inequality was the largest source of world income inequality (Goesling 2001:747). In the closing years of the twentieth century (1980-1995), however, income inequality changed once again (Alderson and Nielsen 2002). Between-nation income differences became less significant while within-nation income differences became more significant. While between-nation income inequality is still the most important factor in the patterns of world income inequality—between-nation inequality still accounts for more than two-thirds of inequality in the world distribution of income—the within-nation income differences are becoming continually more influential in the distribution of world inequality (Goesling 2001:757). The United States now has one of the most unequal income distributions in the world (Keister 2000; Smeeding 1997). This has a profound impact on the life chances of those at the bottom of the stratification system.

Disposable People, Indispensable Body Parts

Global inequality generates social forces that transform some people into commodities for other people to exploit for private gain. If individuals are viewed as commodities or objects during their life, often times expendable commodities at that, this commodification does not end even with death. Organs or skin tissues are sometimes sold by living donors because they are a source of income for individuals who are in desperate straits and must sell their organs or tissues in order to survive (or to help their families survive) (Scheper-Hughes 2000:221). However, at other times the organ harvesting is illegal, and organs are either extracted from a living individual without his or her consent or knowledge, or they are stolen from corpses in places where bodies or body parts are kept. The demand is great for viable organs like heart valves, corneas, eyes, kidneys, and body tissues, because the promised rewards are so handsome for those prosperous enough to be able to afford them (i.e., an extension of life and new abilities and capacities).

> . . . the flow of organs follows the modern routes of capital: from South
> to North, from Third to First World, from poor to rich, from black and
> brown to white, and from female to male. (Scheper-Hughes 2000:193)

What organ trafficking does is to form a temporary relationship based on supply and demand between desperately ill buyers and desperately poor and powerless sellers, both of whom are trying to survive in a place where survival is never guaranteed. "A market price on body parts exploits the desperation of the poor, turning their suffering into an opportunity" (Scheper-Hughes 2000:197).

Multinational Penetration

A crucial factor in understanding a country's inequality is how much it is penetrated by **multinational corporations**, companies that operate in two or more countries at the same time (Alderson and Nielsen 1999:627). Multinationals have no loyalty to any one country, even the ones in which they operate, and they will go wherever they can to make the most money and to find the most hospitable business climate. This often means that deals are made, some legal and some not so legal, between corporate representatives from the core and business elites, governmental leaders, and military officials in countries outside the core. The few are enriched in these non-core countries while the many continue to live their lives in desperate poverty (Braun 1997:157).

> . . . while it may be the best of times for those at the top of the global
> economy, it is not so for the majority of the world's peoples. The pro-cap-
> italist policies of many national governments and international organiza-
> tions have fostered a substantial transfer of wealth from the world's poor
> and working classes to the world's rich and affluent social classes. Social
> injustice in the form of major, and sometimes increasing, inequalities in
> income and wealth can be observed across the globe. (Feagin 2001:2)

One of the objectives of multinational corporations is, quite literally, to keep countries outside the core dependent, helpless, and poor. If a Brazilian restaurant makes a better hamburger than McDonald's, who will flock to the golden arches for their daily fast-food fix? Any effort by a country outside the core to control its economic destiny is fought by multinationals, often with the assistance of the U.S. military and U.S. foreign policy. While multinationals may come to an area with the promise of abundant jobs and higher wages for domestic laborers, the promises are rarely kept. Dominance of a country by multinationals produces long-term financial disaster for the majority of people in the host country (Braun 1997:143), because multinationals always take out of a country in profits more than they put into it in investments (Braun 1997:160).

If underdeveloped countries are to experience genuine economic growth, they must free themselves from the penetration and control of multinationals (Evans 1995). In the advance of international capitalism, the people who suffer the most in these non-core countries are those who already are suffering the most; while the rich get richer, the poor get poorer.

> The mix of world position and penetration is a major force in keeping basic human needs from being met. The more a country is penetrated by multinationals and the further it is from the core, the less able a country is to guarantee the survival of its population. (Braun 1997:181)

Modernization, *if* it is accomplished through foreign assistance and investment, does little to help most of the population in peripheral or semiperipheral nations. What penetration by multinationals does accomplish is a slowing of economic development, injury to the quality of life of most citizens, and increases in political instability and unrest (Bradshaw and Wallace 1996:51). Successful development in underdeveloped countries always requires independence from the control of these countries by multinationals (Alderson and Nielsen 1999:627; Kentor and Boswell 2003:304). This is because foreign investment serves to transfer more wealth *out* of a country than into it.

Global Connections

Globalization is a social process in which people all across the world become increasingly interconnected with one another, socially and culturally. It is more than an economic trend; it is political, technological, and cultural (Giddens 1999:28). Globalization involves the diffusion of similar social practices and cultural beliefs all across the globe (e.g., recreational activities, food, clothing, currency, language, movies, television shows, CDs, music videos). The processes of globalization influence how we live our lives, because they influence family dynamics, schools, the entertainment industry, political and economic institutions, and our cultural understandings. Globalization has forever altered U.S. institutions.

> We continue to talk of the nation, the family, work, tradition, nature, as if they were all the same as in the past. They are not. The outer shell remains, but inside they have changed—and this is happening not only in the US, Britain, or France, but almost everywhere. They are what I call 'shell institutions'. They are institutions that have become inadequate to the tasks they are called upon to perform. (Giddens 1999:36-7)

We now live in a global cosmopolitan society that nobody entirely understands but which still impacts us all (Giddens 1999:25). A sociological imagination allows us to understand what is happening in the world to be able to adjust to the world-system within which we now live.

Globalization can push downward and create opportunities for local regions to grow and develop in independent ways (Giddens 1999:31). **Glocalization** is the term to refer to the interpenetration of the global and the local (hence its name) within which a local region can make its own distinctive accommodation to global processes (Robertson 1994). Communities may work to establish their own separate ethnic, racial, or cultural identities so that they will not be swept up in global processes. This can set the stage for "reverse colonisation" in which non-Western countries influence developments in the West, such as the latinising of Los Angeles (Giddens 1999:34-5). **Grobalization** (Ritzer 2004:73) exists when core nations and/or multinational corporations penetrate a region to increase their own privilege, power, and prestige (hence the name *gro*balization). Grobalization is well-illustrated by the penetration of the McDonald's Corporation into countries all across the world.

The McDonald's Corporation, ever sensitive to the importance of thinking globally and acting locally, adopted the term "global realization" to describe its own involvement with grobalization. McDonald's now earns most of its profits outside of the United States, and McDonald's is the most widely recognized brand in the entire world, more identifiable even than Coca-Cola (Schlosser 2002:229). "The values, tastes, and industrial practices of the American fast food industry are being exported to every corner of the globe, helping to create a homogenized international culture . . ." (Schlosser 2002:229). McDonald's Deutschland, Inc., is far and away the biggest restaurant company in Germany, and traditional German restaurants are rapidly disappearing. McDonald's uses German potatoes in its fries and Bavarian dairy cows in its burgers. The company's most conspicuous and prominent publicist, Ronald McDonald, visits German hospitals and schools to make certain that children are familiar with what McDonald's has to offer (Schlosser 2002:232). McDonald's even has an eatery within walking distance of Dachau, the first concentration camp opened by the Nazis. Schlosser describes his impressions about the restaurant, and the impact of grobalization is easy to recognize.

> This McDonald's was in Dachau, but it could have been anywhere—anywhere in the United States, anywhere in the world. Millions of other people at that very moment were standing at the same counter, ordering the same food from the same menu, food that tasted everywhere the same. (Schlosser 2002:234)

The processes of globalization, especially grobalization, increase the likelihood that people across the planet will become very much alike in a multitude of ways.

Expanding inequality and the ecological risks with which it is associated cannot be blamed solely on the rich. As we have seen, without individuals who are supportive or willing to pay for goods and services, winners would not have won quite so much or quite so often. We must ask not only of the rich but also of others not quite so well placed in the world-system: How much is enough? While the issues are at times murky and reasonable people can disagree, one thing is certainly clear: More is not always better, and certainly not always better for the social world or the natural environment. Runaway consumption is not conducive to a quality life and wholesome relationships if it invites greed and envy with reckless abandon of the planet's ecological system. We consume more than any generation in the history of the world, but it has not necessarily provided a more fulfilling life for us (Durning 1992:36).

If human desires are in fact infinitely expandable, consumption is ultimately incapable of providing fulfillment—a logical consequence ignored by economic theory. Indeed, social scientists have found striking evidence that high-consumption societies, just as high-living individuals, consume ever more without achieving satisfaction. The allure of the consumer society is powerful, even irresistible, but it is shallow nonetheless. (Durning 1992:38)

If runaway consumption and pervasive social inequality continue unchecked, the fate of the earth is in jeopardy. Nobody will prosper on a dying planet.

Human Diversity and Social Deviance

The Social Reality of Deviance

One of the most persistent and common features of all societies is social deviance. Whenever people get together, some of them seem to hurt, annoy, or unsettle others. This does not mean, however, that deviance is an individual dysfunction or abnormality. It is *people acting together* who create social deviance by what they believe, feel, say, and do, and we will find both deviance and deviants practically everywhere we go. Deviance is a matter of social definition, and our understanding of deviance is advanced the furthest by studying who can successfully pin labels on whom (Becker 1963). **Social deviance** exists as a social reality when value judgments are placed on human diversity, which discredits or devalues individuals and what they are or do. Social deviance includes a wide range of things, such as crime and criminal, mental illness and the mentally ill, and even individuals who burp in public. Groups of people identify actions and/or attributes that they do not like, label them as forms of deviance, attach deviant labels to individuals, and subject them to negative sanctions (Becker 1963). As sociologists, we must always understand how groups view both human actions and human attributes and how these conceptualizations work to transform some people into deviants. The study of social deviance is substantially more than a study of a type of behavior or a type of individual; it is a study of social relationships and social perspectives on human behavior and human individuals (Goffman 1963:138).

The Relativity of Deviance

Deviance, like beauty, is in the eye of the beholder (Simmons 1969), and it is the way that people acting together categorize information and understand events that form the basis for the concepts of conformity and deviance (Wilkins 1964:59). Just as "beauty" and "beautiful" have no meaning aside from relationships and social context, neither does "deviance" and "deviant." Deviance changes from society to society, and it changes in any given society over time. At one time or place, drinking alcohol may be perfectly okay, and at another time or place, it may be forbidden; at one time or place, smoking cigarettes may be a sign of maturity and sophistication, and at some other time or place, it may be a sign of immaturity and irresponsibility. The Kágaba Indians of Colombia, for example, have distinctive views about natural sex, and their beliefs are distinctively different from those of people in other lands. They believe that individuals have had sex on every region of earth and that semen has penetrated the ground so much that the land can handle no more.

119

If even one more drop were to fall on the ground, it would open the gates of sickness and ultimately destroy the world. Magical stones must be placed in such a way that they will catch any secretions during sexual acts (Gregersen 1994:4). The Siwa of northern Africa disagree with the Kágaba about sexual secretions. They believe that a woman will find a man irresistible if he secretly ejaculates into her food (Mooney 2000:140).

Human beings are so inventive in assigning positive and negative labels to things that it is impossible to separate deviance from nondeviance in terms of inherent, intrinsic, or objective qualities (Curra 2000). Even the position people use for sexual intercourse varies from place to place, and one position really can't be universally defined as more natural than all others.

> The missionary position (as it is informally referred to, with the partners lying down and facing each other, the man on top) is generally taken for granted in the western world as the most natural in the repertory. When the Bororo Indians of southern Brazil first heard about it, they were deeply offended. "What an insult against the one who is underneath!" exclaimed one Bororo man; another said in astonishment, "But what weight!" The Trobriand Islanders are almost as uncompromising as traditional Westerners: they recognize two natural copulatory positions—neither of these is the missionary position, which they regard as impractical and improper. . . . The Zulu of South Africa judge it [missionary position] to be vulgar and unbecoming in a human being because they claim—quite inaccurately—that it follows "the manner of animals." (Gregersen 1994:4-5)

Sexual practices are learned and sexual tastes vary a great deal, not only from individual to individual, but also from culture to culture and group to group. The meaning of the kiss is not universal (Gregersen 1994:345). While kissing is an important part of love making in some cultures, it is defined as aberrant or unnatural in others (Tiefer 1978:29-37). Kissing has been used as a sign of admiration, respect, farewell, or greeting; but it has also been viewed as a health threat, disgusting, or just plain unnecessary. People in some societies (e.g., Thonga of South Africa) feel about kissing the way an American would feel about sticking his or her tongue in another person's nostril (Tiefer 1978:29-37). Social deviance exists because some groups judge and evaluate what other groups are doing (Matza 1969:41-53).

While we must be concerned with human diversity and come to some understanding of why people in one setting are different from people in another setting, this is not enough. We must also understand the social construction of claims, labels, or definitions that groups use to censure or condemn what they find troubling or upsetting in other people (Spector and Kitsuse 1977:78-81). Because we seek to understand deviance as a social relationship, we cannot only examine the diversity of human behavior and attributes. We must also examine the diversity of claims, labels, or definitions attached to both actions and attributes. Deviance is best viewed as a transaction, negotiation, or relationship in which some individuals come to be viewed by some other individuals as outsiders (Becker 1963:10). Whether a given act is deviant depends partly on what it is (i.e., whether it violates a rule or shared expectation), and partly on what groups do about it (Becker 1963:14). Trespasses are situational and temporary until they become organized into social roles that give them a durability and persistence (Lemert 1951).

Moral Entrepreneurs

Sociologists introduced an important and heretofore neglected subject into the study of deviance: the audience that witnesses some attribute or action.

> Deviance is not a property *inherent in* certain forms of behavior; it is a property *conferred upon* these forms by the audiences which directly or indirectly witness them. Sociologically, then, the critical variable in the study of deviance is the social *audience* rather than the individual *person*, since it is the audience which eventually decides whether or not any given action or actions will become a visible case of deviation. (Erikson 1962:308)

Becker (1963) coined the term **moral entrepreneurs** to help clarify how a witnessing audience can play an important role in the social construction of deviance. Moral entrepreneurs can be divided into two categories: rule creators and rule enforcers. Groups make rules for specific reasons, and sociologists try to understand as much as they can about their reasons for doing so. School boards decide on dress codes for students, and legislators decide on legal codes for citizens. Likewise, we must also understand how rules are enforced, because the groups that create rules are not necessarily the same groups that enforce them. A focus on creators and enforcers shows us as clearly as anything could that deviance is the outcome of a social enterprise (Becker 1963:162).

> Rules are not made automatically. Even though a practice may be harmful in an objective sense to the group in which it occurs, the harm needs to be discovered and pointed out. People must be made to feel that something ought to be done about it. Someone must call the public's attention to these matters, supply the push necessary to get things done, and direct such energies as are aroused in the proper direction to get a rule created. Deviance is the product of enterprise in the largest sense; without the enterprise required to get rules made, the deviance which consists of breaking the rule could not exist.
>
> . . . Once a rule has come into existence, it must be applied to particular people before the abstract class of outsiders created by the rule can be peopled. Offenders must be discovered, identified, apprehended and convicted (or noted as "different" and stigmatized for their nonconformity, . . .). This job ordinarily falls to the lot of professional enforcers who, by enforcing already existing rules, create the particular deviants society views as outsiders. (Becker 1963:162-3)

Nothing automatic exists in regard to the creation and enforcement of rules, and the social construction of deviance is a dynamic, fluid, social process. What is proper and permissible today may be improper and impermissible tomorrow (or vice versa).

Moral Panics and Moral Crusades

Moral enterprises can, of course, be initiated in response to genuinely scary situations, and a moral crusade can sometimes make a group, community, or society a safer place to be (Thompson 1998). However, it is also possible for moral enterprises to transform artificially a mildly troubling social condition into a public issue with epidemic proportions. Moral enterprises can become **moral panics**. A moral panic exists when the level of fear, anxiety, and worry are far out of proportion to the size of the danger that some condition actually poses. Some condition may be exaggerated, while some other condition, one that is actually more dangerous, is overlooked (Altheide 2002). A moral panic can create a new category of danger such as the health hazards of cellular phones or the threat of road rage. More likely, however, an old category is simply relocated, dusted off, and used as the first element in a prolonged attack on some troubling condition (Burns and Crawford 1999:148-50). During moral panics, the search for someone to blame becomes so intense that individuals may be falsely accused and persecuted even though they are undeserving of any scorn whatsoever.

Moral panics are identifiable by a number of key elements (Goode and Ben-Yehuda 1994:33-41). Heightened and widespread concern gets coupled with an increased level of hostility toward a group, category, or condition. It is not enough, however, for something to be seen as a threat; a clearly identifiable group or individual in a society must be held responsible for the troubling event (Goode and Ben-Yehuda 1994:33-4). In this way, social villains are created as they are demonized and contrasted with everybody else. An excellent way to prove one's well-developed moral sensibilities is to become a soldier in the war against evil and punish, correct, or treat other people's wickedness (Cohen 1974:11-12).

> The blacker the villain, the more useful he is to the ordinary man, who might otherwise be hard put to produce the desired contrast effect. For this reason, the wickedness of the villain, like the virtue of the saint, may have to be invented if it is not in fact present in the object. (Cohen 1974:17)

Another element of moral panics is "disproportionality." Members of a society come to believe that more individuals are deviating than actually are and that the deviance is more dangerous than it actually is (Goode and Ben-Yehuda 1994:36). Objective molehills are transformed into subjective mountains (Jones, Gallagher, and McFalls 1989:4). Moral panics tend to be volatile. They emerge abruptly and just as quickly may disappear (Goode and Ben-Yehuda 1994:38-9). Some moral panics, however, get institutionalized or routinized, and they become a relatively permanent fixture on the social landscape (Goode and Ben-Yehuda 1994:38-9). The fear of crime and criminals, drugs and drug addicts, or terrorists and terrorism are prime examples. This durability is most likely when members of what Best (1999) calls the "iron quadrangle"—mass media, government, political activists, experts—promote an interest in some troubling event in mutually reinforcing ways. Individuals and agencies use their values and interests to make claims in order to get resources and to direct attention to their favorite goals and projects (Brownstein 2000:11).

Convergence occurs when two or more activities, traits, or happenings are linked together so that, explicitly or implicitly, they seem more alike than they actually are.

> One kind of threat or challenge to society seems larger, more menacing, if it can be mapped together with other, apparently similar phenomena—especially if, by connecting one relatively harmless activity with a more threatening one, the scale of the danger implicit is made to appear more widespread and diffused. (Hall et al.1978:226)

This convergence increases the danger threshold of the lesser activity. If use of pornography (less menacing) can be mapped with serial murder (more menacing), it makes the use of pornography seem more menacing, too, and the threat potential of pornography is amplified simply by association with serial murder. Any trait or activity that can be plausibly linked or mapped with the word "fiend" will automatically appear dangerous, threatening, and in desperate need of a swift and certain response. The products of one successful moral crusade can be used to gain rhetorical advantage in subsequent moral crusades to ensure that they, too, are successful. Moral crusades can snowball over time. The outcome of one successful crusade can be used to sensitize members of the public to new threats and to desensitize them to the irrationality of participating in every new moral crusade that comes along.

School Violence and Moral Crusades

Near the end of the twentieth century, U.S. schools seemed to be awash in lethal violence. One of the worst incidents occurred April 20, 1999, at Columbine High School, in Littleton, Colorado. Two students (Eric Harris and Dylan Klebold) roamed the school, killing a teacher and twelve students until they finally took their own lives. Incidents like these gave Americans the impression that random, irrational violence was all around and that nobody was safe, even at school (Burns and Crawford 1999). A moral panic swept across the United States as politicians, criminal justice representatives, media spokespersons, and school personnel used the legitimately scary—but infrequent—occurrence of school shootings to further their own personal agendas. Parents became profoundly afraid that their children would be murdered by their classmates at school (Donohue, Schiraldi, and Ziedenberg 1998:3). No school and no child, it was widely believed—and extensively publicized—was safe from random violence. Authorities demanded swifter, more certain, and more severe penalties for juveniles who kill, especially when they were at school. The proposed solutions included demands for additional police in schools, eliminating the minimum age at which children may be tried as adults, ending many of the school-based, after-hours school programs, and extension of the death penalty to juveniles (Donohue, Schiraldi, and Ziedenberg 1998:5).

Individuals who had the interests and the resources were able to take a bad situation and make it worse. They created a moral panic around school shootings and the issue of safety in schools that was both selective and self-serving. Instead of talking about the infrequency of school shootings—remembering that one school shooting is certainly one too many—and the overall safety of schools, most of the individuals who offered opinions chose to portray the shootings as the first sign that a climate of violence in our schools had reached such epidemic proportions that nobody was safe anymore (Burns and Crawford 1999). The issues of "violence" and "school" were linked together (convergence) so that each seemed more troubling than either would have alone. No precise or simple measure of violence in the United States exists, and we do not even agree on a definition of violence or exactly which actions qualify (Brownstein 2000:169). We don't even have good, reliable estimates of the number of youngsters who are killed each year in incidents of school violence. The body count includes both children and adults who are killed, some by other adults, as well as homicides and suicides, and individuals who are killed on school property even if the killings really had nothing to do with school (Donohue, Schiraldi, and Ziedenberg 1998:6). For example, on May 29, 1998, Nichole Weiser, a twenty-six-year-old speech therapist, was gunned down on the grounds of Stranahan High School in Fort Lauderdale, Florida, by her jealous boyfriend (Michael Gramming), who then killed himself. The double killing was classified as a school-related event even though it could in no way be viewed as an indication that our schools are unsafe for students. It could have happened anywhere, and it had nothing to do with a desire to hurt children.

The number of students who are murdered with guns in schools is about half the number of Americans killed each year by lightning (Donohue, Schiraldi, and Ziedenberg 1998:4). Far more children and adolescents are killed by adults than by other juveniles, and practically all killings of juveniles take place *off* of school grounds. Data show that children face about a one-in-a-million chance of being killed at school (Donohue, Schiraldi, and Ziedenberg 1998:4). School shootings, while tragic, are extremely idiosyncratic events and not part of any discernible trend (Donohue, Schiraldi, and Ziedenberg 1998:8). U.S. schools generally provide a safe environment for students, and most juvenile deaths occur near or in the home, not on school grounds, and not during typical school hours (Donohue, Schiraldi, and Ziedenberg 1998:12). The principal factor accounting for the increasing rate of violence in the juvenile population—in school or out—is the change in their use of weapons. Juveniles have stopped using fists or knives as often to settle their arguments and have started using handguns (Blumstein and Rosenfeld 1998:10). One of the best ways to reduce some of the violence that juveniles face is to get guns away from them (Lizotte and Sheppard 2001:6). Longitudinal data (Pastore and Maguire 2004) indicate that schools are still safe places to be, and they have gotten safer with the passage of time. One murder, rape, assault, or robbery in schools—or anywhere else—is one too many, but we must not allow ourselves to be bamboozled into believing that U.S. schools are awash in violence when they really are not.

Degradation Ceremonies and Collective Liability

The successful labeling of behaviors or attributes as "deviant" or of individuals as "deviants" qualifies as a **degradation ceremony** (Garfinkel 1956). To degrade means to lower a person in rank and to humiliate or shame him or her. In a successful degradation ceremony, the "other" is quickly and efficiently separated from everybody else, and the overlap between the accused and the accusers is ignored or explained away. The "other" must be made to appear as if he or she is *essentially* deviant. The threatening nature of what deviants are and what they do is emphasized, not their normality and conformity, and their differentness and dangerousness are selectively perceived and exaggerated. Each member of the deviant group is looked at as more alike than he or she could possibly be and deserving of the same general treatment.

Degradation ceremonies and the social construction of deviance produce a sense of **collective liability**. Each member of the deviant group is held equally responsible for the deviant acts of every other member.

> People might be held collectively liable because of their neighborhood, social class, race, or ethnicity. Crime by young people against adult strangers may have this logic in some cases as well: All adults might be held liable for the conduct of those known personally, such as police, teachers, and parents. Among young people themselves, particularly in large American cities, rival "gangs" may engage in episodic violence resembling the feud in traditional settings, where each member of a feuding group is liable—to injury or even death—for the conduct of the other members. (Black 1998:35)

In the 1940s, when the Nazis were occupying Poland, it was their custom to randomly punish Polish individuals for any wrongdoing done against the Nazis by a Polish national (Black 1998:106). In this case, some Polish people were used as scapegoats by the Nazis to punish other Polish people. Collective liability is a smoke screen that allows all members of some group to be treated and judged as the same. Individual members of a deviant or outside group (e.g., gays, mental patients, sexual deviants, drug users) are hurt through the simple expedient of hurting them all together.

"Sex Fiends," Moral Crusades, and Degradation Ceremonies

The concern with lethal violence in U.S. schools was not the first moral panic to hit the country nor will it be the last. In the 1930s, many individuals in the United States became firmly convinced that the streets were unsafe and that sexual perverts lurked behind every tree, on practically every street corner, waiting to victimize women and children. It was authoritatively claimed that the danger posed by "sex fiends" was great, the number of sex crimes was large and increasing more rapidly than any other crime, and sex crimes were invariably committed by perverts or degenerates who were unable to control their sexual appetites. The only salvation lay, authorities concluded, in the passage of "sexual psychopath laws" and swift and certain incarceration of "sex fiends" in correctional facilities until that time arrived that they were no longer a threat to others (Sutherland 1950:142).

In November 1949, national headlines described in graphic detail the sexual assault and murder of children in three separate incidents.

> On November 14, 1949, Linda Joyce Glucoft, aged 6 years, was sexually assaulted by an elderly relative of the friend she had gone to visit in her Los Angeles neighborhood. When she cried out, her assailant, a retired baker whom the police had already charged in another child molestation case, choked her with a necktie, stabbed her with an ice-pick, and bludgeoned her with an axe, then buried her body in a nearby rubbish heap. Only a few days later, a drunken farm laborer assaulted and mur-

dered a 17-month-old baby girl outside a dancehall in a small town near Fresno. That same week, the Idaho police found the body of 7-year-old Glenda Brisbois, who had last been seen entering a dark blue sedan near her home; she had been murdered by a powerful assailant who had heaved her body 15 feet into an irrigation canal. (Chauncey 1993:161)

The horrific details of these incidents—and their extensive exposure in the U.S. media— gave the average American sufficient reason to conclude that an epidemic of sexual violence had befallen the United States. While sexual assaults were no more common in November 1949 than they had been in previous years, the fear and worry over sex crimes and "sex fiends" took on the elements of a national panic. These crimes were viewed less and less as isolated and tragic events and more and more as a clear sign that "sex fiends" had lost control of their deviant impulses and that no woman or child was safe (Chauncey 1993:161). The gruesome accounts of the murder and raping of children caused groups all across the country to call for state assistance in controlling the wave of sex crimes (Chauncey 1993:164). Laws were passed and commissions were appointed.

The commissions became a driving force in the moral panic. While press reports were responsible for the initial direction of the panic, wherever commissions were created (fifteen state governments established study commissions), they took charge (Chauncey 1993:165). While many different people were represented on the commissions—clergy, police, correctional officials, psychologists, social workers—it was psychiatrists who played the dominant role (Chauncey 1993:165-6). They were successful in convincing other members of the commissions (or alienating them so much that they left), and therefore most everyone else, that sexual deviation should be understood as a medical problem. Psychiatrists insisted that sexual deviance was an indication of a deep-seated pathology or mental disease that could only be cured through science and medicine, not law or religion. The status of psychiatry went up because psychiatrists were able to capitalize on the national panic over sexual deviance to extend their privilege, power, and prestige (Chauncey 1993:166).

The crusade against "sex fiends" in the 1940s and 1950s had serious, negative repercussions for the public image of gays, especially gay men. Some people were willing to believe that gay men were uniquely capable of murdering children of either sex. Gay men found themselves vilified in the press. They were regularly portrayed in the media as perverts and child molesters, dangerous psychopaths strongly inclined to commit reprehensible acts against children (Chauncey 1993:172). What started out as a concern for women's and children's well-being and a fear of sex criminals, eventually crystallized into a generalized and irrational fear of what gay men might do to hurt children. In the absence of a clear way to identify who was gay, public intolerance and fear increased, and the public demanded greater police protection and medical surveillance of gays and other sexual nonconformists (Chauncey 1993:172).

Police and school administrators instituted programs to identify and ferret out sexual nonconformists and then developed programs to keep children away from them. Gays were fired from (or kept out of) any jobs that could bring them into contact with children. Individuals who had been convicted of sex crimes were forced to register with local authorities. Children and their parents were encouraged to be wary of the dangers posed by strangers, even though most of the sexual victimizations experienced by women and children were done by friends, family members, or acquaintances (and still are). Eventually, anyone who violated sex or gender norms was viewed as an actual or potential troublemaker.

> In a Philadelphia suburb in 1950, for instance, a teacher sent the parents of a 9-year-old fourth grader a note warning them that because their son was uninterested in sports the other boys considered him a sissy and there was a danger he might grow up to be a homosexual; she recommended that they get him counseling and force him to play sports. (His parents ignored the advice about counseling, but did set up a basketball hoop in the backyard). (Chauncey 1993:173)

Abnormality was socially constructed, placed squarely on the shoulders of gays and other sexual nonconformists, and associated with dangerous acts and threats to children. Sex murders and murderers came to symbolize the dangers of gender and sexual nonconformity. Denounced by the press, studied by state commissions, and burned into consciousness by public exposure, "sex fiends" became a way to define, by their transgressions, the boundaries of acceptable behavior for anyone who would be sexually normal (Chauncey 1993:178).

The Social Construction of the "Other"

One of the most important things to understand about social deviance is the process by which members of some groups transform members of other groups—or even members of their own groups—into an "other," "outsider," or "enemy." This is one place where those who possess the sociological imagination can make one of their greatest contributions. It does not matter whether we are looking at sex, drugs, violence, mental illness, or some other kind of deviance. Some people are portrayed in such a way that they look wicked or evil, fundamentally different from the rest of us (Scheff 1999:77-78). Both people and happenings may be characterized or caricatured so that a "typical" deviant and "typical" deviance exist in the minds of an audience that witnesses them. Groups with the greatest amount of privilege, power, and prestige are the ones that are best able to construct an "other," even though the rest of us can do so as well ("Who is that weirdo next door?"). This degradation ceremony produces a scapegoat group that can be held accountable both for what they have done and for things over which they have no control whatsoever.

The Politics of Exclusion

In his 1994 presidential address to the American Sociological Association, William Gamson (1995) explored the politics of exclusion. At one extreme, exclusion can take the form of total or partial annihilation of members of one group by members of another group (called genocide). The most-often used example of genocide is the Holocaust, but other examples of localized killings are easy enough to find (e.g., in Hiroshima, Bosnia-Herzegovenia, or Cambodia). At the other extreme is the situation in which reprehensible acts of some people are overlooked or excused, and these individuals are kept within the group (Gamson 1995:3). Sometimes, social exclusion is active and overt, as in genocide; at other times, it is indirect and hidden, as in ignoring or overlooking some group, making them socially invisible (Gamson 1995:4). Once some groups transform other groups into an "other" or "outsider," an important event has occurred. Members of out-groups do not have to be given the same rights and courtesies as are members of in-groups; the universe of obligation in regard to them has changed. It allows any bad things done *by* outside groups to be portrayed as worse than they are, while any bad things done *to* them to be portrayed as justified and necessary.

Using Terrorism

In some cases, construction of an "other" or "outsider" involves more than labeling some group as an "enemy." It actually involves groups or nations provoking—or taking advantage of—terrorist attacks against themselves so that it will make any subsequent violent reactions of their own to outsiders seem justified, a necessary and deserved retaliation (Kelman and Hamilton 1989). "Indeed, it is a matter of public record that the U.S. government and military intelligence apparatus has in the past deliberately provoked acts of terrorism against itself, anticipating massive civilian and military casualties, in order to justify American military action" (Ahmed 2002:322). This is clearly demonstrated in the events surrounding the Japanese attack on Pearl Harbor on December 7, 1941, the attack being a principal cause of the entrance of the United States into World War II.

Franklin Delano Roosevelt, 32nd President of the United States, and his military advisers not only knew in advance that Japan was going to attack Pearl Harbor early in the morning of December 7, 1941, they had taken steps to ensure that it would actually happen. Throughout 1941, provoking a war with Japan (and the other Axis countries of Germany and Italy) was at the core of U.S. relations with Japan (Stinnett 2000:9). Roosevelt was convinced that the only way to stop Axis imperialism was to get the United States directly involved in World War II. He believed that a Japanese attack on Pearl Harbor that appeared unprovoked would rid Americans of their reluctance to join the war. The President knew that the attack on Pearl Harbor would place U.S. military forces— the Pacific Fleet—and the entire civilian population in the Pacific in terrible danger and that the loss of life and property would be enormous (Stinnett 2000:xiii). And it was.

> There were 2,476 Navy, Marine, Army, and civilian personnel killed in the Japanese attacks on December 7. The casualties stretched across the Pacific from Pearl Harbor to Wake Island and Guam. An additional 400,000 residents of the Hawaiian Islands were placed at risk. Japan seized 1,951 Americans as prisoners of war from the military and civilian populations on Guam and Wake, and many of those POWs died while in Japanese custody. (Stinnett 2000:244)

On Oahu alone the attack left 2,273 Navy and Army dead, and 1,119 wounded. Five ships were damaged so severely that they were permanently out of the war, and the Air Force (Army) lost 96 planes, while the Navy and Marine air fields lost 92 planes (Stinnett 2000:248). The attack on Pearl Harbor, portrayed in the United States as unprovoked and totally without warning, provided the spark that was necessary for Americans to demand, and support enthusiastically, U.S. entry into the war in Europe. Practically overnight, opposition evaporated, and Americans were fiercely committed to destroying the Axis powers and winning the war (Stinnett 2000:253-54). What happened at Pearl

Harbor shows that powerful individuals and groups in the United States sometimes have been willing to do practically anything necessary to advance their agenda even if it injures or kills individuals.

We can see some of the same elements playing themselves out if we look at the September 11, 2001, terrorist attack on the United States. The attacks on the World Trade Center and the Pentagon were both a tragedy for individual Americans and a national nightmare. While the United States is no stranger to terrorist attacks, the enormity of the damage of the September attacks simply defies understanding. The loss of life, limb, and property was too much for most Americans to comprehend; certainly it was too much for them to forgive. The attack seemed to be totally without rhyme or reason, unprovoked and unprincipled, the taking of innocent life by a crazed and crazy terrorist group. While this is true, at least in part, there is more to this story than meets the eye. The sociological imagination requires us to critically inspect surface appearances and official interpretations before we accept them as our own. The motifs and methods of sociology make it imperative that we call into question what most other people take for granted. As sociologists, what we value first and foremost is truth.

A study of the September 11 attack and its aftermath by Ahmed (2002) calls into question any simplistic interpretation of what happened and why. What he found, if true, is shocking. His research strongly suggests (but does not prove conclusively) that "significant elements" in the U.S. government, the military, and the intelligence community had "extensive" warnings about the terrorist attack on September 11, 2001. They could have acted either to stop it or, if that effort failed, to lessen its damage substantially (Ahmed 2002:290). These "significant elements" remained silent, however, expecting to benefit from what happened. While the attack produced great losses for many individuals, it also produced great opportunities for other individuals to benefit from what happened. Ahmed (2002:290) concludes that in this case the beneficiaries were the Bush administration, the Pentagon, the CIA and FBI, the weapons industry, and the oil industry.

The U.S. military had been contemplating starting a war with Afghanistan for over a decade (Ahmed 2002:68). September 11 was not so much the cause as it was an excuse for U.S. military presence in the region. Afghanistan is an excellent entry point to Central Asia and the Caspian, a foothold that would allow the United States a position to establish global primacy and cultural hegemony (Ahmed 2002:69). A U.S. presence in Afghanistan allows access to the oil reserves to the north of Afghanistan on the eastern shore of the Caspian Sea, one of the world's wealthiest reserves. A U.S. presence in Afghanistan would also give the United States a gateway to China and the far east (Ahmed 2002:47). Ahmed concluded (2002:255) that the terrorist attack on September 11 actually has been used to justify an invasion of Afghanistan and Iraq that was in the planning stages prior to September 11. The goal was to secure strategic and economic interests abroad with little regard for the lives of Afghans and other indigenous people in the region. While reasonable people can disagree over who or what is really responsible for the terrorist attacks of September 11, few can disagree that they came at a good time for the Bush administration. They made it possible for Bush's presidency to end the crisis of legitimacy that had threatened to topple it and enter the world stage with a new sense of potency and confidence (Ahmed 2002:262). While it is impossible to do justice in this short book to Ahmed's provocative study, let us look at some of the peculiarities of the events surrounding September 11, 2001.

First, U.S. intelligence agencies apparently knew in advance that an attack from the air on key U.S. targets was likely; they even had a fairly good hunch that it would occur on the morning of September 11.

> It is a fact that the American intelligence community received multiple authoritative warnings, both general and specific, of a terrorist attack on the U.S. using civilian airliners as bombs, targeting key buildings located in the nation's capital and New York City, and likely to occur around early to mid-September. (Ahmed 2002:290)

To assume that the intelligence-gathering community was totally in the dark until the attacks occurred strains the limits of both believability and common sense. What's more, it flies in the face of the available information. The FBI had known for years that suspected terrorists with ties to Osama bin Laden were training at flight schools in the United States (Ahmed 2002:103-4; Clarke 2004:237). On July 10, 2001, an FBI agent from Phoenix by the name of Kenneth Williams sent a message to FBI headquarters to alert his superiors that Middle Eastern students were enrolled in an Arizona flight school. He feared that al-Qaeda operatives could possibly be trying to infiltrate the U.S. aviation system. However, his warnings were ignored (Franken 2003:118). By late June, high-ranking officials in the Administration (e.g., Richard Clarke) and at CIA (e.g., George Tenet) were certain that a series of major terrorist attacks was imminent (Clarke 2004:235). "Indeed, the facts on record are sufficient to provide reasonable grounds to believe that the 'intelligence failure' was in fact not a failure at all, but a directive—or rather, the inevitable culmination of carefully imposed high-level directives and blocks that restrained agencies from acting on the very clear intelligence received" (Ahmed 2002:132).

Second, it is very difficult to understand—and most suspicious—why standard operating procedures fell apart on September 11, allowing the attacks on the World Trade Center and the Pentagon to reach their deadly conclusion (Ahmed 2002:144-75). Air traffic controllers followed the flights of the hijacked airliners from start to finish. They were certain that a hijacking had occurred by 8:20 a.m., fifteen minutes *before* the first plane (Flight 11) slammed into the North Tower of the World Trade Center, 43 minutes *before* the second plane (Flight 175) slammed into the South Tower, and 80 minutes *before* the third plane (Flight 77) hit the Pentagon (Ahmed 2002:151-55). No sensible explanation exists for why fighters were not dispatched in time to intercept the hijacked planes and, if necessary, shoot them from the sky. Although it is true that Presidential approval is required to shoot down a civilian aircraft, it is *not* required before scrambling fighter jets to intercept commercial aircraft. In fact, FAA regulations *require* that fighter jets be sent to intercept commercial aircraft in emergencies such as hijackings (Ahmed 2002:157). An F-15 strike eagle could have left McGuire Air Force Base, in New Jersey, and reached the World Trade Center in under three minutes. Yet this did not happen (Ahmed 2002:151). Fighter jets were not scrambled until around 9:40 a.m., too late to do any good.

> For 35 minutes, from 8:15 a.m. until 9:05 a.m., it was widely known within both the FAA and the U.S. military that planes had been hijacked and

had subsequently deviated off their designated flight paths. Despite this, it was not until after Flight 77 smashed into the Pentagon at around 9:40 a.m. that any Washington-based Air Force planes were scrambled to intercept. (Ahmed 2002:159)

Why were no planes dispatched until ninety-five minutes *after* clear evidence existed that a hijacking of commercial airlines was in progress, when fighter planes were fully prepared to intercept, and then only after three crashes and the destruction of the World Trade Center and a section of the Pentagon had already occurred?

Journalists interviewed Vice-President Dick Cheney on "Meet the Press," on September 16, 2001, to learn why fighter jets were not scrambled soon enough to intercept the hijacked planes. His answers do paint a clearer picture of what happened, but they do the Bush administration no good whatsoever. Cheney admitted that when fighter jets were finally scrambled over New York it was explicitly at the direction of leading members of the Cabinet and with Presidential approval (Ahmed 2002:171). Inadvertently, his answers show that the sluggish response of the U.S. Air Force to the terrorist attacks, in violation of standard operating procedures of the FAA and ninety-five minutes too late, was due to decisions by the President and high-ranking members of his Cabinet (Ahmed 2002:171). This failure to act soon enough strongly suggests that "significant, high-level elements of the U.S. military and the Bush administration bear direct responsibility for the terrorist acts that occurred on September 11 on U.S. soil, through what appears to be a combination of deliberate action and inaction" (Ahmed 2002:171).

Third, even after bin Laden was placed on the FBI Most Wanted List and a huge reward was offered for information leading to his location and capture, little pressure was exerted by the State Department on the Taliban to turn him over to authorities (Ahmed 2002:200). In actuality, and contrary to the official line of the U.S. government, Osama bin Laden continues to have close relationships both with his family and the Saudi government (Ahmed 2002:178). The relationship between the Bush administration, the Bush family, and the bin Laden family is apparently a lot cozier than declarations coming out of Washington would suggest.

> Prior to 11th September, President Bush Jr. blocked inquiries into the bin Laden family's terrorist connections. Furthermore, both families were set to benefit financially from the war on Afghanistan that was triggered by the 11th September attacks. This appears to indicate a longstanding financial connection, through the bin Laden family, between Osama bin Laden, the Bush family and the current administration. (Ahmed 2002:187)

It was under contract with the CIA that bin Laden and the family company built the network of multibillion dollar caves in which Osama bin Laden is now apparently hiding (Ahmed 2002:177). According to Clarke (2004:265), the Bush administration was actually less interested in bringing Osama bin Laden to justice and destroying the al-Qaeda network than it was in getting rid of Saddam Hussein, through a protracted war with Iraq if necessary.

Osama bin Laden, al-Qaeda, and the Taliban have been very functional for the Bush administration and other "significant elements" in the United States. "To consolidate and expand U.S. power and cultural hegemony, and to fully counter its Russian, Chinese and European rivals, a massive threat is required, to establish domestic consensus on the unrelentingly interventionist character of U.S. foreign policy in the new and unlimited 'war on terror'"(Ahmed 2002:296). This *does not* mean that U.S. officials staged the attacks or that hijackers were paid by U.S. dollars and told what to do by U.S. officials. This also *does not* mean that the Bush administration knew just how costly the loss of life, limb, and property would be on September 11. However, what it *does* mean—if Ahmed is right—is that "significant elements" in the United States must bear some responsibility for what happened on September 11 and its aftermath.

> . . . the U.S. government, through its actions and inactions, effectively facilitated the attacks, protected those responsible, blocked attempts to prevent the attacks, and maintained close political, financial, military and intelligence ties to key figures who supported those responsible. (Ahmed 2002:293).

Key players in the Bush administration decided in advance of September 11, 2001, that the United States needed another Pearl Harbor, because it would provide the necessary catalyst to justify U.S. military intervention in the Middle East and Asia (Pilger 1/24/04). The Bush administration apparently did some things and overlooked other things so that terrorist attacks against the United States would, or at least could, occur. These attacks were then used in order to justify overt U.S. military operations against terrorist networks wherever they could be found (Floyd 2002; cited in Phillips & Project Censored 2003:44-5). It is not clear that the Bush administration could have done much on September 11 to stop the attacks. It *is clear*, however, that the organizations that were entrusted to protect U.S. citizens did not do so. They failed to get information to the right place at the right time, and they failed to act more courageously to eliminate or at least reduce the threat of terrorist attacks (Clarke 2004:235).

The war on terror has made it possible to manage citizen complaints about U.S. foreign and domestic policy, while it has allowed a crackdown on civil rights, dissent, and free speech; it has given the Bush administration a great deal of power to decide with whom it will wage war (Ahmed 2002:295). The attacks of September 11 made it much easier for the Bush administration to justify its invasion of Iraq. It was not until months after the U.S. occupancy of Iraq that George W. Bush admitted that no evidence existed to show that Iraq had been at all involved in the attacks on September 11 (Clarke 2004:268). The specter of bin Laden and the al-Qaeda network will continue to offer "significant elements" in the United States a golden opportunity to expand into other nations and extend U.S. military, political, strategic, and economic influence abroad (Ahmed 2002:296). The "war on terror" is being used to justify intervention into regions of strategic and economic interest to the United States and to consolidate U.S. hegemony over those regions (Ahmed 2002:298). By keeping the horror of September 11 and the need for increased security always in the public eye, "significant elements" in the United States are likely to reap a cornucopia of rewards in the years ahead.

Enemy Deviants and Criminal Behavior

When we think of criminals it is unlikely that we think of our friends, families, or ourselves; we probably think of people very different from us and the people we know (Kappeler, Blumberg, and Potter 2000:3). An important function of the U.S. criminal justice system is to help construct an "other" in regard to crime (Reiman 2001). Reiman asks us to entertain the idea that the goal of the U.S. criminal justice system is *not* to get rid of crime or to produce social justice. Its goal *is* to project to the U.S. public a visible image that the threat of crime is a threat from the poor (Reiman 2001:1). The criminal justice system must maintain a population of enough poor criminals to be convincing. In order to accomplish this it is necessary that it fail to eliminate the crimes done by the poor and powerless, or even to reduce their number significantly (Reiman 2001:1). On the whole, most of the system's practices make more sense if we look at them as ingredients in an attempt to maintain crime rather than to reduce it (Reiman 2001:4).

> In sum, I will argue that *the criminal justice system fails to reduce crime substantially while making it look as if crime is the work of the poor.* It does this in a way that conveys the image that the real danger to decent, law-abiding Americans comes from below them, rather than from above them, on the economic ladder. This image sanctifies the status quo with its disparities of wealth, privilege, and opportunity and thus serves the interests of the rich and powerful in America—the very ones who could change criminal justice policy if they were really unhappy with it. (Reiman 2001:4)

The criminal justice system's real goal is different from its announced goal (which is why we must use a sociological imagination to understand things clearly). The failure to reduce crime sends a powerful message to the U.S. public, a message that helps and protects the privileged and powerful in our society. It legitimates and reaffirms the prevailing social order with its gross inequalities, while it directs attention and public discontent away from the advantaged in U.S. society toward the poor and the powerless (Chambliss 2000:131). The function that terrorists provide for "significant elements" in the United States on the international front is provided by criminals on the domestic front.

The Orchestration of Social Deviance

Sometimes, powerful groups deliberately orchestrate acts of social deviance because of the benefits it provides them. They purposefully create the social deviance that they complain about so much. On September 5, 1989, then-president George Bush (the father of George W. Bush) delivered his first major prime-time speech to the nation from the Oval Office of the White House. The core of his address was his pledge that he and his administration would achieve a victory over drugs. To show the nation just how accessible drugs are, he held up a clear plastic bag of "crack" cocaine marked "EVIDENCE." He reported to the nation that the bag had been seized by drug enforcement agents in Lafayette Park, directly across from the White House. The implications were clear. No place was safe from drugs. Bush charged that "crack" was destroying our cities by turning them into battle zones and killing our children. A picture of the President, cocaine bag held defiantly aloft, appeared on the front pages of newspapers all across the country (Reinarman and Levine 1997:22).

The President, however, was not telling the truth. His speech writers thought it would enhance his message if he had a prop to show his viewing audience. The President agreed, and he wanted the drug to be seized from Lafayette Park so that he could claim that "crack" was so accessible that it could be purchased right in front of the White House. Reinarman and Levine tell us what happened next.

> White House Communications Director David Demarst asked Cabinet Affairs Secretary David Bates to instruct the Justice Department "to find some crack that fit the description in the speech." Bates called Richard Weatherbee, special assistant to Attorney General Dick Thornburgh, who then called James Millford [sic], executive assistant to the DEA chief. Finally, Milford phoned William McMullen, special agent in charge of the DEA's Washington office, and told him to arrange an under-cover crack buy near the White House . . . . (Reinarman and Levine 1997:22-3)

Unfortunately for the President and his spin doctors, drug agents could not find anyone selling crack or any other drug anywhere near the White House. What to do? DEA agents found someone who was willing to come to the White House to make the sale. They enticed Keith Jackson, an eighteen-year-old African American high school student, to make the trip. He had to be coached, however, because the man did not even know where the White House was, let alone how to get there. Nobody sold drugs near the White House because nobody would be there to buy them; the sale of "crack" was concentrated in the poorer neighborhoods of Washington D.C. The agents did not actually seize the cocaine, either. They bought it from Jackson for $2400 and then sent him on his way (Reinarman and Levine 1997:23). When reality did not conform to the script, the speech, or the wish-es of the President and his advisors, things were done to create a reality that would fit the scripted image (Reinarman and Levine 1997:23).

Elasticity and the Construction of the "Other"

Exclusion of an "other" is not absolute, and groups that were once enemies of the United States no longer are (e.g., the Vietnamese, the Russians, the Germans, the Japanese, the Italians). Social boundaries are group creations that constantly shift. If groups can be excluded, they can also be included. Former enemies are reconstructed as allies, and the relationship between "us" and "them" can change substantially. In the 1980s, for example, Saddam Hussein was a valued ally of the United States, and some of his worst atrocities were committed with full U.S. support or knowledge (Rampton and Stauber 2003:241). Today, however, he is referred to as the "Butcher of Bagdad" and detested for some of what he has done. Once-despised minorities can move toward inclu-sion, while individuals who were once members of our in-group, no longer are. Gays are treated better than they once were; smokers are treated worse; and serial killers are treat-ed pretty much as they have always been. Deviants themselves—gays, criminals, mental patients, drug users, sexual deviants—can do things to affect how they are viewed and treated. U.S. history is filled with examples of devalued groups actively working to end the prejudice and discrimination that they receive in a society.

A Culture of Surveillance

The social construction of both "deviance" and the "deviant"—degradation ceremonies, convergence, moral crusades—must be understood in terms of the growth of what Staples (1997) calls a **culture of surveillance**. More and more of us, in more and more aspects of our lives, are being subjected to "meticulous rituals of power" in which everyone is now watched more closely and more extensively than ever before (Staples 1997:3). Surveillance has shifted from the monitoring of an individual deviant to a generalized monitoring of us all (Staples 1997:6). Everyone is watched because no one is to be trusted (Staples 1997:4).

> . . . as a society we seem to be engaged in a far-reaching attempt to regulate not only the traditional crimes of person and property but also the behaviors, conditions, and lifestyles of substance (ab)use, alcohol and tobacco consumption, "eating disorders," forms of sexual expression and sexual "promiscuity" and "deviance," teenage pregnancy, out-of-marriage births, domestic violence, child abuse, "dysfunctional" families, various psychological or psychiatric disorders and other medical conditions such as "attention deficit disorder," and such diseases as AIDS. (Staples 1997:5)

In the past, the objective of agents of control was to punish a wrongdoer for some specific act. Things are now very different. Individuals are expected to transform themselves from the inside out and become their own monitoring agents (Staples 1997:15). The everwidening culture of surveillance gives individuals the clear impression that they are being watched all the time even if they are not (Foucault 1977). Perception is everything, and, oddly enough, the new culture of surveillance is invisible and overwhelming at the same time (Staples 2000).

Nobody can seriously want to do away with *all* surveillance and social control. Every society includes bad actors who must be rooted out for the betterment of everyone else. Surveillance *does* have a deterrent effect on certain kinds of crime and deviance, making our society safer and more secure (Gillis 1989). However, the expansion of state control and the growth in the culture of surveillance usually has less to do with controlling deviance and crime than it does with the broader objective of controlling the "dangerous classes," defined as those who threaten the status quo (Shelden 2001). Our fears of criminals, sex offenders, drug users, terrorists, and so on are used as the grounds to implement a greater surveillance of us all. We are bamboozled into believing that universal scrutiny is the best and most effective way to achieve a peaceful and safe society.

A culture of surveillance is thriving in U.S. schools. For example, students in Biloxi, Mississippi, are recorded all day, every day, by some seven hundred video cameras. They are filmed in gymnasiums, hallways, cafeterias, and classrooms. Cameras have also been installed in many of the school buses. The only places that are free from surveillance are the bathrooms and the locker rooms. The heavy cost of the equipment—$2.5 million—and the loss of privacy are justified because they supposedly contribute to greater security and safety for victims—actual or potential—of criminal acts. Supporters of the creeping surveillance claim that all people in a school benefit, even individuals who might be inclined to deviate, because their anxiety over not knowing if someone is watching is a powerful deterrent. If surveillance made schools safer by deterring murders, rapes, assaults, robberies, and other serious crimes, it might be a worthy addition to a school's technology of control. However, it is far more likely that overzealous or tyrannical administrators will use the new technology to mark for attention and control those who are weird, friendless, despised, unlucky, or simply disruptive of the status quo, not the truly dangerous.

While the cameras are relatively new, the philosophy of discipline on which they are based is centuries old. In 1791, Jeremy Bentham, British utilitarian philosopher, wrote about what he called the Panopticon. This was a central tower surrounded by cells within which the subjects to be controlled were kept. Bentham thought that it did not matter if the subjects were violent criminals, petty thieves, insane, incorrigible, idle, helpless, sick, or uneducated—all would be forced to change their ways and become law-abiding, hard-working, healthy, and respectable members of society. Why? Because an inspector could sit in the central tower and not be seen, but could see everyone else. Subjects in the Panopticon were not really under constant surveillance, they just thought that they were. The subjects held captive in the Panopticon, being anxious about their constant visibility to an inspector, were supposed to monitor and discipline themselves, eventually becoming the kind of person the inspector desires (Foucault 1977). As more and more people fall under the "gaze" of inspectors (Foucault 1977), it threatens to turn the United States into a surveillance society.

Wilding in America

Sociologists are as aware as anyone of the damage and hurt caused by deviants. Even though we study deviance as a social relationship instead of a pathological condition—looking at labels and social constructions—it does not mean that we romanticize deviance. Deviance can be, and often is, a nasty, brutal business. One rape, murder, or assault is one rape, murder, or assault too many. A sociological concern with deviance, then, goes beyond the study of labels and reactions to a study of how sociocultural factors can and do cause people to act in ways that are hurtful, damaging, or annoying to others.

Perhaps no term better summarizes a deeply disturbing feature of American life than **wilding**, any activity that individuals use to deliberately hurt others to help themselves (Derber 2002:11-12). On April 19, 1989, a large group of teenagers entered Central Park in New York, perhaps as many as thirty. They threw rocks and bottles at passing motorists, and then they knocked down a Hispanic man, covered him with beer, and stole his food. They then started attacking other people they met. (They did not attack everyone, as a dating couple was spared.) In all, eight individuals were assaulted, one a forty-year-old teacher and another an ex-marine (Meili 2003:13). However, the savagery of wilding came to be associated almost exclusively with one particular attack that night, the assault on an individual initially known only as the Central Park Jogger (her actual name is Trisha Meili). The following is a description of some of what happened to her.

> On April 19, 1989, a group of teenagers aged 14 to 16 went into Central
> Park . . . . According to police at the time, the youths came upon a young
> woman jogging alone past a grove of sycamore trees. Allegedly using

rocks, knives, and a metal pipe, they attacked her. Some pinned her down while others beat and raped her. Police reported that one defendant, 17-year-old Kharey Wise, held the jogger's legs while a friend repeatedly cut her with a knife. They then smashed her with a rock and punched her face. (Derber 2004:2)

The Jogger was discovered more than three hours after the attack by two men who thought they had found a beaten and bound man in the woods. When police arrived at the scene, they found the fallen female jogger. She was naked except for her bra (which had been pushed above her breasts). She had been gagged with her running shirt, and her hands had been tied in front of her face. She was comatose and bleeding profusely. One eye was swollen almost shut. She was rushed by ambulance to the emergency room at Metropolitan Hospital.

Examination by physicians provided more information about the extent of her injuries. She had been raped, assaulted, and sodomized (Meili 2003:103). She was in deep shock. Physicians were unable to get an accurate blood pressure reading because it was so low. Her temperature was recorded at eighty-five degrees, and she could not breathe on her own. She was bleeding from several deep cuts and gashes on her forehead and scalp, her skull was fractured, and her eyeball had to be inserted back into its socket. Her arms and legs were gyrating wildly, evidence of the massive brain damage she experienced from the beating; attending physicians were convinced that her brain damage would be permanent. Last rites were administered to her (Meili 2003:14-15). Miraculously, the woman did recover and more quickly than anyone thought possible. She even wrote about the attack and her journey to heal herself in body and spirit, and it is a moving and inspirational tale (Meili 2003). In fact, six-and-a-half years after her attack, she ran in the New York City Marathon and completed the twenty-six mile race in four hours, thirty minutes, and one second (Meili 2003:214).

What was so alarming about the crime was not only the extreme violence—the savagery of the attack was memorable enough—it was the attitude of the attackers. They showed neither guilt nor regret over what they did. It was fun for them, something to do, something to pass the time (Meili 2003:13). If it was indeed amusing for the teenagers, few other people could understand their fascination. The attackers, it was reported, were smug and arrogant about the brutality that they had visited upon an innocent individual. Wilding, a word that the attackers themselves used to describe their crimes, came to represent any violence that was random, irrational, and savage, all done without guilt or remorse. It seemed closer to the feeding-frenzy of sharks than it did to anything human. The fear of wilding became a fear of individuals who had been blocked from achieving the American Dream and willing to take revenge on those who were more fortunate or industrious than they were (Derber 2004:3).

While the attack on Ms. Meili was real enough, the public's rage may have been directed toward the wrong individuals. On December 19, 2002, New York State Justice Charles J. Tejada of Manhattan's State Supreme Court took only five minutes to vacate the convictions of the teenagers who had been arrested and incarcerated for the attack on the Central Park Jogger. Another man, Matias Reyes, already serving thirty-three years to life for murder and rape, confessed to the attack and rape in Central Park (Meili 2003:1). (He may have confessed because he knew the statute of limitations had expired so he could not be charged with the crimes.) The man's DNA matched the DNA taken from a semen stain on the Jogger's sock as well as a cervical swab taken from her after the rape (Meili 2003:165). The teenagers may have been coerced by police to confess to a crime that they did not commit (Derber 2004:3).

The sociological imagination gives us a distinctive way to think about wilding (Derber 2004:17-20). Groups of individuals construct normative systems that are at odds with the normative systems of other groups. Juveniles may reduce their commitment to legal norms and law-abiding groups and identify with delinquent subcultures because it gives them a sense of self-worth that they have been unable to find in conventional society (Kaplan and Johnson 2001). Wilding is not simply some aberrant, individual act; it is a *social* phenomenon.

> The resulting behavior does not reflect a failure to socialize individuals but, instead, an oversocialization in American values of competition, individualism, and materialism. This excessive greed of "wilding" behavior is evident in both government and business. It is demonstrated in novels, television, movies, and popular music and rewarded in schools. Little wonder, then, that given such role models, Americans are increasingly pursuing personal goals with little regard for their effects on others. (Ball 1998:32)

The wilders in Central Park were not so much out of control—although some of that certainly did occur—as they were constructing their own **normative system** that was focused on the moment. The normative system that they constructed encouraged a defiance of authority and an indifference and insensitivity to others whom they met. Their normative system also made them indifferent to the consequences of their actions, even for themselves, as they thought little about the legal consequences of the evening's wilding. They were indifferent, too, to the normative system that demanded civility, lawfulness, and compassion toward others and respect for private property. By looking at the social meaning of wilding for its perpetrators, we can see that it represents defiance of authority, temporary relief from alienation, revenge against an "other" (society or individual), ego enhancement, sexual gratification, male bonding, and posturing for their peers, not the result of some slobbering senility. Adolescent males are no strangers to violence. They are involved as perpetrators and victims, with strangers and intimates, and in ways that hurt themselves and others (Hagan and Foster 2001:874). A strong relationship exists between masculinity, adolescence, and violence (Messerschmidt 2000).

Conclusion

One of the most consequential features of human social experience is that our groups, communities, institutions, and societies are characterized by a great deal of social stratification or inequality. This inequality exists when social positions and the individuals who occupy them are ranked and then differentially rewarded with privilege, power, and prestige. The positions at the top of the hierarchy are more highly rewarded than those at bottom. Because nobody can be at the top unless lots of people are at the bottom, a system of inequality is based on exploitation and opportunity hoarding as groups and individuals jockey for better positions in a society. Even though capitalist societies have a great deal of both upward and downward social mobility, a system of inequality does endure over time. One of the principal reasons is that advantaged groups use all the resources they can to maintain, or even increase, their high standing.

Social mobility in a society is affected by the nature of both human and social capital. Some individuals are smarter, harder working, more energetic, more attractive, or stronger than other individuals, and these characteristics will often make the difference between success and failure. Social capital is also very important. This refers to the connections among individuals and the social networks and norms of reciprocity that exist. Practically everyone who lives in a well-connected society will benefit from the experience because both the collective and individual rewards will be greater. U.S. culture has tended to exaggerate the role of the individual in determining what happens to him or her and to negate or overlook the power of the group in the creation of social stratification.

Not only are people in a society interdependent, but entire societies are, too. What happens in one part of the world affects what happens in other parts. Economic interconnections are becoming stronger, even while political interconnections are becoming more fragmented. A world-system does exist, and globalization is continually transforming how people across the planet live their lives. These global processes create a system of world inequality with both winners and losers. Some nations experience a great deal of prosperity—and their impact on the world stage is great—while other nations do not. The processes of globalization—glocalization and grobalization—will continue to transform the conditions of our lives in the years ahead.

Whenever some humans identify and evaluate other humans, this sets the foundation for the social construction of deviance. Some groups come to look at other groups as evil, sick, sinful, rude, disgusting, or just plain weird, and they act accordingly. It is people acting together who create social deviance by what they believe, feel, say, and do. Groups identify actions and/or attributes that they do not like, label them as forms of deviance, and attach these labels to specific acts and actors. The sociological imagination requires that we strenuously avoid classifying deviance as an individual pathology or aberration. To understand deviance, we must focus on the audiences that witness some troubling event. Moral entrepreneurs are responsible for making and enforcing rules, and moral enterprises can easily evolve into moral panics. These exist when our collective fears are disproportionate to the actual danger posed by some social condition.

Sociologists make one of their greatest contributions to an understanding of deviance by explaining the processes by which an "other" or "outsider" is created. Some groups and individuals are portrayed in such a way that everything about them looks wicked and evil, and they are defined as fundamentally different from everyone else. When these degradation ceremonies are successful, the gap or divide between an accused "other" and everyone else looks far greater and more significant than it actually is. Sometimes this social exclusion is total and absolute, involving efforts to kill off members of some out-group. At other times, the social exclusion is less extreme, and the "other" may be kept within the boundaries of the group but separate and alone. The social construction of an "other" changes the universe of obligation in regard to members of the out-group. Bad things that are done *to* them can be explained away and justified, and good things done *by* them can be overlooked and ignored. Exclusion of an "other" is not rigid and unchanging. Groups that were once enemies no longer are, and once-friendly nations can go to war with one another. The relationship between "us" and "them" can change dramatically as once despised minorities work to be incorporated into the way of life of the in-group.

U.S. society is characterized more and more by a culture of surveillance. The focus of attention has shifted from a monitoring of an individual deviant to a generalized monitoring of us all. Our fears have been turned against us. We are nudged in the direction of believing that the best and most effective way to produce a safer and more secure society is to embrace the culture of surveillance even while we are scrutinized in more and more aspects of our lives. As the net of surveillance expands more and more, this makes us all susceptible to greater control and stigmatization.

The sociological imagination cannot stop with a study of how claims, labels, and definitions are created by groups and applied to outsiders. We must also understand how sociocultural factors can produce the social arrangements or human actions that hurt or upset others. Wilding is a self-oriented, self-serving act that deliberately hurts others while damaging the social fabric. It is done without guilt or remorse by its participants. While wilding can be caused by individual envy or greed, it is caused more often by sociocultural factors. Individuals develop subcultural systems that emphasize competition, materialism, and self-interest. They may encourage individuals to do what is smart, effective, fun, or easy instead of what is right. Wilding is not so much a result of some slavering senility or drooling derangement as it is a defiance of authority, a search for revenge, ego enhancement, a disregard for others, and a posturing for one's peers.

References

Adams, Annemarie and Peta Tancred. 2000. *"Designing Women": Gender and the Architectural Profession*. Toronto: University of Toronto Press.

Ahmed, Nafeez Mosaddeq. 2002. *The War on Freedom: How and Why America was Attacked, September 11th, 2001*. East Sussex, UK: Institute for Policy Research and Development.

Alderson, Arthur and François Nielsen. 2002. "Globalization and the Great U-Turn: Income Inequality Trends in 16 OECD Countries." *American Journal of Sociology* 107:1244-1299.

Alderson, Arthur and François Nielsen. 1999. "Income Inequality, Development, and Dependence: A Reconsideration." *American Sociological Review* 64:606-631.

Altheide, David. 2002. *Creating Fear: News and the Construction of Crisis*. New York: Aldine de Gruyter.

Arrow, Kenneth, Samuel Bowles, and Steven Durlauf. 2000. *Meritocracy and Economic Inequality*. Princeton, NJ: Princeton University Press.

Art, Lee and Bren Ortega Murphy. 2000. *Cultural Hegemony in the United States*. Thousand Oaks, CA: Sage.

Ball, Michael. 1998. "Evil and the American Dream." Pp. 31-44 in *The American Ritual Tapestry: Social Rules and Cultural Meanings*, edited by Mary Jo Deegan. Westport, CT: Greenwood.

Becker, Howard. 1963. *Outsiders*. New York: Free Press.

Beckfield, Jason. 2003. "Inequality in the World Polity: The Structure of International Organization." *American Sociological Review* 68:401-424.

Best, Joel. 1999. *Random Violence: How We Talk About New Crimes and New Victims*. Berkeley, CA: University of California Press.

Black, Donald. 1998. *The Social Structure of Right and Wrong*, revised edition. San Diego, CA: Academic Press.

Blau, Joel. 1999. *Illusions of Prosperity: America's Working Families in an Age of Economic Insecurity*. New York: Oxford University Press.

Blumstein, Alfred and Richard Rosenfeld. 1998. "Assessing the Recent Ups and Downs in U.S. Homicide Rates." *National Institute of Justice Journal* 237:9-11.

Bourdieu, Pierre. 1991. *Language and Symbolic Power*, translated by Gino Raymond and Matthew Adamson. Cambridge, MA: Harvard University Press.

Bradshaw, York and Michael Wallace. 1996. *Global Inequalities*. Thousand Oaks, CA: Pine Forge.

Braun, Denny. 1997. *The Rich Get Richer: The Rise of Income Inequality in the United States and the World*. Chicago: Nelson-Hall Publishers.

Brownstein, Henry. 2000. *The Social Reality of Violence and Violent Crime*. Boston, MA: Allyn and Bacon.

Burns, Ronald and Charles Crawford. 1999. "School Shootings, the Media, and Public Fear: Ingredients for a Moral Panic." *Crime, Law & Social Change* 32:147-168.

Burris, Val. 2001. "The Two Faces of Capital: Corporations and Individual Capitalists as Political Actors." *American Sociological Review* 66:361-81.

Chambliss, William. 2000. *Power, Politics, and Crime*. Boulder, CO: Westview.

Charbeneau, Travis. 1992. "Ragged Individualism: America's Myth of the Loner." *Utne Reader* 51:132-33.

Chauncey, Jr., George. 1993. "The Postwar Sex Crime Panic." Pp. 160-178 in *True Stories from the American Past*, edited by William Graebner. New York: McGraw-Hill.

Clarke, Richard. 2004. *Against All Enemies: Inside America's War on Terror*. New York: Free Press.

Cohen, Albert. 1974. *The Elasticity of Evil: Changes in the Social Definition of Deviance*. Oxford, UK: Oxford University Penal Research Unit.

Collins, Chuck and Felice Yeskel. 2000. *Economic Apartheid in America: A Primer on Economic Inequality & Insecurity*. New York: The New Press.

Cotter, David, Joan Hermsen, and Reeve Vanneman. 1999. "Systems of Gender, Race, and Class Inequality: Multilevel Analyses." *Social Forces* 72:433-460.

Cowie, Jefferson. 1999. *Capital Moves: RCA's Seventy-Year Quest for Cheap Labor*. New York: Cornell University Press.

Curra, John. 2000. *The Relativity of Deviance*. Thousand Oaks, CA: Sage.

Derber, Charles. 2004. *The Wilding of America: Money, Mayhem, and the New American Dream*, third edition. New York: Worth.

Donohue, Elizabeth, Vincent Schiraldi, and Jason Ziedenberg. 1998. *School House Hype: School Shootings and the Real Risks Kids Face in America*. Washington, DC: Justice Policy Institute.

Durning, Alan Thein. 1992. *How Much Is Enough? The Consumer Society and the Future of the Earth*. New York: W.W. Norton.

Erikson, Kai. 1962. "Notes on the Sociology of Deviance." *Social Problems* 9:307-314.

Evans, Peter. 1995. *Embedded Autonomy: States and Industrial Transformation*. Princeton, NJ: Princeton University Press.

Feagin, Joe. 2001. "Social Justice and Sociology: Agendas for the Twenty-First Century." *American Sociological Review* 66:1-20.

Feagin, Joe and Karyn McKinney. 2003. *The Many Costs of Racism*. Lanham, MD: Rowman and Littlefield.

Fernandez, Roberto. 2001. "Skill-Biased Technological Change and Wage Inequality: Evidence from a Plant Retooling." *American Journal of Sociology* 107:273-320.

Firebaugh, Glenn. 1999. "Empirics of World Income Inequality." *American Journal of Sociology* 104:1597-1630.

Floyd, Chris. November 1, 2002. "Into the Dark." *CounterPunch* (www.counterpunch.org/floyd101.html). Cited in Project Censored 2004, 1/14/04 (http://www.projectcensored.org/publications/2004/4.html).

Foucault, Michel. 1977. *Discipline and Punish: The Birth of the Prison*, translated by A.M. Sheridan. New York: Pantheon.

Fredrickson, George. 2002. *Racism: A Short History*. Princeton, NJ: Princeton University Press.

Franken, Al. 2003. *Lies (And the Lying Liars Who Tell Them): A Fair and Balanced Look at the Right*. New York: Dutton.

Gamson, William. 1995. "Hiroshima, the Holocaust, and the Politics of Exclusion: 1994 Presidential Address." *American Sociological Review* 60:1-20.

Garfinkel, Harold. 1956. "Conditions of Successful Degradation Ceremonies." *American Journal of Sociology* 61:420-424.

Giddens, Anthony. 1999. *Runaway World: How Globalization Is Reshaping our Lives*. New York: Routledge.

Gillis, A.R. 1989. "Crime and State Surveillance in Nineteenth Century France." *American Journal of Sociology* 95:307-341.

Goesling, Brian. 2001. "Changing Income Inequalities Within and Between Nations: New Evidence." *American Sociological Review* 66:745-761.

Goffman, Erving. 1963. *Stigma: Notes on the Management of Spoiled Identity.* Englewood Cliffs, NJ: Prentice-Hall.

_____. 1971. *Relations in Public.* New York: Harper and Row.

Goode, Erich and Nachman Ben-Yehuda. 1994. *Moral Panics: The Social Construction of Deviance.* Oxford, UK: Blackwell.

Gould, Roger. 2002. "The Origin of Status Hierarchies: A Formal Theory and Empirical Test." *American Journal of Sociology* 107:1143-78.

Gregersen, Edgar. 1994. *The World of Human Sexuality: Behaviors, Customs and Beliefs.* New York: Irvington.

Grodsky, Eric and Devah Pager. 2001. "The Structure of Disadvantage: Individual and Occupational Determinants of the Black-White Wage Gap." *American Sociological Review* 66:542-567.

Halaby, Charles. 2003. "Where Job Values Come From: Family and School Background, Cognitive Ability, and Gender." *American Sociological Review* 68:251-78.

Hall, Stuart, Chas Critcher, Tony Jefferson, John Clarke, and Brian Roberts. 1978. *Policing the Crisis: Mugging, the State, and Law and Order.* New York: Holmes and Meier.

Hagan, John and Holly Foster. 2001. "Youth Violence and the End of Adolescence." *American Sociological Review* 66:874-899.

Hodson, Randy and Robert Kaufman. 1982. "Economic Dualism: A Critical Review." *American Sociological Review* 47:727-39.

Jones, Brian, Bernard Gallagher, III, and Joseph McFalls, Jr. 1989. "Toward a Unified Model for Social Problems Theory." *Journal for the Theory of Social Behavior* 19:337-56.

Kaplan, John and Robert Johnson. 2001. *Social Deviance: Testing a General Theory.* New York: Kluwer Academic/Plenum.

Kappeler, Victor, Mark Blumberg, and Gary Potter. 2000. *The Mythology of Crime and Criminal Justice*, third edition. Prospect Heights, IL: Waveland.

Keister, Lisa. 2000. *Wealth in America: Trends in Wealth Inequality.* Cambridge: Cambridge University Press.

Kelman, Herbert and V. Lee Hamilton. 1989. *Crimes of Obedience: Toward a Social Psychology of Authority and Responsibility.* New Haven, CT: Yale University Press.

Kentor, Jeffrey and Terry Boswell. 2003. "Foreign Capital Dependence and Development: A New Direction." *American Sociological Review* 68:301-313.

Knapp, Peter, Jane Kronick, William Marks, and Miriam Vosburgh. 1997. *The Assault on Equality.* Westport, CT: Praeger.

Koggel, Christine. 1998. *Perspectives on Equality: Constructing a Relational Theory.* Lanham, MD: Rowman and Littlefield.

Lareau, Annette. 2002. "Invisible Inequality: Social Class and Childrearing in Black Families and White Families." *American Sociological Review* 67:747-76.

Lemert, Edwin. 1951. *Social Pathology: A Systematic Approach to the Theory of Sociopathic Behavior*. New York: McGraw-Hill.

Lizotte, Alan and David Sheppard. 2001. "Gun Use by Male Juveniles: Research and Prevention." *Juvenile Justice Bulletin*. Washington, DC: Office of Juvenile Justice and Delinquency Prevention.

Lucas, Samuel. 2001. "Effectively Maintained Inequality: Education Transitions, Track Mobility, and Social Background Effects." *American Journal of Sociology* 106:1642-1690.

Mark, Noah. 1998. "Beyond Individual Differences: Social Differentiation From First Principles." *American Sociological Review* 63:309-330.

Matza, David. 1969. *Becoming Deviant*. Englewood Cliffs, NJ: Prentice-Hall.

Mayer, Susan. 2001. "How Did the Increase in Economic Inequality between 1970 and 1990 Affect Children's Educational Attainment?" *American Journal of Sociology* 107:1-32.

McCall, Leslie. 2000. "Gender and the New Inequality: Explaining the College/Non-College Wage Gap." *American Sociological Review* 65:234-255.

McMurrer, Daniel and Isabel Sawhill. 1998. *Getting Ahead: Economic and Social Mobility in America*. Washington, D.C.: The Urban Institute Press.

Meili, Trisha. 2003. *I Am the Central Park Jogger: A Story of Hope and Possibility*. New York: Scribner.

Messerschmidt, James. 2000. *Nine Lives: Adolescent Masculinities, the Body, and Violence*. Boulder, CO: Westview.

Mooney, Shane. 2000. *Useless Sexual Trivia: Tastefully Prurient Facts About Everyone's Favorite Subject*. New York: Fireside/Simon and Schuster.

Pastore, Ann and Kathleen Maguire, editors. Access date: 12/9/2004. *Sourcebook of Criminal Justice Statistics*. Online. Available: http://www.albany.edu/sourcebook/ (Table 3.47).

Paxton, Pamela. 2002. "Social Capital and Democracy: An Interdependent Relationship." *American Sociological Review* 67:254-277.

Phillips, Peter, & Project Censored. 2003. *Censored 2004: The Top 25 Censored Stories*. New York: Seven Stories Press.

Pilger, John. 1.24.04. "Pilger in Print." http://pilger.carlton.com/print/124759.

Putnam, Robert. 2000. *Bowling Alone: The Collapse and Revival of American Community*. New York: Simon and Schuster.

Rampton, Sheldon and John Stauber. 2003. "Weapons of Mass Destruction." Pp. 231-45 in *Censored 2004: The Top 25 Censored Stories*, by Peter Phillips & Project Censored. New York: Seven Stories Press.

Reiman, Jeffrey. 2001. *The Rich Get Richer and the Poor Get Prison: Ideology, Class, and Criminal Justice*, 6th edition. Boston, MA: Allyn and Bacon.

Reinarman, Craig and Harry Levine. 1997. "The Crack Attack: Politics and Media in the Crack Scare." Pp. 18-51 in *Crack in America: Demon Drugs and Social Justice*, edited by Craig Reinarman and Harry Levine. Berkeley, CA: University of California Press.

Reskin, Barbara. 2003. "Including Mechanisms in Our Models of Ascriptive Inequality: 2002 Presidential Address." *American Sociological Review* 68:1-21.

Ridgeway, Cecilia, Elizabeth Heger Boyle, Kathy Kuipers, and Dawn Robinson. 1998. "How Do Status Beliefs Develop? The Role and Resources and Interactional Experience." *American Sociological Review* 63:331-50.

Ritzer, George. 2004. *The Globalization of Nothing*. Thousand Oaks, CA: Pine Forge.

Robertson, Roland. 1994. "Globalisation or glocalisation?" *Journal of International Communication* 1:33-52.

Rogers, Jackie Krasas. 2000. *Temps: The Many Faces of the Changing Workplace*. New York: Cornell University Press.

Scheff, Thomas. 1999. *Being Mentally Ill: A Sociological Theory*, 3rd edition. Chicago: Aldine.

Scheper-Hughes, Nancy. 2000. "The Global Traffic in Human Organs." *Current Anthropology* 41:191-224.

Schlosser, Eric. 2002. *Fast Food Nation: The Dark Side of the All-American Meal*. New York: Perennial/HarperCollins.

Schwarz, John. 1997. *Illusions of Opportunity: The American Dream in Question*. New York: W. W. Norton.

Scott, John. 2001. *Power*. Cambridge, UK: Polity Press.

Sewell, William, Archibald Haller, and George Ohlendorf. 1970. "The Educational and Early Occupational Status Attainment Process: Replication and Revision." *American Sociological Review* 35:1014-27.

Shelden, Randall. 2001. *Controlling the Dangerous Classes: A Critical Introduction to the History of Criminal Justice*. Boston, MA: Allyn and Bacon.

Simmons, Jerry. 1969. *Deviants*. Santa Barbara, CA: Glendessary Press.

Smeeding, Timothy. 1997. "The International Evidence on Income Distribution." Pp. 79-103 in *The Political Economy of Redistribution*, edited by Jon Neill. Kalamazoo, MI: Upjohn Institute for Employment Research.

Spector, Malcolm and John Kitsuse. 1977. *Constructing Social Problems*. Menlo Park, CA: Cummings.

Staples, William. 1997. *The Culture of Surveillance: Discipline and Social Control in the United States*. New York: St. Martin's.

_____. 2000. *Everyday Surveillance: Vigilance and Visibility in Postmodern Life*. Lanham, MD: Rowman and Littlefield.

Stinnett, Robert. 2000. *Day of Deceit: The Truth About FDR and Pearl Harbor*. New York: Touchstone/Simon and Schuster.

Sutherland, Edwin. 1950. "The Diffusion of Sexual Psychopath Laws." *American Journal of Sociology* 56:142-8.

Thompson, Kenneth. 1998. *Moral Panics*. New York: Routledge.

Thurow, Lester. 1970. *Investment in Human Capital*. Belmont, CA: Wadsworth.

Tiefer, Leonore. 1978. "The Kiss." *Human Nature* 1:29-37.

Tilly, Charles. 1998. *Durable Inequality*. Berkeley, CA: University of California Press.

Vela-McConnell, James. 1999. *Who Is My Neighbor? Social Affinity in a Modern World*. Albany, NY: State University of New York Press.

Walker, Henry, Phyllis Moen, and Donna Dempster-McClain. 1999. "Introduction." Pp. 1-11 in *A Nation Divided: Diversity, Inequality, and Community in American Society*, edited by Phyllis Moen, Donna Dempster-McClain, and Henry Walker. New York: Cornell University Press.

Wallerstein, Immanuel. 1974. *The Modern World System*. New York: Academic Press.

_____. 2000. *The Essential Wallerstein*. New York: The New Press.

_____. 2001. *Unthinking Social Science: The Limits of Nineteenth-Century Paradigms*, second edition with a new preface. Philadelphia: Temple University Press.

Webster, Jr., Murray and Stuart Hysom. 1998. "Creating Status Characteristics." *American Sociological Review* 63:351-78.

Warren, John Robert, Robert Hauser, and Jennifer Sheridan. 2002. "Occupational Stratification Across the Life Course: Evidence from the Wisconsin Longitudinal Study." *American Sociological Review* 67:432-455.

Weber, Max. 1968. *Economy and Society: An Outline of Interpretive Sociology*, edited by Guenther Roth and Claus Wittich. New York: Bedminster Press.

Weiss, Linda. 1998. *The Myth of the Powerless State*. New York: Cornell University Press.

Wilkins, Leslie. 1964. *Social Deviance*. London: Tavistock.

Zeitlin, Maurice and L. Frank Weyher. 2001. "'Black and White, Unite and Fight': Interracial Working-class Solidarity and Racial Employment Equality." *American Journal of Sociology* 107:430-67.

Chapter Five: Knowledge and Power in Society and the Future of the Present

Troubles with Knowledge: Just Because It's True Doesn't Make It So

Grasping the World Theoretically and the Criticisim of Everything Existing

The Prospects for a Critical Sociology and its Most Vital Trends

The Issue Of Social Change And Peering Into The Future

Conclusion

Notes

References

Chapter Five: Knowledge and Power in Society and the Future of the Present
Troubles with Knowledge:
Just Because It's True Doesn't Make It So

All cultures contain forms of knowledge that are false or that distort reality. Much of accepted Western history is laced with such falsehoods and myths. Let's look at a few. No one named Christopher Columbus ever set sail to prove the world was round (almost universally known by mariners in Europe of 1492). Rather, Christoforo Colombo tried to reach India in a hunt for gold, slaves, and prized commodities by going west because the Turks had cut off the eastern trade route. Colombo needed an alternate route and, thinking the world smaller, he blundered into the discovery of the "New World" (Zinn 1980:2).[1] The Puritans did *not* support religious freedom and did *not* come to America fleeing British persecution. "The most famous congregation of Separatists, fleeing royal wrath, departed for Holland in 1608," writes historian Thomas Bailey (1971:23). "During the ensuing twelve years of toil and poverty, they were increasingly distressed by the 'Dutchification' of their children. They longed to find a haven where they could live and die as Englishmen," Baily concludes, somewhat generously. After first fleeing to Holland, the Puritans found the Dutch's tolerance and liberality intolerable, and they feared for their and their children's souls. The Puritans fled Holland and came to America to escape *liberal* society and religious *tolerance*. They wanted a narrowly restrictive and austere society based on their own religious code and free from the religious beliefs of others. George Washington was *not* the first President of the United States. The United States was officially a country under the *Articles of Confederation*, and though this document ultimately failed, it was the legal structure of the newly minted confederation of states.[2] Under that structure, the first President was John Hanson (1781) —others have claimed it was Peyton Randolph (1774), Elias Boudinot (1783), Thomas Mifflin (1784), Richard Henry Lee (1785).Washington (1789) was the first president under the *Constitution of the United States of America*. Several others, none named Washington, succeeded Hanson. Washington even wrote him a note of congratulations on his election to the presidency. Abraham Lincoln did *not* abolish slavery in the United States. His "Emancipation Proclamation" only freed those few slaves in rebel territory captured by the Union. In this document, Lincoln declared that "all persons held as slaves within any State or designated part of a State the people whereof shall then be in rebellion against the United States shall be then, thenceforward, and forever free."[4] Those states remaining loyal to the Union would not have their slaves liberated. The Proclamation is a *military doctrine* with two goals: redefining the war as a war over slavery in order to prevent England and France, dependent on southern agricultural goods, from entering the war on the side of the South; and providing for the liberation of slaves in conquered territory and their incorporation into Union ranks.

Culturally accepted truths are not always in line with the facts. Other accepted truths crumble on inspection, too. Are men really stronger than women? It all depends on what you mean by strength. Males are less resistant to pain than females. Males get sick more often than females. Males die at younger ages than females. Is humanity composed of many races? Anthropologists long ago abandoned categories of race because no consistent set of criteria to distinguish the races could ever be found. Genetic studies have demonstrated that no uniform genetic markers of separate races exist.[5] People vary genetically as much within racial categories as they do between them. Is hard work the key to success? Most people remain in the class they were born into, irrespective of effort, and most of the great stocks of wealth have been inherited. As these examples show, humans' assumptions about the world, their culture, and the relationships between the forces and events around them do not necessarily have to be true to be believed and to function socially. This is easy to see in other societies' stories, myths, and fables, but we often are reluctant to see the fallacies or inconsistencies of our own.

Every society uses stories to tell its members who they are and from where they came. As forms of cultural knowledge, these stories become embedded in institutions. They are regularly repeated and reaffirmed to such an extent that they eventually come to pass for what is right and good, or true and untrue. Knowledge is almost always a **contested terrain**, changing slowly or quickly as individuals and groups struggle over its meaning. The slower a social system changes, the less likely its institutionalized form of knowledge will face challenges from contrary ideas, making it more likely a relatively rigid system of knowledge. When societies change, the power of the institutional structure is shaken loose, creating new cultural knowledge and opportunities for individuality and personal freedom. New rules have not yet developed and neither has an institutional apparatus to enforce them. Those who control social resources have a better chance to get their views of truth and reality accepted by others, sometimes even if the evidence for their claims is questionable or nonexistent.

Grasping the World Theoretically and the Criticism of Everything Exisiting

The **capitalist mode of production** has become the dominant method for producing and distributing goods and services in the world. Sociologists have long asked about this system's origins, structure, and future. Though its roots are found in the collapse of feudal society, capitalism tends to extend itself to more and more areas of social life. In their attempts to understand this system, sociologists have appealed to the study of history, mathematics, political economy, anthropology, and law. Marx, Weber, and Durkheim, for example, studied a variety of thinkers—such as Jacques Rousseau, Adam Smith, Herbert Spencer, William Shakespeare, Georg Hegel, and Charles Darwin—and subjects—such as the French Revolution, early religious systems, the division of labor, the rise of bureaucratic organization, trade policies, and the problems of infinitesimal calculus. Each of sociology's founders demonstrated a level of virtuosity that was common among **Enlightenment** thinkers. Sociologists, like other thinkers in the Enlightenment tradition, hold the assumption that **human reason** can be harnessed to improve the human condition. Projecting capitalism forward in the imagination in the context of a more democratic social structure, Marx concluded that progress could be made toward a more **egalitarian society**. Such progressive social change, he thought, requires a scientific discourse that qualifies as a "ruthless criticism of everything existing" (Marx 1844b). Sociologists have often adopted a similar posture, for example, by forwarding debunking, relativistic, unrespectable, and cosmopolitan discourses. The vigilance required by science and the progressive social change facilitated by social critique necessarily entails focusing on ruling institutions. This line of thinking and form of social analysis "must not be afraid of its own conclusions, nor of conflict with the powers that be" (Marx 1844b:13). Marx, Weber, and Durkheim agreed: conflict with ruling-class, political or religious authorities should not stop or limit studies or inquiries into sociological questions. This is the charge sociologists have inherited from their founders.

The Politics of Multiple Realities: Social Domination and the Shaping of Discursive Knowledge

In *An Invitation to Sociology*, Peter Berger (1963) reminded his readers that there are multiple layers of reality in society. However, he neglected to develop the idea that such benefits are distributed in ways that lead to inequalities in power, wealth, status, well-being, and autonomy for different social groups. This means that the social construction of reality is influenced by variables such as class, status and power. As long as inequality exists and "the seemingly most intimate details of private existence are actually structured by larger social relations" (Ross and Rapp 1997:153), socially constructed definitions of reality will be contested by groups. The personal is always political (Hanisch 1969). When it comes to the relationships between inequalities in power, status, and class and how reality is defined, sociologists are apt to ask: What sort of interests are being served? Whose definition of reality dominates? and Who loses out and to what effect? Analysis of both material and ideological structures of domination provides answers to these questions.

Structures of Domination and Power: The Power Elite, Capitalist States, and the Military-Industrial Complex

Sociologists are often interested in understanding powerful and influential social structures. The three dominant and most powerful social structures in modern society are the power elite, capitalist states, and the military industrial complex. Each is discussed below.

The Power Elite

The concentration of wealth in capitalist society and the growth of bureaucracies provide the structural basis for the existence of a "power elite" (Mills 1956). This is an upper-level strata of society composed of a clique of several hundred families, descended from the original wealth holders in America, that has coalesced into a relatively identifiable class of corporate owners and managers, civic leaders, and policy makers. Members of this power elite rule the largest corporations, run the machinery of state, and direct the military establishment (Domhoff 1979, 1983; Mills 1956). The structural position of this non-elected elite translates into its control of the world's largest political and economic organizations and relegates the public largely to the role of spectators. However, though not everyone participates in the process of ruling, the elite's decisions affect everyone. Elites direct state and industrial policy, including decisions on the rate and amount of the extraction of resources, the supply of jobs, the prices at which things are sold, the levels of immigration, and whether the country moves to war. Non-elites provide the labor, the taxes and the soldiers to supply the resources necessary to execute the policies on which elites depend (Tilly 1975, 1981). There is nothing democratic about this; nor are sacrifices and benefits equally shared.

This elite exists on an international level, too. This loosely organized global cohort is relatively conscious of themselves as cultural, economic, and political managers. They meet regularly. They enact policies to sustain their position of power, deliberate on trade and monetary policy, discuss impending threats to the market, and work out the political-military strategies to preserve the system as a whole.[6] Several overlapping groups represent this elite, including the Trilateral Commission, the World Bank, the IMF, the Bilderberg Group, the Council on Foreign Relations, and the Business Roundtable (Domhoff 1979, 1983; Palast 2003). Members of the Trilateral Commission, for example, include the heads of state of the most powerful nations in the world, the largest financial and industrial moguls, and select academic spokespersons (Sklar 1980). More recent elite organizations include the International Monetary Fund (IMF), the World Bank, and the World Trade Organization (WTO). Their power is extensive, though rarely discussed in popular culture.

Disagreements over specific policies among the elite do occur and they cannot always act in concert and/or with impunity. Capitalist organizations shift in complexity over time, creating conflicts and fragmentation within the capitalist class (Davis, Diekmann, and Tinsley 1994; Palmer et al.1995; Stearns and Allan 1996). Contrary interests exist between different industries. For example, car manufacturers would be harmed *less* than oil companies by technology that made gasoline unnecessary. Also, individual capitalists and their firms often hold contrary views on government policy and might even support or fund competing candidates and/or policies (Burris 2001). The fact that individuals and firms exist across spatial, political, and national boundaries, makes concerted action something that is possible *only under specific conditions*, and any that are achieved are hard to sustain (Akard 1992). Further, the economic growth elites need and desire leads the public to greater expectations of affluence, consumption, and cultural participation and this leads to the public's greater expectations of democratic participation in decision-making (Muller 1995). The failure of providing greater access to democratic participation often leads to resistance from non-elites (Boswell and Dixon 1993). Popular resistance, or the anticipation of it, results in attempts to co-opt, discipline, and control citizens and workers (Foucault 1977; Parenti 1999; Stepan-Norris and Zeitlin 1995). For such reasons, consensus is difficult to achieve within and across the capitalist class as a whole, though this does not mean it is never attempted or reached.

An **interlocking directorate** occurs when a person or persons sit on the board of directors of more than one company. The greater the number of interlocks, the greater the concentration of power of the capitalist class, though this power is unevenly distributed across this class. Use of financial power by banks and corporations to shape the political process attains different levels of success depending on their level of interlocking directorates (Fligstein and Brantely 1992). Banks gain more advantages from such interlocks than do manufacturing firms (Mizruchi 1989), making them more powerful politically. However, elites are not puppet-masters, nor can they be. Their continual need to periodically meet, plan, and create new organizations (e.g., the World Trade Organization) and their split over major policies (e.g., the Iraq-U.S. war) testifies to this lack of omnipotence and unity. Capitalism is a dynamic system that no one group can control. However, elites try to control as many variables as possible that effect their power and wealth. Where capitalists invest their money in the political-process often determines the policies pursued by governments. Capitalists must also confront the size and the level of organization of workers, students, and the politically active. These are important factors determining the range of the state's options, and it is important for elites to undermine resistance they might receive from these groups. Understanding these relationships goes a long way to understanding real historical events.

The elite possess the most significant influence on how things happen in modern society. The institutions that are ostensibly set up to provide people an increasing awareness of their options in life are also those that increasingly are used to prevent the public from understanding the powerful forces that affect them. The elite and their representatives own the mass media. The owners and editors they hire set the agenda for what gets discussed in the media and *how* it gets discussed (Bagdikian 1992; Herman and Chomsky1988; Parenti 1986). They run most agencies in the government, control the military, and staff the most powerful and wealthy corporate firms in the world. Tax shelters of the rich, disguised as philanthropic organizations, provide funds for much of what gets studied in the laboratory and the classroom (Sears 2003). The policies elites set out affect the vast majority of the world's populations, with those effected having little, if any, direct say in these same policies. Most other professionals work for them and/or serve their interests. Corporations pay legions of lawyers to sue, countersue, and file patent applications on things such as plants, genes, and even species in order to ensure that their interests are protected. They fund the political parties, and these groups control the contours of state policy. Though they are not elected by any deliberative body nor answerable to any identifiable voting bloc, the legal ownership of private property hands corporations political power. The public only has its wallets, its labor, its feet, and its voice to vote with in return, though it often remains only dimly aware of this power or that of the elite (Burris 2001; Domhoff 1967, 1970, 1973; Jessop 1982; Palast 2003; Parenti 1988, 1995; Perucci and Potter 1989).

Capitalist States and the Military-Industrial Complex

If capitalist firms fail to accumulate capital, they fail as business enterprises and, if these fail, both workers and capitalists are all the poorer. So, market players—both capitalists and laborers—are ruled by a coercive economic force that is external to them but nevertheless is difficult for either to escape (Marx 1867:151, 257, 293). The search for ever-more profits—the all-consuming logic of the representatives of capital—increasingly shapes other social institutions. Take the state, for example. Capitalists as a class maintain a measure of control over state policy through funding **the political process**, as well as universities, think tanks, and foundations (Kerbo 2003:180-186). Also, some states possess strong militaries. Military power can be used when capitalist interests are threatened. Profitability requires that vital markets be kept open, labor be kept relatively weak, leaders of weaker states be made cooperative, and the flow of goods and services allowed to continue uninterrupted (Wallerstein 1982, 1983). A weak and acquiescent labor force is ideal for capitalists because, where no unions exist, wages can be kept low, productivity high, and employers can be relieved of offering pensions, health care, worker benefits or the obligation to follow environmental laws. Such conditions allow for higher profits, especially if production facilities operate in areas where labor costs are low, and firms can export to areas with affluent consumers (Greider 1997).

To ensure an adequate supply of cheap labor and raw materials conducive to the needs of multinational corporations, formally democratic-capitalist countries have often supported dictatorships in other countries, particularly in the "Third World" (Blum 1995). Former President Dwight D. Eisenhower, in his last presidential address, warned that a "military-industrial-complex" had emerged that threatened American society with the "acquisition of unwarranted influence, whether sought or unsought."[7] These were the sort of interrelationships that concerned him. When they perceived oil interests were at stake, the United States, through its CIA, overthrew a democratically elected government in Iran in 1953, installed the Shah and his secret police, who terrorized the population to such an extent that it played a major role in the subsequent storming of the U.S. Embassy and the hostage crisis of the 1979-1981 period. The United States has supported similar dictator-ships in the Philippines, Brazil, Nicaragua, Honduras, Panama, South Africa, Haiti, El Salvador, Indonesia, and Guatemala (Chomsky 1988). This explains the finding that very weak and very strong states exercise violence more often than do states of moderate strength (Cooney 1997). Historically and globally speaking, states have been neither neutral nor particularly democratic, but rather have served a particular function—that is, the pursuit of capitalist interests.

Max Weber (1946), largely agreeing with Marx's critique of capitalism, added **bureaucracy** to the list of forces of social domination in modern societies. Bureaucracy, as a form of social organization, coordinates (or is able to coordinate) large numbers of people to achieve specific goals, whether they be fighting a war, building a railroad, running a hospital, or operating a postal service. Bureaucracy served the needs of both industry and the state. The problem with bureaucracy is that it ultimately becomes irrational and dehumanizing. It traps people within a narrow set of means-to-ends calculations. It controls people instead of people controlling it, and the individual becomes "a small cog in a ceaseless moving mechanism" (Weber 1978:988). Under the rule of both bureaucracy and the power of money, capitalist market relationships take on a power of their own over individuals and society as a whole. We become trapped in an **iron cage** of our own making (Weber 1978), a cage from which it is difficult to escape.

Weber's iron cage metaphor includes both individuals and society as a whole. As more and more of institutional life is centered in large, bureaucratic organizations, legal rules come to ensnare individuals in the machinery of state. Their only escape may be to "break the law." This happened during Gandhi's struggles in India and the civil rights movement in the American South, embodied in the peaceful resistance strategies of Martin Luther King, Jr. Both King and Gandhi encouraged their followers to impede the power of the state and industry by placing their bodies in such a way that it interfered with their daily operations, and they absorbed the violence unleashed by these forces when they refused to move. Today, we consider Gandhi's and King's causes to be admirable, just, and right. Still, changing the world in the manner they did required them to break laws, that is, commit crimes. Though rules, regulations, and the dictates of organizations can come to dominate us and limit our freedom, both physically and mentally, there is no reason to assume today's laws will necessarily be tomorrow's. But in the present, our thought processes can become as rigid as the rules we are taught, forcing our minds into their own cages. Escaping the cage requires actions that are defined as criminal, courageous, or even insane (most people did not join the Civil Rights Movement even though they heard of it).

Ministries of Truth: Religious Institutions, Educational Apparatuses, and The Mass Media

Sociologists have come to understand that social institutions regularly serve the interests of one social bloc over another through control of things such as law or ideology. In modern, free societies, government-sponsored violence and propaganda are not the leading method of enforcing the power of the elite. The validity of any society's authority structure is based on whether individuals believe it is **legitimate**, that is, whether a relationship of domination is just, right, and therefore acceptable (Weber 1947:124-132). The process of **legitimation** may be understood as the "ways by which [the institutional world] can be 'explained' and justified" (Berger and Luckmann 1967:61). Not just any explanation will do, however. Legitimacy is more likely to be sustained when the public sees the world in a way that is harmonious with the views and interests of elites. Through socialization, obedience and submission to power relations can produce beliefs and behavior that seem, to those enacting them, as the free exercise of their reason, independent from the influence of others. Such training is very often located in popular social institutions such as families, schools, churches, synagogues, mosques, and the media. By funding them, staffing them, or even threatening them, the world-view of those with political-economic power tends to be disseminated. In this way, the official world-view of public institutions tends to be shaped by the ruling class and tends to reflect its interests. When a world-view propagated by elite institutions is internalized, citizens adopt an elite's world-view. This helps elites to maintain their **hegemony** or social domination (Gramsci 1971). Legitimacy is, therefore, often granted through voluntary submission where "the appropriate attitudes will exist, and the corresponding practical conduct ensue" (Weber 1947:324-326). Needing legitimacy, elites rarely leave this issue to chance. In the past, religion was the most important agent of social control and domination. In the modern era, religion has had to compete and/or cooperate with newer institutions, namely the educational apparatus and the mass media. These three social institutions have proved incredibly effective at setting the bounds of debate and access to information available to the public. The vision of the world that these institutions put forth, in part, establishes the grounds for what is public knowledge and respectable discourse.

Religious Institutions

Gods, sociologically speaking, are **collective representations**, or abstract figures created by humans to tell them their society's story and to regulate their behavior (Durkheim 1915). For Durkheim, religion was an emblem of a human collective and depicted its values and images of itself *to* itself, integrating people into a larger world of shared meanings. This explains why religious criticism is so closely associated with criticism of popular culture. To the extent that a religion stands as a symbol of those in a culture who practice it, religious critique threatens the sanitized images a society projects of itself through its myths, stories, and official history. Like money, once invented, the Gods as social facts become captive players in human life. Earlier human groups saw a world active with powers and spirits to be negotiated by the shaman. Over time as social structures changed, beliefs multiplied and Gods were specified. The institution of **religion** developed which, by presenting itself as the path to a type of freedom intended by a human-like creator, functioned to shape people within a socially determined framework. Besides assigning basic social taboos on murder, theft, and lying, religion can regulate what people wear, how they cut their hair, what they eat or don't eat, how they walk, bow, and pray; how they have sex, how they give birth, and who they marry. However, in modern society as whole, with its mix of multiple religions amid secularizing trends, often little agreement exists on what the proper beliefs and behaviors are.

Marx (1844a:53), like Durkheim, also believed that "Man makes religion, religion does not make man." In his view, religious systems represent a humanity divided against itself, fundamentally alienated, or otherwise **estranged** from its real existence as a species. Religion, in this perspective, arises because of human suffering. Like Durkheim, Marx believed that religion persists because it functions to soothe the alienating social conditions of which it is an expression.

> Religious suffering is, at one and the same time, the expression of real suffering and a protest against real suffering. Religion is the sigh of the oppressed creature, the heart of a heartless world, and the soul of soulless conditions. It is the opium of the people. (Marx 1844a:54).

This is Marx's most well-known comment on religion, though he has many others. Marx says that in a world that produces suffering, religion provides it some meaning. Human suffering might be caused by the forces of nature. It might come from the inhumanity among individuals. In a natural and social world indifferent to individual well-being, religion fills that void with humanly interpretable and meaningful traits (e.g., a heart and soul). The world is thus humanized. However, like opium, despite the help religion gives people to get through painful times, it does nothing to cure the conditions that account for the pain in the first place. The sociological point to understand is that the function of religion is not necessarily to bring *Truth* to a believer but rather to help him or her manage the affairs of this world.

If a religion is to manage its own affairs, grow and survive, its belief structure must not disrupt the dominant power relationships in its host society. Thus, religion is an important variable in the sociology of power. Religions that hold beliefs that undermine the power of a ruling class are likely to be suppressed or even crushed. For instance, usury, the charging of interest on money lent, is considered sinful by both the Old and the New Testaments of the Christian Bible. People without money are the ones who need to borrow it; for those who have money to ask for more in return than what is lent out is to exploit the vulnerable. Usury is therefore antisocial and is no basis for a cohesive set of social relations. Maintaining usury as a sin would have been in conflict with the needs of the rising capitalist market, a fact that eventually dawned on Church authorities. As the religious powers of Christianity learned to forget about this sin over time, so has the experience of people in the West lost touch with this Biblical sin (though sections of the Islamic world still forbid usury). The rising banking and commercial interests of early modernity were too powerful for established religion to challenge, and a world in which usury was an official sin had been destroyed. Few people, if any, in the West today experience their relationship to banks, credit cards, and car/student/housing loans as a violation of Biblical scriptures. Dominant

Christian denominations have long made their peace with the ruling class powers that be. In fact, Christianity is practiced by many in the ruling class. Religions, often starting as a rebellion against them, come to express the ideas and the interests of the ruling class in this way.

In his book, *The Sacred Canopy*, Peter Berger (1967) argued that when individuals interpret the world in their society's terms, they have internalized the external institutional world as their own world-view. Religious concepts arise as humans attach **sacred** meanings to special social relationships and institutions, meanings that become part of who the person *is*. "Our" social institutions always seem sacred. "Their" social institutions do not. This can be articulated in a variety of ways. In the years after America's founding, for example, a **civil religion** emerged and became a central theme in many Americans' view about the purpose of their government, their selves, and their history (Bellah 1970). "What we have," explains Bellah (1970:175), "from the earliest years of the republic is a collection of beliefs, symbols, and rituals with respect to sacred things and institutionalized in a collectivity," where one of the goals of the nation is "the obligation, both collective and individual, to carry out God's will on earth" (Bellah 1970:172). This civil religion has its own religious prophets (the Founding Fathers), its own religious symbols and icons (the flag, the Statue of Liberty), its own rituals where "God" is invoked (the inauguration), its own martyrs and myths (The Minute Men, Abraham Lincoln, John F. Kennedy, Dr. Martin Luther King, Jr.), and its days of remembrance and celebration (Memorial Day, the Fourth of July). Such a mix of the secular and the sacred is possible because "the average American saw no conflict between the two. In this way, the civil religion was able to build up without any bitter struggle with the church powerful symbols of national solidarity and to mobilize deep levels of personal motivation for the attainment of national goals" (Bellah 1970:180-181). Invasion and adventurism in foreign lands has often been explained as defending things that can be seen as the tenets of the American civil religion—e.x., abstract things such as "freedom," "democracy," "free markets," or "our national interests." Such policies often become endorsed by religious leaders who putatively preach a mission handed down from the ministry of Jesus Christ. In this way, what American leaders do by definition is considered "God's work." Those in positions of authority and power in the United States have continually relied on this civil religion and the belief in American superiority and moral rightness to mask their policies.

> The theme of the American Israel was used, almost from the beginning, as a justification for the shameful treatment of the Indians so characteristic of our history. It can be overtly or implicitly linked to the idea of manifest destiny that has been used to legitimate several adventures in imperialism since the nineteenth century. Never has the danger been greater than today. The issue is not so much one of imperial expansion, of which we are accused, as of the tendency to assimilate all governments or parties in the world that support our immediate policies or call upon our help by invoking the notion of free institutions and democratic values. Those nations that are for the moment "on our side" become "the free world." (Bellah 1970:181-182)

Historically, politicians in the United States have consistently depicted their actions as part of a larger religious mission. Slavery was depicted as bringing "civilization" to "savages" and serving the larger purpose of "Christianizing" the world, or the "white man's burden" (Jordan 1974). Deployment of U.S. soldiers is routinely depicted as necessary to fight against evil in the world and to preserve "our freedom," regardless of the real level of threat. In the nineteenth century, the seizure of Mexico and the destruction of Native-American cultures were interpreted as part of a "manifest destiny" providentially sent. The unilateral U.S. attack on the Philippines, condemned by Mark Twain in the national press, was painted by its defenders as a divine or sacred duty.[8] In order to halt the "evil spread of communism," in the late 1970s there began an onslaught of civilians by mercenary armies funded by the U.S. and controlled by right-wing dictatorships in Guatemala, El Salvador, Nicaragua, and Honduras, which lasted well into the 1980s, and in Columbia, well past the year 2000. Ronald Reagan depicted "the Contras" in Nicaragua as "freedom fighters" while they conducted operations against relatively defenseless and terrified Nicaraguan villagers (Chomsky 1988). The U.S. invaded Panama in December 1989 to depose military despot Manuel Noriega (a former ally) whose supposed drug offenses put U.S. national security and freedom at risk. The first President Bush depicted dictator Saddam Hussein (also a former ally) as "worse than Hitler" and the second President Bush explained his invasion of Iraq as both fighting terrorists (none were known to exist in Iraq) and preserving American's freedom, and even claimed that he had prayed to be an agent for God's will on Earth. How far from the Crusades have we really come? With the United States on a permanent war-time economy and with the rise of the national-security apparatus (i.e., CIA, National Security Agency, the Joint Chiefs of Staff, the Department of Homeland Security), there must always be new contenders for the leading evil in the world and/or the newest threat to freedom. As the interests of the elite shift over time, so do the threats. In the next one-hundred years, who will be targeted as the enemy? France? Germany? Canada? It only *seems* impossible.

The Educational Apparatus

Though defined differently across the world, all societies have standards for what passes for intelligence. Historically, formal education has been the most systematic way to cultivate it. Education systems have multiple functions, some intended and others unintended. One important function is that an educational system should provide individuals with the basic rudimentary tools of intelligent thinking, a standard that changes with societal changes. In ancient Greece and Rome, instruction in military arts was considered an essential part of education. The growth of scientific knowledge in the modern world brought with it increased needs for rudimentary knowledge of mathematics and writing skills. Modern educational systems teach the standards of cultural knowledge in a society, including its history, major cultural figures, and achievements. Individuals learn the official story a society tells about itself, a story that may not be entirely, or even remotely, true. Many American history texts used in high schools, for instance, demonstrate a pattern of error, omission, and distortion about its past (Loewen 1995). In terms of early U.S. history, the "first Thanksgiving" is usually depicted as something the Pilgrims provided to the Indians, a reversal of the actual course of events. In fact, most of the food served was native to the region, and thus foreign to the Pilgrims. Most texts never discuss the diseases brought by the Europeans and the effect this had on the Indians, nor how the Pilgrims thanked their God for bestowing this tragedy on its hapless victims (Loewen 1995:85-90). Neither are the genocidal tendencies in Columbus's behavior (e.g., rape, murder, pillage, and enslavement, without regard to age or sex) nor the cannibalism of the earlier Jamestown settlements (e.g., with one man murdering his wife and devouring her corpse) usually discussed in conventional accounts (Zinn 1980).

Another function of an educational system is to reproduce the relationships of power in a society. Though the rules of basic math, language, and abstract thinking apply equally to rocket science or car repair, as a social institution, education must still provide an adequate supply of students for both life in college and life as wage-laborers. The **formal curriculum**—that is, what is apparent from the list of classes, syllabi, schedules, and texts—is geared toward producing specialists in both symbolic and manual labor, with the tendency of the latter being more poorly paid and of a lower social status. A **hidden curriculum** also exists that is both intentionally and unintentionally structured into the educational system. To cultivate desired attitudes toward authority, early mass schools were structured to teach the discipline required for laboring under a schedule, so students were organized to resemble a workforce, with similar uniforms, shift changes on a signal like a factory's whistle or bell, and the answering to the authority of teachers, vice-principals, and principals. Students being prepared for college are taught the basics of institutional management and the tastes and desires associated with affluence. Other students are inculcated with the expectations appropriate for the working-class. Tracking, vocational schools, and the teaching of "marketable skills" instruct young students what to expect out of life, not to demand more and, if necessary, to be happy with less. Understood as such, the institutional function of schools in capitalist society is to reproduce the class structure (Bowles and Gintis 1976).

The educational apparatus as an institution is bound up in relationships of power and knowledge. Data support the assertion that the cabinets of the earliest chief executives in the United States and England were dominated by members from the upper class, most of whom had attended exclusive schools (Aronson 1964; Miliband 1969; Mills 1956). While there is no doubt that a fine education can be attained at universities such as Brown, Harvard, Princeton, Yale, Cornell, and Columbia, it is not unreasonable to ask: For the comparative cost, is the actual education at elite universities *that* much better than an education at State University? Is it really the *education itself* at these elite schools that opens the doors to lucrative careers for graduates? Elite universities have important functions in capitalist society, which, more than the quality of education, explain their exclusivity and cost. Entrance to such schools is tightly limited by admission standards and the expense of tuition. The faculty and student body at the most prestigious schools are usually qualified, at least on paper, for their high-status positions, though whether only they represent the best is a different issue. Only so many positions exist, and it is doubtful that the Ivy League will have room for all those who excel in their discipline, nor does every outstanding professor *want* to be in the Ivy League. While excellence in teaching might be enhanced by an active research agenda, excellence in publication does not ensure excellence in teaching, and an excellent teacher-student experience is one of the things for which a person desiring an *education*, rather than just a *diploma*, is paying.

There are some things students acquire at elite schools that are more difficult to get at State University. Two of the most important are *connections* and *lessons in comportment*. Making connections begins long before college, as parents search for prestigious grade schools and high schools for their children that more easily open the doors to the Ivy

League (Domoff 1978, 1983). After admission to an Ivy League school, students are introduced to a world of people who are being trained for the upper reaches of cultural, state, and industrial management. Educational institutions like those represented by the Ivy League were created, in part, as a training ground for each new generation of the elite. It is important to make sure this group of people learns to see the world in a way that justifies the investments made in them by the benefactors of these institutions (Chomsky, in Achbar and Wintonick 1992). This is why places such as Harvard save a certain percentage of their openings for "legacy" students, that is, children of alumni. The next generation of power holders must be trained, meet others, establish vertical and horizontal connections, and start "networking." That is, they must start accumulating the necessary social and cultural capital appropriate for maintaining and reproducing their class position. Once graduated, the diploma carries a reputation that will open more doors, many at higher paying jobs, than one could open with a diploma from State University. Elite schools function as the training ground for this career advancement. Therefore, it is important that individuals learn the right way to think, act, talk, and interact, and with whom to do so. New generations must be able to conduct themselves in a manner acceptable to the standards dear to what Mills called "the higher circles" (1956:3-29). It is *less* the education and *more* the status of the diploma, learning the right manners, and developing the connections that make people willing to pay the high costs of elite universities.

The Mass Media

Historically, knowledge has been passed down most often by word of mouth. Cave paintings, pottery, clothing, amulets, and other assorted social and bodily adornments followed. With growing complexity of the division of labor, efforts at communicating across time and space rested with various monks and priests and other associated specialists. In what we now know as the West, ever since the Gutenberg Bible at least, there have been constant efforts to make sure that the masses in modern society receive the knowledge that corresponds with their roles in society. As modern society became technologically developed, various modes of mass communication emerged and spread— for example, postal services, the telegraph, the telephone, and into the globally interconnected era of the computer. Understanding the implications of the process, twentieth century corporate leaders spent significant amounts of money in an attempt to influence the world's discourse. They bought publishing houses, newspapers and broadcast media, hired compliant editors, paid for the printing of textbooks pushing the corporate message, poured money into learning the techniques of advertising, and produced movies that depicted a particular vision of the world (Ewen 1976). Ownership of mass media organizations translates into a powerful influence over the vision of the world that is relevant to political decisions made by the population (and the decisions made by politicians that must be endured by the population). The mass media, whether liberal or conservative, functions as spokesperson for a world-view that is conducive to interests, needs, and outlooks of those who own it. To assume otherwise is to misunderstand the nature of both capitalism and its organizational structures. Capitalists are not in the habit of owning organizations that undermine their property, wealth, and social power.

In the United States, the mass media include the major networks (ABC, NBC, CBS, FOX), the largest newspaper publishers (*New York Times, Washington Post, Chicago Tribune, Chicago Times, LA Times*), the wire services (Associated Press, Reuters, United Press International), book publishers, and movie producers. Most of these are large corporations, and many of them are owned by larger, multinational corporations. Between 1982 and 1992, "the number of companies controlling most of the national daily circulation [shrank] from twenty to eleven. In magazine publishing, a majority of the total annual industry revenues, which had gone to twenty firms, now goes to two; in book publishing, what had gone to eleven firms now goes to five" (Bagdikian 1992:ix-x). Bagdikian later expands on the concentration of control of sources of information, ideas, and public discourse:

> Predictions of massive consolidation are based on extraordinary changes in recent years. At the end of World War II, for example, 80 percent of the daily newspapers in the United States were independently owned, but by 1989 the proportion was reversed, with 80 percent owned by corporate chains. By 1981 twenty corporations controlled most of the business of the country's 11,000 magazines, but only seven years later that number had shrunk to three corporations. Today, despite more than 25,000 oulets in the United States, twenty-three corporations control most of the business in daily newspapers, magazines, television, book, and motion pictures. (Bagdikian 1992:4)

In 2000, Bagdikian updated his book. It opens with this passage: "As the United States enters the twenty-first century, power over the American mass media is flowing to the top with such devouring speed that it exceeds even the accelerated consolidations of the last twenty years. For the first time in U.S. history, the country's most widespread news, commentary, and daily entertainment are controlled by six firms that are among the world's largest corporations, two of them foreign" (Bagdikian 2000:viii, xxxviii). It is important here to pause and consider the many reasons why this tendency toward concentration of media ownership has significant implications for democratic society. Two interrelated reasons are most relevant.

First, democracy requires free access to a diversity of opinion and information. **Democratic theory** is based, in part, on the idea that people should be able to meaningfully participate in the process of making decisions that will significantly impact their lives. In relation to the mass media, democratic theory also assumes that democracy in practice requires a cantankerous and skeptical press that checks on those who wield power and makes its findings freely available to the public. Increasing levels of concentration in media ownership translates into fewer alternatives and choices, reducing the odds of the media successfully fulfilling its function. (The explosion of the Internet as an information resource tempered the Orwellian march of media concentration in the late twentieth century.) A decline of informational sources available to the public is a decline in its ability to check the "facts" offered by its leaders. The general theory is that the more free and open public discourse is, the stronger democratic institutions can be made. Access to vital informational resources has typically been secured when social institutions of power accept and honor principles of both **intellectual freedom** and the **freedom of the press**. The continuing concentration of ownership of popular and news media firms works against this ideal of a free marketplace of diverse opinion and fact. Increased media concentration brings the West closer and closer to the authoritarian conditions that existed in the Soviet Union during the Cold War. This is not a simple irony of shifting historical math in relation to the number of media institutions—that is, the West now has as few sources of information as did the Soviet Union. Rather, this trend replays the real, legitimate warnings and fears the West broadcast against Communism: fewer sources of information and ideas undermines the democratic ideal. With the vast majority of the public constantly exposed to a mantra that accuses the media of a "liberal" bias, the claim that the media functions as spokespersons for its capitalist owners is a hypothesis taken seriously only in the academy and on the political left. The hypothesis that the mass media functions to undermine democracy in favor of the ruling class, however, should not be too readily dismissed.

Second, fewer media choices increases the likelihood that the media functions as **propaganda**, which, in authoritarian societies, is clearly obvious to consumers of "news." In the Soviet system, for instance, centralized, government-controlled information was hardly hidden, a situation that Western discourse during the Cold War constantly and accurately depicted as anti-democratic, anti-social, malformed, and generally undesirable. The influence of capitalists' search for mass markets in the media, however, has produced an institution characterized by bland conformity and self-censorship (Barak 1995). Though the formally free Western market place of ideas is not obstructed by governmental agencies, concentrated wealth, the search for affluent markets, the manipulation of news agencies by governmental bureaus, and the socialization of media operators into institutional roles, all function to shape U.S. and European media products into exercises in propaganda. Liberal media critics see the conservative, pro-capitalist bias of the media as quickly as conservative critics spot the media's liberal bias. That the media offers a world view that endorses conventional ideology (e.g., the civil religion) containing both liberal and conservative biases is a conclusion that is often left unconsidered in conventional media criticism. Propaganda works best when it presents itself as coming from a free and skeptical press (Chomsky, in Achbar and Wintonick 1992; Herman and Chomsky 1988).

Critics often accuse "the free marketplace of ideas" of serving as an institution of propaganda. The business community, primarily conservative on political and economic issues, makes the decisions that allow the broadcast media to function as it does, which, unless it is the Public Broadcasting System (PBS), National Public Radio (NPR), or community radio, is always as a **for-profit** enterprise. Media representatives want to reap the largest income that they can from advertising revenue. The owners and decision-makers are going to make sure they take care of their **market position** first and foremost. They do not want a media that would undermine their political-economic interests. Owners of news media tend to select editors who share their outlook on the world, or at least those who are not in conflict with them. Reporters, if they are to advance in their careers, must make sure that both what they report and how they report it are acceptable to their editors. A top-down socialization process exists where reporters learn to write what they think will please their editors. Reporters who internalize the dominant set of institutional values then practice a conscience-free self-censorship in which they feel immune to external coercion from their employers on what to report and how to report it. Governmental organizations and businesses provide press releases and news conferences to make sure their story and their visions of reality dominate the airwaves. They give reporters press-kits with the information that they want available for public consumption. Commercial television also has its own constraints. Not only is there a similar process of professional socialization among producers and directors, but news segments are wedged between commercials, and this reduces ideas, analysis, and content into a form in which complex issues are reduced to thirty-second sound-bites. Information that does not fit conventional wisdom and prevailing world views receives no serious hearing. News becomes propaganda (Chomsky, in Achbar, Wintonick 1992; Herman and Chomsky 1988; Parenti 1986; Postman 1986).

The propaganda function of U.S. media must be understood in light of the general freedom of the press and thought enjoyed in the United States. Even its critics admit a measure of respect and appreciation for the freedom of the U.S. press in comparison to other modern industrial societies (Palast 2003:182-196). The existence of formal freedoms and the legal protection of the press and individual consciousness must nevertheless be translated into an actual skeptical press that checks those in power and informs the public. Sociologically speaking, however, it is quite possible that the level of formal freedoms in the U.S. media makes its propaganda function even more effective, though more subtle. It will surprise no one that sociologists believe their tools—a commitment to empirical research, the experimental model, forms of logical reasoning, a skeptical disposition toward official truths—forged in the fire of science, provide an effective antidote to these problematic forms of information and knowledge about the world.

The Prospects for a Critical Sociology and its Most Vital Trends

The ministries of truth can impede a more complete understanding of the most important events in the world. It is the ways these and other institutions distort our thinking that provides sociology its cosmopolitan spirit of debunking and relativizing assumed knowledge, which bestows upon its practitioners a modicum of unrespectability in the eyes of the public. Sociology is mainly an academic discipline dependent on external funding, and, as such, it must justify its use of resources in the same way that the educational system must compete with other organizations for a share of social resources. In attempts to stay relevant, a not-insignificant number of academics, sociologists included, have attempted to make themselves useful to state functionaries and planners (Diesing 1991). Often socially **liberal** in outlook and **reformist** in politics, such sociologists often gear their work toward "policy analysis" and "advising" and work for goals embedded in state agencies. The field also attracts critics and skeptics, individuals whose study and personal experiences have led them to a more **critical** stance toward social and political relationships of the modern world. "Whose side are we on?" became a battle cry of sociological critics uninterested in either policy analysis or advising state planners (Becker 1967). Should sociologists or their research help state functionaries and others in positions of power, or should they use their skills to tell the story of the marginalized and the powerless? Are these mutually exclusive programs? The debates have been contentious. Critical sociologists stand somewhere between reformism and radicalism. They are reformist in that they see a need for our social institutions to change in important ways, such as bringing more women and non-whites into positions of power. They are radical in the sense that they see the problems of the world resolvable only through sweeping social change. These poles—that is, liberal skepticism and reform versus radical critique and social transformation—bound the outlooks of significant numbers of those in the discipline.

The Problems of Political-Economy: Neo-Marxism and the Continuing Critique of Capitalism

The fall of both the Soviet Union and the former Eastern Bloc regimes was embraced and greeted with optimism by many people. The Soviet system was viewed by most Western Marxist sociologists as a form of repression and as an example of how distorted and deformed a workers' **revolution** could become. Most of them welcomed its fall. Unfortunately, the almost universal interpretation—even held by some self-identifying Marxists as well as many sociologists—was that the fall of official communism proved that Karl Marx was wrong, and his ideas were no longer relevant. But not so fast. Marx's specific contribution to sociological thought had little to do with "communism." The contributions of Marx and Engels to sociological knowledge have to do with the **dialectical method** of inquiry, the development of materialist theory, the use of **class analysis**, and the study of **the political-economic structure** of capitalism. None of these concerns was informed in any way by the existence of the Soviet Union, communist China, or communism in general. Therefore, their fall and/or transformation is largely irrelevant to an assessment of Marx's contribution to sociology. Sociologists influenced by Marx believe that capitalism as a system produces knowledge that is ill-suited to providing the insight we need to fundamentally understand life in this society. Historically, capitalism has produced significant levels of poverty, hunger, war, and environmental destruction. Capitalism exacerbates things like sexism and creates systemic racism by dividing up labor and reward through the **ascribed statu**s of sex and ethnic category. If problems such as poverty, prejudice, and environmental destruction are to be solved, capitalism must be fundamentally transformed, as each social problem is now internally related to this system and the growing severity of its overall problems.

The Problems of Power: Machiavellian Dramaturgy in Political Life

Social research inherently involves the issue of **power**, whether it be from conservatives in classical and contemporary thought (Hobbes 1651; Locke 1688; Dahl 1961, 1979; Parsons 1963) or more recent critical perspectives (Jessop 1982; Lukes 1974; Miliband 1983; Perrucci and Potter 1989; Poulantzas 1969, 1978). Critical perspectives most often view power from the point of view of repression, violence, and dominance of political-economic institutions by elite groups. The usefulness of Niccolo Machiavelli's work (1515), *The Prince*, which examines the strategies used in the exercise of power, has been recently put to creative use by members of this tradition (Foucault 1978). His analysis provides insight into how political-economic power is exercised through the **management of impressions** by those in power (Goffman 1959; Paolucci, Holland, and

Williams 2004; Prus 1999). *The Prince* is not concerned with the moral implications of the strategies used by the powerful, only with what has or has not worked in defeating enemies, controlling subjects, and holding on to power. Everyday morality used to regulate inter-personal behavior has nothing to do with the proper strategies involved in exercising and keeping power. However, a prince will nevertheless be judged by his subjects on the basis of the public's morality. **Dramaturgical** sociology recognizes a similar principle, one which focuses on how the legitimacy of the individual in a social role is fostered by whether or not he or she performs it in conformity with an audience's expectations. "When an actor takes on an established social role, usually he finds that a particular front has already been established for it. . .[and therefore must] sustain the standards of conduct and appearance that one's social grouping attaches thereto. . .[and provide] an effort to give the appearance that his activity embodies certain standards" (Goffman 1959:27, 75, 107). As a dramaturgic actor, a prince "will have to forego or conceal action which is inconsistent with these standards" (Goffman 1959:41). This means that a prince, regardless of actual behav-ior or designs, wants to make sure he or she *appears* to the public in a manner that con-forms with its expectations about human morality— "In the end, they won out over those who tried to act honestly" (Machiavelli 1515:49).

A prince's goal is like any actor's in a social role, that is, "to control the conduct of the others" (Goffman 1959:3). There are several strategic techniques of impression man-agement a prince can employ. Because there are "vices that enable him to reign," "a prince must learn how not to be good" (Machiavelli 1515:46, 44). A prince must manipulate his **presentation of self** in order to reduce the problems he encounters if his domestic subjects observe the gap between their standards of morality and the vices exemplified by his actions. For example, Machiavelli (1515:20), while advising a prince to use "the example of his actions," also holds that a prince must "be a great liar and hypocrite," "skillful in hid-ing his intentions," and should learn "how craftily to manipulate the minds of men" by using "the pretext of religion" (Machiavelli 1515:50, 21, 49, 63). These strategies assist in making sure an "idealized impression is offered by accentuating certain facts and conceal-ing others," and "In this way an impression of infallibility, so important in many presenta-tions, is maintained" (Goffman 1959:43, 65). Because of these techniques, "Everyone sees what you seem to be, few know what you really are" (Machiavelli 1515:47).

Those who control what passes for the official **definition of the situation** often find themselves in a position to significantly influence, even control, social relationships. Accordingly, those in power who fail to learn how to manipulate others will suffer threats to their rule. In formally democratic societies, those in power have long learned to use pub-lic relations firms and advertising agencies to shape public discourse, to project the desired images of candidates, to depict political enemies in the worst fashion possible, and to har-ness images in an effort to harvest as many votes as possible. By providing an interpretive framework to understand such facts, the sociological imagination provides individuals a powerful tool of critical analysis. It facilitates a way to understand how the perceptions and behaviors of others are shaped through techniques of manipulation. Understanding both the rules of power and the methods of presentation of self provides tremendous insight into the behavior of those who wield state power. For example, during the build-up to its war in Iraq, the Bush administration consistently concealed major facts about its plans and reasoning, used religion as a pretext, and set up offices of "strategic information" in order to influence the discourse over the war and to shape the public's perception of it. Language to describe the level of threat represented by the Iraqi dictator changed almost daily, as did the terms used to describe his weapons, which went from "weapons of mass destruction" to "weapons programs" to "weapons programs related activities." Bush even allowed erroneous information to make it into his State of the Union Address, claiming that Saddam Hussein had tried to purchase "yellow cake"—a component of nuclear weapons production—in Africa. This discredited assertion was something for which he was eventually taken to task. Investigation reveals that members of the Bush Administration in fact were schooled under at least one intellectual, Leo Strauss (1899-1973), who had mastered Machiavellian ideas and found in them a useful and powerful political philosophy (Drury 1988, 1997). The skeptical bent asked of sociologists makes them sensitive to such information.

Race Studies and Feminism

In its first century, sociology concentrated much of its energy on issues that animated or plagued European societies. Those who dominated Europe's institutions of learning and knowledge spoke first, and it was capitalism's rapid emergence on the European continent that dominated their discourse. This brought on a confrontation with religion, partly due to growth of the natural sciences and how they influenced social thought. Older, deep-seated relationships of power, such as those based on sex and ethnic identity, only received partial and incomplete attention in classical sociological thought (Adams and Sydie 2002). When these topics *were* addressed, they were often dealt with through assumptions that were biased in favor of **heterosexist, patriarchal, white-supremacist thought** (hooks 1989, 2000). These biases had to be extracted from the social sciences if they were to achieve more valid explanations of the social world.

In the 1950s, African Americans began demanding that state officials enforce civil rights legislation. This stimulated an interest in sociology on **racial discrimination** and the history of **race relations**. These studies brought new knowledge to the social sciences, a knowledge that did not always flatter dominant groups in modern society (Cox 1976; Frazier 1962; Fredrickson 1981; Genovese 1976; Graves 2001; Harding 1993; Jordan 1974; Wilson 1987). Both the civil rights movement and the emerging scholarship on race and racism forever changed the political-intellectual landscape, inside and outside of the academy. No longer do the social sciences treat issues of race as secondary or minor issues in the field. Slightly later, women organized to challenge the structures of **patriarchy**, from men's domination of social institutions to the sexist knowledge about gender contained in religion, science, and culture. These struggles started in the class-privileged sectors of core capitalist countries but over time a generalized **feminist** rebellion spread to countries outside the core. The women's movement now cuts across many different ethnicities and class structures world wide and a vibrant feminist scholarship exists (Collins 1990; de Beauvoir 1974; Friedan 1963; Greer 1970). In 1995, in Beijing, China, women held their first global conference to explore how sexism affected them. It was a historic event.

Scholarship on race and gender brought new ways of thinking to the sociological imagination. One lesson is that science itself could be political and used to marginalize some groups and enhance the power of others. Another lesson is that the study of social inequalities in modern societies could not focus only on issues of class, but had to include categories of race, ethnicity, sexuality, and gender. Sociologists studying these issues argued that eliminating class exploitation would provide no guarantee that inequalities of gender, race, ethnicity, or sexuality would also be eliminated. The social sciences historically had been guilty of neglecting these issues. With the rise of studies in social inequalities in the social sciences combining with the ways associated political movements have changed the world, it is doubtful that questions of gender, race, or sexuality will be neglected or unanswered ever again.

Post-Industrial Society, Post-Colonial Theory, Post-Structuralism and Post-Modernism

World War II was a traumatic experience for the human community, affecting all of the planet's regions, all of its ethnic groups, and all of its institutions. It signaled so many things, including humanity's ability to be cruel, hateful, brutal, and destructive. It also signaled the end of one era and the beginning of another. The ending of the war brought the power of the atom into public consciousness and in the United States made way for the rise of the greatest economic and military power the world had yet seen. With the creation of the United Nations, the Marshall Plan, the World Bank, the International Monetary Fund, and NATO, powers in the United States and Europe rebuilt the world-economy in a manner to solidify capitalist political-economic institutions and relationships. With core states' withdrawal from regions they formerly controlled, the world-system was prepared to shift into an era that was new in some ways, and very familiar in others.

From Post-Industrial Society to Post-Colonial Theory

The post-World War II era brought on a period of **Pax Americana** where U.S. capital led in the reconstruction of the world-economy. This spurred a growth of industrial and technological innovation in which the United States and Western Europe began to shift over to more information-based industries and less manufacturing of durable goods. Academic spokespersons began to announce the arrival of **post-industrial society** where value and wealth were based less on physical labor and more on providing services and manufacturing ideas (Bell 1976). Though such analyses were profoundly mistaken about the decline of industry, they were perceptive that the economic base of core-capitalist societies was being transformed by the rise of new technologies, service industries, and information systems. Such analyses were often overly sanguine about the prospects for the average working class person, however. Real standards of living and hours of work versus hours of leisure have actually gotten worse since the start of the "post-industrial" age (Collins, Leonard-Wright, and Sklar 1999).

A group of scholars from former colonial societies came to the attention of Western scholarship in the 1990s. Many of these scholars focused on how forms of knowledge, culturally held and institutionalized in both science and political-economic agencies (e.g., the World Bank, the IMF, UNICEF), portrayed people in these colonies as exotic, savage, ignorant, or otherwise requiring tutelage in the ways of modernity (Said 1979; Spivak 1999; Crush 1995; Escobar 1995). A central feature of criticism from **post-colonial theory** is that even though many former colonizers have withdrawn militarily, many former colonies are still subjected to foreign power, this time through capitalist and monetary agencies, rather than direct occupation by the armies of foreign states. Post-colonial relationships nevertheless subject people in these societies to modern forces of power through economic imperialism (again), but this time through agencies that exist beyond the level of the nation-state. It is a *post-colonial* form of domination based on the power of capitalists to dictate the rules of the global free market that trap peripheral nations into a perpetual state of subordination. Modern theories of power recognize that forces of domination have expanded beyond the level of the most powerful nation-states.

Post-Structuralism and Post-Modernism

The French academy has contributed significantly to the history of social thought. In the late 1950s, a trend dubbed **post-structuralism** emerged (Dreyfus and Rabinow 1982). This approach to social thought argued that many social realities cannot be reduced to structural explanations alone. Instead, there exist many arenas of power rather than a central source, like capital or the state. Each arena of power has its own logic and effects, which may or may not intersect with the others. Power is a "capillary" or dispersed phenomena, not one with a centrifugal force or a singular organizing principle (Foucault 1980). For example, while capitalism was influential in the rise of modern sexuality, other social institutions were equally influential, such as the fields of science, medicine, law, and religion (Foucault 1978). Power involved more things than simply the repression of bureaucratic machines or repressive Victorian moralities. It involved the production of human subjects through the forces of knowledge (Foucault 1983).

Another trend, often referred to as **postmodernism**, also emerged in this period. One strand of postmodern thought critiques **grand narratives** such as Marxism or psychoanalysis for being too unwieldy (Lyotard 1984). Another view sees capitalism as being transformed by the rise of the artificial simulations and foundationless imagery (**simulacra**) in industry, media, and entertainment. With the social construction of the human as a consumptive unit, the production of brand loyalty, the use of advertising firms to run political campaigns and manipulate public consciousness, and the mangling of historical truths in movies, television, and print media, social life is seen as being centered on things that are unreal, concocted and ultimately only imaginary. From this perspective, such forms of cultural discourse, as opposed to more traditional roots in shared laboring or class relationships, are interpreted as the contemporary basis of modern social relationships (Baudrillard 1981, 1989). Disney World, a world of false images and fantasy, is a central analogy for this perspective. Truth in the world only refers to images and simulations, not real history or facts. Political ads refer to images of candidates that have little association with reality but rather other false images. For example, during the build-up to the second Gulf War, vice-president Cheney consistently asserted that Iraq had weapons of mass destruction and ties to bin Laden's terrorist organization. Neither claim was true, and each one was contradicted by other members of the administration (Paolucci, Holland, and Williams 2004). In his 2004 election campaign, George W. Bush used his appearance at the wreckage of the World Trade Center to prove his leadership. However, his actual presence right after the attack on the WTC was unknown to a nervous nation for several hours. And later, in a Machiavellian-dramaturgical fashion, he did little more at the site than pose, talk, and have his picture taken. The mass media constantly referred to his campaign as a "re-election bid," though he was never officially elected but rather was appointed by the Supreme Court and had a minority of the popular vote.

A third strand of postmodern thought strives to **deconstruct** forms of knowledge in a search for their hidden biases and assumptions (Derrida 1997). For example, there are many interpretations of the idea of "freedom." There is freedom of conscience, freedom of movement, and freedom of the press. There is freedom from fear, freedom from tyranny, and freedom from want. Whether people should have a freedom *from* religion has been per-haps debated less often. For the founders of the modern democratic state, freedom meant the freedom to own private property in the form of land, machinery, stocks, and other forms of great wealth (Parenti 1995). This freedom often is in conflict with the other freedoms. So, those with great wealth have often used their power to conflate their freedom to own productive resources, to buy labor, and to sell its products with the freedoms enjoyed and/or supported by the public at large, such as freedom of religion and freedom of speech. In fact, the Supreme Court of the United States has provided free speech rights to corporations by giving them the legal status of individuals. By deconstructing the assumptions associated with the social meanings of "freedom," one can better see how public discourse can be manipulated to service narrow interests in society. Though often over-stated in their claims and aims, postmodern perspectives have contributed to the ongoing efforts to establish both theoretical and empirical bases for continuing the critique of relationships of power and domination that still mark modern society.

Though intellectuals are often jealous of their professional boundaries, sociologists once saw their discipline as being the queen of the sciences. In Chapter One, we argued that, as a discipline, sociology required its practitioners to master a wide range of ideas and other disciplines. While the field has continued this tradition, professionals in academia often tend to specialize, and this has worked against the broad-ranged approaches handed down from our classical roots. In reference to the continuing relevance of sociology, what seems to have happened is that our classical roots have been pillaged by other disciplines, ironically, to both our pleasure and chagrin. This has made more disciplines sociological in outlook but without elevating the discipline or its practitioners to a higher level of academic or social respectability. Sociologists as cosmopolitan skeptics are skilled at debunking official knowledge and relativizing social facts, all of which does little to dislodge the level of unrespectability they have cultivated over the historical course of their discipline. Still, more and more social scientists have come to agree with a sociological truism handed down from the classics: any study of society must draw on the sociological imagination if any sense is to be made out of the modern world.

The Issue of Social Change and Peering Into the Future

Where are we going? This is not an unreasonable question to ask, and, in fact, this question is constantly asked. The question is at the heart of politics. It is in between the lines of newspaper print. Universities have programs that address the question called "pub-lic policy," "public administration," and "philosophy." The question is pondered over by pundits, poets, priests, and prognosticators. Sociologists ask this question, too, though their success in predicting what lies ahead has only been slightly better than the average. The social world does not follow laws in the same way as does the physical world, making predictions about society's shape in the future a precarious undertaking. What forces are changing society today? How are they changing it? Where might these changes take us?

The Rise of the Global Period

From about 1550 until around 1700, the capitalist **world-economy** was dominated by agriculturally based concerns and from then until the early 1800s, entrepreneurial capitalists, that is, the shop keepers and merchants, came to the fore (Wallerstein 1974). After this period until the early 1900s, those entrepreneurial firms that were the most cunning in strategy and located in vital markets thrived and produced an industrial explosion. With the rise of the great trusts in banking, steel, oil, and railroads in the 1910 to 1940 period, an era of **monopoly capitalism** predominated (Sweezy 1966). While some of these monopolies were broken up by federal power, the period of the two world wars (1900-1945) stimulated industrial growth through the mass production for war efforts. This occurred in all regions of the world-system. After the war period, the largest remaining firms were in a position to grow, and they did, expanding globally at a rapid pace. Capitalists became a true **transnational class** (Barnet and Muller 1974). Ever since, their size and mobility have grown at an astounding rate and to an enormous degree (Greider 1997; Kolko 1988). By the twenty-first century, several hundred of these capitalist firms had grown to the point where they possessed more financial resources than most governmental structures of the world's nation-states. Many state-functionaries found that the traditional relationship between state institutions and the structure of capital was being transformed. The most powerful capitalists were influential enough to dictate the terms of trade and labor policies to states, as well as policies in energy, education, health, and welfare. Only state structures in the United States, Western Europe, Australia, Russia, and China were able to resist these capitalist pressures, even if only to varying degrees. With their interests represented in key positions in the United States and Europe, capitalists were able to use their control of the state in core societies to reduce the power of states elsewhere (e.g., the Gulf Wars). With capitalists themselves as a supra-national class with growing power, the number of members on the list of societies able to resist the power of the largest capitalist interests is likely to grow smaller over time. Today, the largest capitalist firms are no longer located in any one geographical state but rather enjoy global mobility. This makes them *an outright global social fact*, something that has been called **globalization** (Chase-Dunn, Kawano, and Brewer 2000). Globalization is a process that has significant implications for the future of human life on planet earth.

Human Ecology and Perils of Globalization: Indications of Environmental Collapse

The magnitude of environmental destruction is something that is often not immediately felt or understood. Growing amounts of data and an increasing consensus in the scientific community suggest that the planet's ecology is in terrible jeopardy. Extinction risks are growing for many species and current levels of social development and consumption are unsustainable in the face of possible ecological collapse. A brief survey of the state of earth's ecology as it relates to human life reveals global warming;[9] the loss of rainforests, arable topsoil, and supplies of fresh water; tons of nuclear waste; holes in the ozone layer; rising levels of sickly oceans;[10] increasing amounts of heavy metals and carcinogens in water and food supplies; unhealthy levels of air pollution;[11] melting glaciers; and a partial break-up of the ice-shelf in Antarctica.[12] Biologists claim that a "mass extinction" of plants and animals is occurring worldwide.[13] There are rising levels of cancer and birth defects in humans and millions of excessive annual deaths attributable to environmental causes worldwide. By the year 2004, there had been little *significant and concerted* global action to reverse any of these trends. That which has been done to the environment already cannot easily be undone; those policies that do get enacted to protect the environment can easily be dismantled when power relationships change in the political-economic system. The global warming that has taken place is due to gasses released by industry and automobiles over a decade earlier. Therefore, any steps taken to arrest or reverse the process of global warming will not have immediate effects. Worse, dealing with each environmental crisis in a piecemeal fashion deflects attention away from the human assault on the environment as a whole. These are society-wide or even worldwide problems that must be dealt with through fundamentally changing our most powerful social institutions. Though evidence suggests that the number of treaties and organizations addressing environmental issues has grown (Frank, Hironaka, and Shofer 2000), any approach that settles for only reforming what and how individuals consume will not be enough. With the world's population at six billion and expected to reach nine billion by 2050, these conditions foretell a perilous future. We should remember that Mother Nature has had a way of ridding herself of species that threaten the integrity of an ecosystem. Assuming that this principle is not operative on a global level is a huge gamble.

Tribalism, Fundamentalism, and Terrorism

In a book that received wide attention and comment, Benjamin Barber (1996) argued that the world is increasingly being pulled toward two opposing but mutually dependent poles, which he termed "Jihad" and "McWorld."

> The first scenario rooted in race holds out the grim prospect of a retribalization of large swaths of humankind by war and bloodshed: a threatened balkanization of nation-states in which culture is pitted against culture, people against people, tribe against tribe, a Jihad in the name of a hundred narrowly conceived faiths against every kind of interdependence, every kind of artificial cooperation and mutuality; against technology, against pop culture, and against integrated markets; against modernity itself as well as the future in which modernity issues. The second paints that future in shimmering pastels, a busy portrait of onrushing economic, technological and ecological forces that demand integration and uniformity and that mesmerize peoples everywhere with fast music, fast computers, and fast food—MTV, Macintosh, and McDonald's—pressing nations into one homogenous global theme park, one McWorld tied together by communications, information, entertainment, and commerce. Caught between

> Babel and Disneyland, the planet is falling precipitously apart and coming reluctantly together at the very same moment. (Barber 1996:4)

The capitalist market has created a need for consumerism, and mass marketing has turned consumerism into a phenomenon planetary in scope. With nation-states willing to subjugate peoples outside their borders, indigenous people sometimes fight back for their own protection and/or to promote their own vision of the world. Sometimes other communities in the world find these visions unfamiliar or dangerous and they fight against them (such as calls for an Islamic state by fundamentalist Muslims). Those peoples who are subjugated often view the forces of modernity with an equal amount of horror and fascination, condemning them for immorality (e.g., the availability of alcohol and pornography) while becoming dependent on their conveniences (e.g., Nike's shoes, Microsoft's software, and Toyota's automobiles). This is most often true when their older cultural values have remained intact during their introduction to modern society. Indeed, the modern world has developed unevenly but interdependently and is threatened with being pulled apart by great institutional forces that in reality, if not in the minds of the people subject to these same forces, express a contradictory compatibility.

A case can be made that many of the world's poorest peoples have been subjected to harsh repression. Sometimes, this has often been at the hands of imperial powers. Other times this has come at the hands of their neighbors. But even then, the most powerful nation-states have often played a significant role. Those living in the island nations of East Timor and Aceh have had the military might of Indonesia inflicted upon them, a military funded and trained in large part by Western resources and expertise. After the Cold War, the peoples in the Balkans of Central Europe turned on one another. In Rwanda, between April and July (1994), the Hutus attacked Tutsis with genocidal ferocity, killing upwards of 800,000 people, made possible in part by European assistance. The Kurds and Palestinians have frequently been attacked by neighbors and abandoned by former allies, situations that the world's greatest powers could resolve but chose to ignore. The forces of McWorld have proven themselves as interested in looking after their own provincial interests as the forces of Jihad. The United States has one of the world's highest percentage of religious fundamentalists (Harding 2000), is xenophobic toward outsiders (even Canadians and, especially, Mexicans, their closest neighbors), and has supported military dictatorships worldwide (Blum 1995). There is little reason to assume that McWorld contains no Jihad of its own or that both McWorld and Jihad will refrain from violence and irrational ultranationalism any time in the near future. The differences between these two trends should not make us confuse or ignore their very telling similarities. That is, both McWorld and Jihad express a certain fanaticism and irrationality that are not harmless or inert but rather portend an ominous future.

World War III

Though he was referring to a conflict between the United States and the former Soviet Union in his work, *The Causes of World-War Three*, C. Wright Mills (1959:54) argued that the "immediate cause of World War III is the preparation for it," a warning that is still relevant today. If the structural relationships that caused the first two world wars remain in place, then it is toward those relationships that the sociological imagination would first be directed. In a system of unequal exchanges across regions containing multiple states, each armed with conventional and unconventional weapons, locked within the framework of a global world-economy, one thing to know is how preparation for war is structured into the political-economic framework. In the capitalist world-economy, wars are often fought between core-powers divided against one another as semi-peripheral societies align with the contending sides. Fighting typically breaks out over control of resources. The leading firms world-wide are oil and gas companies, weapons manufacturers, and advanced technology industries. Their struggles over reserves of oil and gas and the everyday business operations of weapons industries are preparing us for a third world-war. Their interests lead in the direction of getting more weapons into more hands in more countries. The market does not reward either altruism or loyalty beyond temporary expediency. Former animosities and grievances have historically been overlooked for the sake of temporary advantage, immediate threat, or long-term gain. What are the likely sources of a world war if it erupts sometime between 2005 and 2025? If it breaks out amongst the greatest powers armed with nuclear weapons, it will probably produce global destruction.

After the election of 2000, the second Bush administration adopted policies that forced a decline in the power and relevance of NATO and the United Nations, two institutions designed to avert another global war. During the Cold War, the goal of successive administrations was to prevent the powers of Europe from deciding that anything other than a capitalist system was against their interests (Wallerstein 2002). It is still important for the U.S. elite to prevent a Russian-European axis. With communism no longer a significant social force, the market ascendant, and the United States' power unrivaled, why would Paris, twice invaded by Germany, *not* now align with Berlin, Moscow, or even Beijing? The United States probably cannot rely on nuclear power to prevent this. Pakistan, North Korea, India, and Israel all have nuclear capabilities, too. Pakistan has made its technology available for export, and North Korea continues to threaten to do so. Further, the collapse of the USSR, among all its meanings and effects, removed a disciplining power wielding over potentially aggressive militarism against the United States by rogue enemies. Today, there are too many potential players and only one target at the top—that is, the United States—for the United States to rely on nuclear exchanges to intimidate potential enemies. China is also not likely to want to go to war against the United States because it needs the United States as a market for its exports. If the United States fails to keep incomes high enough to support global demand, it will lose a major card that it holds in soliciting patience from temporary, convenient, and/or marginal allies and staving off military threats from rivals. Britain's alignment with the United States during the second war in Iraq will keep it closely attached to U.S. elites' shifting interests. As these change, so will the direction and tenor of Britain's policies. The joint inability of the United States and Britain to pacify opposition in Iraq will signal to others that resistance is possible. States such as North Korea are likely to read this as a vulnerability. Totalitarian states with nuclear weapons such as this are likely to do anything, as are terrorists, who are likely to continue their attacks, with each new "success" upping the ante for the next group of putative martyrs for the cause. The trajectory of the planet is ominous indeed.

Much of what happens is dependent on events in the Middle East and the flow of oil. Many regional conflicts are likely to continue to erupt around Arab and African areas of the world-system as oil supplies dwindle. None of the nation-states is self-sufficient enough or technologically prepared to engage in conventional conflict without access to worldwide oil resources. This was a major reason for the second Bush administration's push toward the second Iraq war. This was not a war over oil so much as it was over what military force and a compliant regime in the oil fields could bring one particular faction of U.S. elites. Because of its increasing ties with the former Soviet republics in Central Asia, historic ties with Israel, military dominance of Kuwait and Afghanistan, and the war with Iraq, the United States became a force to be bargained with in the Middle East. OPEC's survival is threatened by this set of events, and its breakup would benefit the interests of U.S. elites. If a world war were to break out beginning in the Middle East, the NATO alliance would fracture. With its geographic and political position, Turkey would be a major variable in the degree of its breakup. Though an alliance with the United States would prevent it from being invaded by it outright, the years of the United States supplying arms to the military autocracy running Turkey may turn into another case of "blow-back," where a former ally turns its arms on its former sponsor (Johnson 2000). Given its position as lone, global, core state, the United States may spread itself so thinly that a coalition of several strategically placed adversaries could bring it disaster. This is one reason why its unilateralist, "go it alone" posture in the second Iraq war was so foolish. Surrounded by enemies instead of friends, a paranoid and entrapped nuclear power losing its singular global economic dominance would bring no benefit to the world community, nor to Americans themselves. The further one projects events into the future, of course, the more difficult it is to calculate possibilities.[14] However, another world war will likely emerge from the same causes as the previous two world wars.

Overwork, Mass Consumerism and the Reinvigoration of Feudalism and Fascism

Capitalism is a contradictory economic system. It is able to produce an abundance of commodities. Its capacity for technological innovation dramatically reduces the number of labor hours needed to produce products and services. However, historically and globally, capitalism has also brought increased amounts of time spent at work under supervision and for inadequate wages. More and more commodities are being produced ever more efficiently, but people are working more and more hours for less and less pay. The period of leisure and affluence enjoyed by working- and middle-classes in core capitalist regions has receded in the face of the processes of globalization. With the intensity of work up and pay down, more workers are taking on multiple jobs. Workers worldwide increasingly cannot afford the products and services they produce. In the peripheral societies that supply much of the world's food, labor, and raw materials, starvation has increased. These societies are also bearing the brunt of the ecological crisis. As the divide between those who own private resources and those who do not continues to increase, all will suffer.

One of the reasons the United States, Britain, and the Soviet Union fought the second world war was to defeat **fascism**. The traits associated with fascism were not unique to the leaders of fascist Italy, Germany, and Japan, however. They were not the product of some "evil genius." Hitler could not have acted alone. The Nazis needed help to come to power, which they received from religious and business leaders (Black 2001; Cornwell

1999). Fascism is no fleeting aberration. Rather, the traits indicative of fascism arrived with the market itself and have ebbed and flowed with the market's dynamics. The defeat of fascism in World War II therefore, did not guarantee the defeat of fascism generally.. The ground it grows in is still fertile, and its seeds are capable of flourishing again. How will we know fascism when it comes? Studies of fascist states show they were characterized by several traits, including a glorification of state and corporate power; strong nationalism and militarism; a controlled mass media; the use of sexism, racism, and xenophobia to unify the population; an obsession with national security; a disdain for intellectuals and human rights; the union of religion and government; and widespread corruption, evidenced in things like fraudulent elections (Adorno 1950; Britt 2003). Nothing in the above list requires a new evil genius on the scale of Hitler, Mussolini or Tojo. If these researchers have located the relevant characteristics, then fascism in capitalist society is *something always there, something whose presence is simply a matter of degree.* If the forces that keep fascism in check—such as strong working-class consciousness, participatory democracy, open social debate, checks and balances on the powerful—are weakened, then the probability that fascism will re-emerge and thrive is increased.

Economic Collapse

The Achilles heal of the capitalist system—its ultimate contradiction—is that it is a system that produces more value in goods and services than the total relative value its workers are paid for their labor. Therefore, the total amount laid out by capitalists in wages is, on average, insufficiently large enough to allow workers to buy all the commodities that they produce. A good way to understand this problem is to look at a bank, which is a sort of microcosm for the capitalist system as a whole. Before the reforms enacted after the Great Depression, federal insurance for banks did not exist. This left them susceptible to rumors and runs. People withdrew their money because they believed their bank had insufficient funds. If too many people pulled out their money, then the bank's funds would evaporate, leaving it vulnerable to instability and collapse. Banks stay solvent by having enough cash on hand to cover demand for daily withdrawal. Their cash on hand never equals or exceeds the total amount of wealth invested by clients. A market is like a bank: if the prices of all the commodities for sale are added up, then that total should exceed the total value of wages available to purchase these same commodities. Workers are paid less in wages than the total value of the commodities they produce, and thus consumers as a class do not possess enough money to pay for the total goods produced by capitalist activities. Because of this, capitalism is a system that suffers from an **overproduction of goods**. When overproduction hits a certain magnitude, profit rates begin to drop first for firms, but if a general decline in profit rates is not stopped, profit rates can drop across the capitalist system as a whole. Moderate dips in the market that last for over a year cycle are often called **recessions**, and more severe, long-term declines in market value are called **depressions**. If such periodic economic downturns are not reversed, the system eventually grinds to a halt. Much like the way the value of wealth in a bank can "dry up," the vast quantities of wealth in the capitalist system are always threatened with a potential loss of their value. The market system, under its own logic, could fall from its own weight if an economic crisis is not solved. What is likely to happen in, during, or after such a situation is really anyone's guess.

If history is any guide, the sudden loss of economic power is likely to be followed by a military reaction by elites in an attempt to save a dying system. The media will likely portray something like that as a police or military response to criminals, rebels, or terrorists. Regardless of the likelihood of this scenario, the prospect of economic collapse is a regular fear as stock market investors attempt to avoid it personally every trading day. Because investors' behaviors are institutionalized and enacted right out in the open, we often forget that their daily ritual to prevent personal bankruptcy is a future possibility awaiting the system as a whole.

The Slow Decline

If you want to boil a frog alive, you cannot put it in a pot of boiling water. When the frog feels the heat, it will immediately jump from the pot. However, if you put a frog in a pot of cold water and bring up the heat very slowly, the frog will not notice the gradual change and will fail to jump out of the pot and die. It is similar in society. Slow changes are less likely to be noticed and, when they are, they may already be too far along to do much about. Capitalism, too, has proven itself to be able to survive its own contradictions. As well as impacting the livelihood of uncountable numbers of people, recessions also wash out inefficient firms, leaving a fewer number of stronger firms at the next upward tick of the market. New products produce new industries unforeseen a generation earlier (e.g., computer technology). Innovations such as credit expand the purchasing power of consumers and businesses. Human and natural disasters (e.g., wars and earthquakes) produce incredible opportunities for the weapons, construction, and medical industries. Fatty, salt-laden food is very profitable for both its producers and industries associated with heart disease and cancer. Clearly, capitalism is a constantly changing, constantly expanding system. When its changes are rapid, when people remember a better day, people are likely to question the system and the prerogatives of its beneficiaries. They might even organize and work for social change. When its changes are rapid and people remember days that were much worse, capitalism is praised as the panacea for all economic ills. Sociologists do well to make themselves immune to such swings of prejudice and opinion. Theirs is a more reasoned path.

Critics of capitalism saw its constantly expanding and intensifying cycles as creating so much disparity between the wealthy and the poor that it would reach one great moment of working-class resistance. It was hypothesized that this would sound the death-knell of capitalism. However, it could just as easily happen that, like a swarm of locusts moving from field to field, those firms that find an economy-of-scale profitable enough to continually globe-hop for the cheapest labor, resources, and compliant workforce will do so. In its real history, investment has moved from regions in Europe, to the United States and to Mexico, and from there to China. If the Chinese will not work for less than a dollar a day, prisoners can be made to do so. A logical extension of the globalization process is to move industries from the lowest wage areas of the world to prisons. If this becomes a real, widespread, and successful policy, then the further merging of industry and prisons, like old company towns, will find willing takers in the investing classes. And if prisoners in the United States can be made to work, then it will be easer to make prisoners all over the world do so. Capital worldwide, in a scramble for profitable opportunities, drives labor to the lowest common denominator, leaving workers with little spending power. Though the rich continue to get richer and the poor poorer, there are limits to how far this can go. Capitalism might simply exhaust itself. Rather than one moment of upheaval, capitalism might experience a gradual winding down where, like locusts moving from field to field, it devours everything in its path until the whole can no longer survive. Going into the prisons for cheaper labor is likely part of this process. If the process is slow, then people, like the boiled frog, are unlikely to notice what afflicts them until after it is too late.

Protest, Revolution, and the Autonomous Movements

Forms of power that are organized and institutionalized only can be changed through a similarly organized counteracting power. Citizens worldwide still do have ways to struggle for their interests and well-being, as they can simply withdraw their willingness to work and consume. Social protest, boycotts, and general strikes—as old fashioned as they seem—are still some of the most powerful weapons people have to defend themselves. Voting candidates from the dominant political parties into office has proven itself a very limited strategy, and reforms won through the ballot box are easily dismantled by the next administration. As capitalism has gone global, the opposition to it has grown, too. Issues of race, gender, and sexuality have converged with the ongoing struggle over labor and environmental issues. The levels of global protest against free trade policies and environmental degradation have grown. Protest against war by core powers has also grown in scope, sometimes occurring *prior* to the outbreak of war (Chomsky 2003). For example, it took several years for the policies in Vietnam to become known to the American public, and it took some time after that before sentiment and protest turned against the war in a significant way. This experience of facing widespread social unrest, Chomsky (1991) argues, effectively drove U.S. foreign policy throughout Central America into a more covert phase during the 1980s, a measure of the fear policy planners had of public protest. Additionally, in both of the wars the United States waged against Iraq, protests began *before* the bombing, a significant change over previous periods.

In the early twenty-first century other forces emerged, forces that Wallerstein refers to as **anti-systemic movements** (Wallerstein 1982, 1983). One of the most significant is the **anti-globalization movement**, a loose coalition of union activists, environmentalists, church workers, indigenous peoples, human rights activists, students and professors, and other concerned citizens. Their central objective is to combat the creation of both unregulated global markets and those supranational institutions that set the rules of trade and environmental policy. This coalition of groups contends that labor rights, environmental health, and democratic practice are all being undermined and sacrificed for the benefit of capital in the global market. There has also been a growing tide of resistant antisystemic movements that have been referred to as **autonomous movements**. There are several of them world-wide.[15] While far from uniform in their objectives, these movements tend to rely on grassroots organizations and oppose foreign control of their political institutions and economic resources. They urge people to resist and to form collectives and communities that will provide them some space and freedom outside of markets, outside of police states, and outside of oppressive institutions so that they can regain control of their lives.

Conclusion

The modern world has developed as a series of institutions that both inform and misinform the public on the most important issues that impact their lives. The class structure undermines both political democracy and everyday people's ability to control their own economic destinies. Religious institutions have succumbed to the power of the dominant classes, as have the institutions of the educational apparatus and the organizations of mass media. As the world's ecological balance continues its decline, and humanity's social institutions teeter on the edge of dysfunction and breakdown, most of the world finds the forces of production a treadmill they cannot escape. To the extent that they are aware of their predicament, the iron cage of bureaucracy stands as a persistent obstacle. The health of the organism that is the world-system appears poor and due to get worse.

What would we think of biology as a science if its practitioners never turned their tools toward disease? Knowledge for knowledge's sake means little unless it makes itself relevant to the human world of meaning and experience. Sociological knowledge that is too abstract does little to help scientists make their work relevant to the daily problems of existence in the social world. Though he is not a sociologist, Noam Chomsky constantly reminds us that it is real human beings who live lives of privilege or deprivation that we study: the real decisions made in real institutions by real people with real power play a real part in who lives and succeeds and who does not. Sociologists are obligated by the nature of their discipline to discover fundamental inequalities, dangers, and injustices and educate others about them. Armed with the tools they have and their access to information, intellectuals have a responsibility to expose lies and to tell the truth (Chomsky 1967). If our observations tell us that social roots of human existence are under attack, then sociologists have a responsibility to explain as clearly and as fairly as they can why they have come to such a conclusion.

What is at stake? Earth? Probably not. The planet will discipline and maybe even destroy us before we destroy it. Humanity? No. Even with dire ecological conditions and a possible collapse of the political-economic system, it is likely that human life will continue, though on a smaller scale. If humans survive, so will their forms of social organization. What is actually at stake are all the things that modernity has made possible but has not made accessible to all people: freedom from superstition, exploitation, and toil; access to resources; democracy and freedom; and free inquiry. All those things for which modernity has been praised, especially its advancement of human reason, stand to be destroyed by the development of the system that assisted the historical evolution of human thought itself. Whether humanity's social existence and faculties of reason will be traits that destroy its host species and prove to be an evolutionary oddity is what is at stake.

Notes

1.
See:

http://www.bnl.gov/bnlweb/pubaf/pr/2002/bnlpr072902a.htm

2.
See:

http://www.law.ou.edu/hist/artconf.html

3.
See:

http://www.straightdope.com/mailbag/mprez1st.html

For a series of debates on this issue, see:
http://www.uspresidency.com/johnhanson.net/
http://members.tripod.com/~earthdude1/washington/washington.html
http://www.marshallhall.org/hanson.html
http://www.issues2000.org/askme/confederacy.htm
http://www.beyondbooks.com/gop00/2.asp?pf=on
http://www.uspresidency.com/2.uspresidency.com/

4.
See:

http://www.nps.gov/ncro/anti/emancipation.html
http://www.archives.gov/exhibit_hall/featured_documents/emancipation_proclamation/

5.
See:

Natalie Angier. "Genome Researchers Discover Race Little More Than Skin-Deep." New York Times News Service. Published in, *Lexington Herald-Leader*, August 22, 2000.

6.
See:

http://www.hiddenmysteries.com/item300/item387.html

7.
See:

http://coursesa.matrix.msu.edu/~hst306/documents/indust.html
http://www.museumstuff.com/articles/art1097910607203341.html
http://www.yale.edu/lawweb/avalon/presiden/speeches/eisenhower001.htm
http://mcadams.posc.mu.edu/ike.htm

8.
See:

http://www.boondocksnet.com/ai/ail/ailbib_twain.html

9.
See
http://www.cosmiverse.com:
"World Heads for Warmest Year Yet." Reuters, London. Thursday, August 1, 2002.
Science News. "Last Three Months in U.S. Warmest in History." February 22, 2002.

10.
See:
Michael Christie. "Record Sea Temperatures Threaten Great Barrier Reef." Reuters, Sydney. Thursday, July 25, 2002.

11.
See:
Anthony Brown, Environmental Editor. "Asian Cloud Heating Europe, Says UN." Times Online. August 12, 2002.

12.
See:
Joseph B. Verrengia, AP Science Writer. "Antarctic Ice Shelf Collapses." Associated Press, Tuesday, March 19, 2002; Paul Recer, AP Science Writer. "Kilimanjaro Snow Cap May Melt Soon." Associated Press, Washington. Thursday, October 17, 2002; Eric Pianin. "Alaskan Glaciers Melting at Unexpectedly Fast Rate." *The Washington Post*. Republished in, *The Lexington Herald-Leader*. Friday, July 19, 2002; "Huge Iceberg Breaks From Antarctica." Associated Press, Washington. March 23, 2000.

13.
See:
Gary Polakovic. "Earth Can't Sustain Human Activity Rate, Study Says." Los Angeles Times. Republished in, *The Lexington Herald-Leader*. June 27, 2002; Christopher Doering. "World Plants Near Extinction Close to 50 Pct.-Study." Reuters, Washington. Thursday, October 31, 2002; Joby Warrick. Staff Writer. "Mass Extinction Underway, Majority of Biologists Say." *Washington Post*. Tuesday, April 21, 1998, page A4; Worldwatch Institute. 1998. "Worldwatch Report: Fastest Mass Extinction in Earth History." Los Angeles Times Syndicate. Wednesday, September 16, 1998.

14.
See:
http://www.newamericancentury.org/
http://www.newamericancentury.org/statementofprinciples.htm
http://www.newamericancentury.org/iraqmiddleeast.htm

15.
See:
http://www.wogan.org/NYCflyer.pdf
http://scan.dorja.com/scan/
http://www.frac.ws/aboveandbelow.html
http://slash.autonomedia.org/analysis/02/05/13/0130213.shtml
http://www.eroseffect.com/books/subversion_download.htm
http://flathat.wm.edu/2003-11-14/story.php?type=1&aid=6
http://zena.secureforum.com/Znet/zmag/articles/clayrev.htm

References

Achbar, Mark, Peter Wintonick and Noam Chomsky. 1992. *Manufacturing Consent: Noam Chomsky and the Mass Media.* Zeitgeist Films.

Adams, Bert N. and R. A. Syide. 2002. *Classical Sociological Theory.* Thousand Oaks, CA: Pine Forge Press.

Adorno, Theodor. 1950. *The Authoritarian Personality.* New York: Harper.

Akard, Patrick J. 1992. "Corporate Mobilization and Political Power: The Transformation of U.S. Economic Policy in the 1970s." *American Sociological Review* 57:597-615.

Aronson, Sidney H. 1964. *Status and Kinship in the Higher Civil Service: Standards of Selection in the Administrations of John Adams, Thomas Jefferson, and Andrew Jackson.* Cambridge, MA: Harvard University Press.

Bagdikian, Ben. 1992 (2000). *The Media Monopoly.* Boston: Beacon Press.

Bailey, Thomas A. 1971. *The American Pageant: A History of the Republic.* Lexington, MA: D. C. Heath and Company.

Barak, Gregg, editor. 1995. *Media, Process, and the Social Construction if Crime: Studies in Newsmaking Criminology.* New York: Taylor & Francis.

Barber, Benjamin. 1996. *Jihad v. McWorld.* New York: Ballantine Books.

Barnet, Richard J. and Ronald Muller. 1974. *Global Reach: The Power of the Multinational Corporations.* New York: Simon and Schuster.

Baudrillard, Jean. 1981. *For a Critique of the Political Economy of the Sign.* St. Louis, MO: Telos Press.

_____. 1989. *America.* New York: Verso.

Becker, Howard. 1967. "Whose Side are We On?" *Social Problems* 14: 239-248.

Bell, Daniel. 1976. The Coming of Post-Industrial Society: A Venture in Social Forecasting. New York: Basic Books.

Bellah, Robert. 1970. "Civil Religion in America." Pp. 168-189 in, Beyond Belief: Essays on Religion in a Post-Traditional World. New York: Harper & Row. Originally published as in *Daedalus* 1967, 96:1-21.

Berger, Peter. 1963. *Invitation to Sociology: A Humanist Perspective.* Garden City, New York: Anchor Books / Doubleday Company.

_____. 1967. *The Sacred Canopy.* Garden City, New York: Doubleday.

Berger, Peter and Thomas Luckmann. 1967. *The Social Construction of Reality.* Garden City, New York: Anchor Books / Doubleday & Company.

Black, Edwin. 2001. *IBM and the Nazis: The Strategic Alliance Between Nazi Germany and America's Most Powerful Corporation.* New York: Crown Publishers.

Blum, William. 1995. *Killing Hope: U.S Military and CIA Interventions Since World War II.* Monroe, ME: Common Courage Press.

Boswell, Terry and William J. Dixon. 1993. "Marx's Theory of Rebellion: A Cross-National Analysis of Class Exploitation, Economic Development, and Violent Revolt." *American Sociological Review* 58:681-702.

Bowles, Samuel and Herbert Gintis. 1976. *Schooling in Capitalist America: Education Reform and the Contradictions of Economic Life*. New York: Basic Books.

Britt, Lawrence. 2003. "Fascism Anyone?" *Free Inquiry* Spring (23:2):20.

Burris, Val. 2001. "The Two Faces of Capital: Corporations and Individual Capitalists as Political Actors." *American Sociological Review* 66:361-381.

Chase-Dunn, Christopher, Yukio Kawano and Benjamin D. Brewer. 2000. "Trade Globalization Since 1975: Waves of Integration in the World-System." *American Sociological Review* 65:77-95.

Chomsky, Noam. 1967. "The Responsibility of Intellectuals." *New York Review of Books*. February 23, 1967.

_____. 1988. *The Culture of Terrorism*. Boston: South End Press.

_____. 1991. *Deterring Democracy*. New York: Hill and Wang.

_____. 2003. *Hegemony or Survival: America's Quest for Global Dominance*. New York: Metropolitan Books.

Collins, Chuck, Betsy Leondar-Wright and Holly Sklar. 1999. *Shifting Fortunes: The Perils of the Growing American Wealth Gap*. United for a Fair Economy.

Collins, Patricia Hill. 1990. *Black Feminist Thought: Knowledge, Consciousness, and the Politics of Empowerment*. Boston: Unwin Hyman.

Cooney, Mark. 1997. "From Warre to Tyranny: Lethal Conflict and the State." *American Sociological Review* 62:316-338.

Cornwell, John. 1999. *Hitler's Pope: The Secret History of Pius the XII*. New York: Viking.

Cox, Oliver. 1976. *Race Relations: Elements and Social Dynamics*. Detroit: Wayne State University Press.

Crush, Jonathan. 1995. *The Power of Development*. New York: Routledge.

Dahl, Robert. 1961. *Who Governs?* New Haven, CT: Yale University Press.

_____. 1979. "Who Really Rules?" *Social Science Quarterly* 60 (1):150.

Davis, Gerald F., Kristina A. Diekmann, and Catherine H. Tinsely. 1994. "The Decline and Fall of the Conglomerate Firm in the 1980s: The Deinstitutionalization of An Organizational Form." *American Sociological Review* 59:547-570.

de Beauvoir, Simone. 1974. *The Second Sex*. New York: Vintage.

Derrida, Jacques. 1997. *Deconstruction in a Nutshell: A Conversation with Jacques Derrida*. New York: Fordham University Press.

Diesing, Paul. 1991. *How Does Social Science Work? Reflections on Practice*. Pittsburgh: University of Pittsburgh Press.

Domhoff, G. William. 1967. *Who Rules America?* Englewood Cliffs, NJ: Prentice Hall.

_____. 1970. *The Higher Circles*. New York: Random House.

_____. 1979. *The Powers that Be: Processes of Ruling Class Domination in America*. New York: Vintage Books.

_____. 1983. *Who Rules America Now?* New York: Touchstone Books.

Dreyfus, Hubert, and Paul Rabinow. 1982. *Michel Foucault: Beyond Structuralism and Hermeneutics*. Chicago: University of Chicago Press.

Drury, S. 1988. *The Political Ideas of Leo Strauss*. New York: St. Martin's Press.

_____. 1997. *Leo Strauss and the American Right*. New York: St. Martin's Press.

Durkheim, Emile. 1915. *Elementary Forms of the Religious Life*. New York: Free Press/Macmillan.

Escobar, Arturo. 1995. *Encountering Development: The Making and Unmaking of the Third World*. Princeton, NJ: Princeton University Press.

Ewen, Stuart. 1976. *Captains of Consciousness: Advertising and the Social Roots of the Consumer Culture*. New York: McGraw-Hill Company.

Fligstein, Neil and Peter Brantley. 1992. "Bank Control, Owner Control, or Organizational Dynamics: Who Controls the Larger Modern Corporation?" *American Journal of Sociology* 98 :280-307.

Foucault, Michel. 1977. *Discipline and Punish: The Birth of the Prison*. New York: Vintage.

_____. 1978 (1980). *The History of Sexuality, Volume I*. New York: Vintage.

_____. 1983 (1982). "Afterword: The Subject and Power." Pp. 208-226 in *Michel Foucault: Beyond Structuralism and Hermeneutics*, edited by Hubert Dreyfus and Paul Rabinow. New York: Harvester-Wheatsheaf.

Frank, David John, Ann Hironaka and Evan Schofer. 2000. "The Nation-State and the Natural Environment Over the Twentieth Century." *American Sociological Review* 65:96-116.

Frazier, E. Franklin. 1962. *The Black Bourgeoisie*. New York: Collier Books.

Fredrickson, George. 1981. *White Supremacy: A Comparative Study in American and South African History*. New York: Oxford University Press.

Friedan, Betty. 1963. *The Feminine Mystique*. New York: Norton.

Genovese, Eugene. 1976. *Roll, Jordan, Roll: The World the Slaves Made*. New York: Vintage Books.

Goffman, Erving. 1959. *The Presentation of Self in Everyday Life*. New York: Anchor/Doubleday.

Gramsci, Antonio. 1971. *Selections from the Prison Notebooks*. New York: International.

Graves, Joseph. 2001. *The Emperor's New Clothes: Biological Theories of Race at the Millenium*. New Brunswick, NJ: Rutgers University Press.

Greer, Germain. 1970. *The Female Eunuch*. London: MacGibbon and Kee.

Greider, William. 1997. *One World, Reader or Not: The Manic Logic of Global Capitalism*. New York: Simon & Schuster.

Hanisch, Carol. 1979 (orig. 1969). "The Personal is Political." Pp. 204-205 in, *Redstockings Collective, Feminist Revolution*. New York: Random House; also see: Hanisch, Carol. 1971 (1969). "The Personal is Political." Pp. 152-155 in *The Radical Therapist*, edited by Jerome Agel. New York: Ballantine.

Harding, Sandra, editor. 1993. *The "Racial" Economy of Science*. Bloomington: Indiana University Press.

Harding, Susan Friend. 2000. *The Book of Jerry Falwell: Fundamentalist Language and Politics*. Princeton, NJ: Princeton University Press.

Herman, Edward and Noam Chomsky. 1988. *Manufacturing Consent: The Political-Economy of the Mass Media*. New York: Pantheon.

Hobbes, Thomas. 1651 (1988). *Leviathan*. New York: Penguin Classics.

hooks, bell. 1989. *Talking Back: Thinking Feminist, Thinking Black*. Boston, MA: South End Press.

_____. 2000. *Where We Stand: Class Matters*. New York: Routledge.

Jessop, Bob. 1982. *The Capitalist State: Marxist Theories and Methods*. New York: New York University Press.

Johnson, C. 2000. *Blowback: The Costs and Consequences of American Empire*. New York: Henry Holt.

Jordan, Winthrop. 1974. *The White Man's Burden: Historical Origins of Racism in the United States*. New York: Oxford University Press.

Kerbo, Harold R. 2003. *Stratification and Inequality: Class Conflict in Historical, Comparative, and Global Perspective*. Boston: McGraw-Hill.

Kolko, Joyce. 1988. *Restructuring the World Economy*. New York: Pantheon.

Loewen, James W. 1995. *Lies My Teacher Told Me: Everything Your American History Textbook Got Wrong*. New York: The New Press.

Locke, John. 1688 (1960). *Two Treatises of Civil Government*. Cambridge: Cambridge University Press.

Lukes, Steven. 1974. *Power: A Radical View*. New York: MacMillan.

Lyotard, Jean Francois. 1984. *The Postmodern Condition: A Report on Knowledge*. Minneapolis, MN: University of Minnesota Press.

Machiavelli, Niccolo. 1515 (1977). *The Prince*. Translated and edited, Robert M. Adams. New York: W.W. Norton & Company, Inc.

Marx, Karl. 1844a (1978). "Contribution to the Critique of Hegel's *Philosophy of Right*: Introduction." Pp. 53-66 in *The Marx-Engels Reader*, edited by Robert Tucker. New York: W. W. Norton & Company.

_____. 1844b (1978). "For a Ruthless Criticism of Everything Existing." Pp. 12-15 in *The Marx-Engels Reader*, edited by Robert Tucker. New York: W. W. Norton & Company.

_____. 1867 (1992). *Capital, Volume I: A Critical Analysis of Capitalist Production*. New York: International.

Miliband, Ralph. 1969. *The State in Capitalist Society*. New York: Basic Books.

_____. 1983. *Class Power and State Power*. London: Verso.

Mills, C. Wright. 1956. *The Power Elite*. New York: Oxford University Press.

_____. 1959. *The Causes of World-War Three*. London: Secker & Warburg.

Mizruchi, Mark S. 1989. "Similarity of Political Behavior among Large American Corporations." *American Journal of Sociology* 95 :401-424.

Muller, Edward. 1995. "Economic Determinants of Democracy." *American Sociological Review* 60:966-982.

Palast, Greg. 2003. *The Best Democracy Money Can Buy: The Truth about Corporate Cons, Globalization, and High-Finance Financiers*. New York: Plume.

Palmer, Donald, Brad M. Barber, Xueguang Zhou, and Yasemin Soysal. 1995. "The Friendly and Predatory Acquisition of Large U.S. Corporations in the 1960s: The Other Contested Terrain." *American Sociological Review* 60:469-499.

Paolucci, Paul, Micah Holland, and Shannon Williams. 2004. / Forthcoming "The Mayberry Machiavellians In Power: A Critical Analysis of the Bush Administration through a Synthesis of Machiavelli, Goffman, and Foucault." *Current Perspectives in Social Theory* 23.

Parenti, Christian. 1999. *Lockdown America: Police and Prisons in the Age of Crisis*. New York: Verso.

Parenti, Michael. 1986. *Inventing Reality: The Politics of the Mass Media*. New York: St. Martin's.

_____. 1988. *The Sword and the Dollar*. New York: St. Martin's Press.

_____. 1995 (1974). *Democracy for the Few*. New York: St. Martin's Press.

Parsons, Talcott. 1963. "On the Concept of Political Power." *Proceedings of the American Philosophical Society* 6:232-262.

Perrucci, Robert and Harry Potter, editors. 1989. *Networks of Power: Organizational Actors at the National, Corporate, and Community Levels*. New York: Aldine de Gruyter.

Postman, Neil. 1986. *Amusing Ourselves to Death: Public Discourse in the Age of Show Business*. New York: Penguin Books.

Poulantzas, Nicos. 1969. "The Problem of the Capitalist State." *New Left Review* 58:67-78.

_____. 1978. *State / Power / Socialism*. London: Verso.

Prus, Robert. 1999. *Beyond the Power Mystique: Power as an Intersubjective Accomplishment*. Albany: State University of New York Press.

Ross, Ellen and Rayna Rapp. 1997. "Sex and Society: A Research Note From Social History and Anthropology." Pp. 153-168 in *The Gender / Sexuality Reader: Culture, History, Political Economy*, edited by Roger N. Lancaster and Micaela di Leonardo. New York: Routledge.

Said, Edward. 1979. *Orientalism*. New York: Vintage Books.

Sears, Alan. 2003. *Retooling the Mind Factory: Education in a Lean State*. Aurora, Ontario: Garamond Press.

Sklar, Holly. 1980. *Trilateralism: The Trilateral Commission and Elite Planning for World Management*. Boston: Sound End Press.

Spivak, Gaytari Chakravorty. 1999. *A Critique of Postcolonial Reason: A History of the Vanishing Present*. Cambridge, MA: Harvard University Press.

Stearns, Linda Brewster and Kenneth D. Allan. 1996. "Economic Behavior in Institutional Environments: The Corporate Merger Wave of the 1980s." *American Sociological Review* 61:699-718.

Stepan-Norris, Judith and Maurice Zeitlin. 1995. "Union Democracy, Radical Leadership, and the Hegemony of Capital." *American Sociological Review* 60:829-850.

Sweezy, Paul (With Paul Baran). 1966. *Monopoly Capital: An Essay on the American Economic System*. New York: Monthly Review Press.

Tilly, Charles. 1975. *The Formation of National States in Western Europe*. Princeton, NJ: Princeton.

_____, editor. 1981. *Class Conflict and Collective Action*. London: Sage.

Wallerstein, Immanuel. 1974. *The Modern World-System*. New York: Academic Press.

_____. 1982. "Crisis as Transition." Pp. 11-54 in *Dynamics of Global Crisis*, edited by Samir Amin, Giovanni Arrighi, Andre Gunder Frank, and Immanuel Wallerstein. New York: Monthly Review.

_____. 1983. *Historical Capitalism*. New York: Verso.

_____. 2002. "The Eagle Has Crash Landed." *Foreign Policy* 131 (July/August):60-68.

Weber, Max. 1946. "Bureaucracy." Pp. 196-239 in *From Max Weber*, edited by H.H. Gerth and C. W. Mills. New York: Oxford University Press.

_____. 1947. *The Theory of Social and Economic Organization*. A.M. Henderson and Talcott Parsons, translators. New York: Oxford University Press.

_____. 1978 (1921). *Economy and Society*. G. Roth and C. Wittich, editors. Berkeley: University of California Press.

Wilson, William J. 1987. *The Truly Disadvantaged: The Inner City, the Underclass, and Public Policy*. Chicago: University of Chicago.

Zinn, Howard. 1980. *A People's History of the United States*. New York: Harper & Row.

Index

Index

Index

Index

Index

Index